# A SAFETY HANDBOOK for SCIENCE TEACHERS

## Fourth edition

**K. EVERETT &
E. W. JENKINS**

**JOHN MURRAY**

© K. Everett and E. W. Jenkins 1991

First published 1973
by John Murray (Publishers) Ltd
50 Albemarle Street
London W1X 4BD

Second edition 1977
Third edition 1980
Fourth edition 1991

Photoset by Rowland Phototypesetting Ltd
Bury St Edmunds, Suffolk

Printed by Butler and Tanner Ltd, Frome and London

**British Library Cataloguing in Publication Data**
Everett, K. (Kenneth)
    A safety handbook for science teachers. – 4th. ed.
    1. Great Britain. Schools. Laboratories. Safety measures
    I. Title   II. Jenkins, E. W. (Edgar William) *1939–*
    371.7756
    ISBN 0-7195-4645-1

# Preface to the Fourth Edition

In the decade that has elapsed since the publication of the third edition of this Handbook, there have been important changes both in the education service and in the relevant Health and Safety legislation and advice.

The introduction of a national curriculum and, more particularly, of broad and balanced science curricula for all, will lead to more pupils studying science and extend the range of the work undertaken. It may also lead to a greater number of science teachers teaching outside their own subject specialisms. In addition, the advent of systems of local management in schools has placed new responsibilities upon many governing bodies and changed the relationship between them and the local education authorities who, in the case of county, voluntary-controlled and special agreement schools, remain the employers of teachers.

The changes to the legislative and advisory framework relating to the safe practice of school science teaching have been numerous and wide-ranging. Examples include the COSHH *Regulations*, revised standards governing work with micro-organisms and with ionising radiations, advice relating to AIDS, new guidance on electrical safety in schools, and the *Animals (Scientific Procedures) Act 1986*. In addition, a number of hazards associated particularly or uniquely with school science teaching have been reported.

In the present edition, we have sought to reflect these changes as fully as possible while retaining an essential feature of a Handbook, that of offering advice and information in a compact but readily accessible form. Several topics, e.g. microbiological hazards are treated in greater detail than in earlier editions whereas material relating to the COSHH *Regulations*, and a number of other sections, is necessarily entirely new. The Appendix, listing accidents reported in *The School Science Review* and *Education in Science* has been brought up to date and a new index has also been prepared.

The University of Leeds K. Everett
E. W. Jenkins

# ACKNOWLEDGEMENTS

Particular acknowledgement is given to the University of Leeds for permission to use material that first appeared in various editions of the University of Leeds *Safety Handbook*.

We are grateful also to Dr R. J. Lock, University of Birmingham, for helpful comments on chapter 3.

Appendix B is based upon work originally undertaken by Mr S. C. Wilson.

Copyright material is reproduced by permission of:
Health and Safety Executive (COSHH logo, p. 11)
St John Ambulance Association (logo, p. 90, illustration, p. 93, adapted from *Emergency Aid in Schools*)

Diagrams by RDL Artset

Cartoons by David Anstey

# CONTENTS

# INTRODUCTION

The prevention of accidents in laboratories is the duty of every individual using or entering them. For teachers, ensuring the safety of others as well as of themselves is of particular importance.

At the least, accidents result in wasted time, spoiled materials or broken apparatus. If there is also personal injury, then pain and suffering are involved. Clearly, it is the duty of all teachers to organize their classes in ways that reflect both their responsibility for the welfare of their pupils and their commitment to teaching pupils appropriate safety-conscious attitudes and behaviour.

Safety is to be regarded as a *positive factor* in science teaching and one that forms an integral part of lesson planning. This planning requires (i) knowledge of the level and nature of the risks in a given situation, (ii) adequate experimental design, (iii) correct and appropriate laboratory techniques and (iv) identification of the safest, rather than less safe, procedures consistent with the educational objectives of the lesson. Such identification is often facilitated by answering the following three questions.

1. What is the most likely accident in a given situation?
2. What is the 'maximum credible accident'?
3. How can the accidents referred to in questions 1 and 2 be prevented?

It is also important to keep the level of risk in science teaching in perspective, although it is not possible to quantify that risk with any precision. How, for example, is an accident to be defined? Should such a definition include the most minor burns and scratches as well as more obviously serious injuries that subsequently cause a child to be absent from school for a period of time? In addition, up-to-date and reliable national data seem to be unavailable. There is good reason to believe, however, that school science laboratories are among the safer places in a school. A survey of *The Health of the School Child* (published in 1969) defined an accident as an incident that kept a pupil away from school for at least half a day. Using this definition, the school science laboratory was about 60 times safer than the playground. There seems to have been no significant change in the level of risk by 1975 when an analysis of 70 000 accident report forms by Her Majesty's Inspectorate

**Table 1.1**  Sources of school laboratory accidents

| Category | Number | Percentage |
|---|---|---|
| Chemicals on the body: | | |
| in eyes | 177 | 22.8% ⎫ |
| elsewhere | 161 | 20.6% ⎬ 43.4% |
| | 338 | |
| Cuts | 158 | 20.3% |
| Burns—flames, hot objects, scalds | 113 | 14.5% |
| Dropping, falling, slipping, knocking, lifting | 57 | 7.3% |
| Chemicals in mouth | 32 | 4.1% |
| Inhalation | 29 | 3.7% |
| Animal bites | 22 | 2.8% |
| Explosions | 12 | 1.5% |
| Fainting | 12 | 1.5% |
| Electric shock | 5 | 0.6% |
| | n = 778 | |

of Schools revealed that only about 2% of these referred to laboratory-based accidents. In a sample survey in South Warwickshire in 1983, laboratory accidents almost certainly accounted for only a very small proportion of the 10% of attendances at the accident and emergency departments of hospitals that were required by injuries sustained at school. This percentage should be set alongside the 45% of such accidents that occurred in the home.

A survey carried out by the CLEAPSS development group and reported in 1981 confirmed that at that time, 'The general accident record of school science teaching [was] good.' The most interesting aspect of the survey, however, was its analysis of the nature of the accidents involving staff and pupils. The analysis is summarized in Table 1.1.

It is possible that some contemporary developments in school science teaching may pose something of a threat to the safety record referred to above. Some open-plan laboratories may be less safe than others of more traditional and secure designs. The move towards integrated science, coupled with an enduring shortage of science teachers, may require teachers to teach topics that lie beyond their immediate professional and academic expertise. New science courses often demand new materials and new techniques. In addition, a commitment to investigative work may make it difficult, particularly for inexperienced pupils, to draw the line between legitimate inquiry and hazardous exploration. These developments and the growth in understanding of the hazards associated with often familiar materials or procedures mean that the case for continued vigilance and professionalism in matters of school safety is overwhelming. Good professional practice that identifies and accommodates the risks inherent in an undertaking is the key to safe laboratory practice. This book reflects the view that most accidents in school laboratories usually result from errors of omission or of commission, rather than from, for example, equipment failure. Such accidents, therefore, can be regarded as incidents which could have been prevented by adequate forethought.

This view acknowledges that pupils do not have the instinctive feeling for experimental work that a teacher will have acquired as a result of training and experience. As a result, what is common sense to the teacher may well be totally outside the experience of pupils and, therefore, be far from obvious to them. It also entails the notion that a minor accident can develop into something much more serious if it is not dealt with in an appropriate manner. Safety in science teaching, therefore, depends upon effective and informed planning that embraces the action that would need to be taken when, for whatever reason, an accident occurs.

If there is an accident, your duties are as follows.

1. Assist any casualties.
2. Take appropriate steps to control the emergency.
3. Avoid becoming a casualty yourself.
4. Inform the appropriate authority (HM, LEA) that an accident has occurred. Many LEAs have a standard form on which accidents have to be reported.

### Action to be taken in an emergency

There are certain points that apply to all emergencies.

1. Commit to memory the standing orders for action in an emergency. You will not have time to read them in an emergency. You must also know the lay out of the school —the location of fire-fighting equipment and how it works, ways of getting out of a room or building, where telephones are sited and first aid arrangements.
2. You are expected to act in the spirit of the instructions. There is no substitute for informed common sense.
3. The most important consideration at ALL times is human safety.
4. Act quietly and methodically. This is likely to be the most effective way of retaining class control.
5. Ensure pupils do not rush or attempt to pass others when leaving the scene of an accident.
6. As a teacher you must assume control of the situation, ensuring, if necessary, the safe evacuation from the premises of all pupils in your charge to an agreed assembly point.

Be prepared to warn the fire brigade, etc. of any known special hazards such as gas cylinders or radioactive sources.

7. Remember that if you become a casualty someone must rescue you, possibly at personal risk to the rescuer.
8. An accident to a teacher may be a major emergency. Contingency plans should take account of this possibility: (a) by prevention by using safety screens, etc.; (b) by instructing pupils what to do.

## Use of telephone in an emergency

When telephoning for assistance in an emergency, give the following information:

(i) the precise location from which you are telephoning;
(ii) the type of emergency and the kind of assistance required;
(iii) the place where the assistance is required.

Ensure that the message has been correctly received by asking for it to be repeated to you.

## Water emergencies, flooding

Attention is drawn to the very large variations in water mains pressure that occur at certain time of the day in large buildings. It is essential that pupils are taught to use screw clips or wire to secure condenser tubing. Water-cooled apparatus likely to be left unattended for any length of time must be fitted with an appropriate 'fail-safe' device to accommodate any failure in the water supply.

Every teacher must have ready access to the mains water tap in any laboratory in which he or she is teaching. This tap, along with other mains controls (gas, electricity, steam) should be located near the exit door of the laboratory. Note that a laboratory floor, made slippery by the spillage of quite a small quantity of water, constitutes a significant hazard.

# 2 SAFETY IN LABORATORIES AND WORKSHOPS

## General

Apparatus not in immediate use should be put away, either in a store room or in a cupboard. Do not place quantities of flammable or other dangerous materials near exits. In ground-floor laboratories, ensure that apparatus or other items do not block or obscure emergency escape routes.

ALWAYS KEEP THE QUANTITIES AND VARIETY OF DANGEROUS MATERIALS TO A MINIMUM.

Note that some Local Education Authorities specify the maximum quantities of individual substances that schools of various types may hold in stock.

Passages between benches and pieces of equipment should permit free circulation under normal working conditions. Obstruction of passages or interference with access to switches, fire extinguishers or other emergency equipment should not be permitted. Controls, switches, taps, etc. should always be between the teacher and any apparatus being used for demonstration purposes.

A correct height for a working surface is an underestimated factor in laboratory safety. For advice, see DES Building Bulletin No. 50, *Furniture and Equipment, Working Heights and Zones for Practical Activities*, HMSO, 1973. Also of interest are DES, Building Bulletin No. 62, *Body Dimensions of the School Population*, HMSO, 1985 and Building Bulletin No. 63, *Craft, Design and Technology: Accommodation in Secondary Schools*, HMSO, 1986.

Guard against overhanging or jutting items. Lengths of metal or glass tubing must not be allowed to jut out into gangways.

## Workshops

The British Standards publication, BS 4163 (1984), *Recommendations for Safety in Workshops of Schools and Colleges of Education*, should be available in every school with workshop facilities. During any demonstration of workshop techniques, great care must be taken to ensure that students do not lean over machines or tools in order to obtain a better view. Teachers should also consult Chapter 5 of *Safety in Further Education*, DES Safety Series No. 5, HMSO, 1976. For advice on safety in workshops relating to woodworking, metalworking, ceramics, etc. see the bibliography on page 120.

**Offices, libraries and general areas**

Offices are the scene of a substantial number of serious accidents every year. Most of these accidents are avoidable. The amount of machinery in offices is increasing (duplicators, guillotines, word-processors, photocopiers, printers, etc.) and such machinery should be operated only in accordance with the manufacturer's instructions. Only maintenance personnel should remove the enclosing panels of machines.

Portable electric fires and fans should be fitted with approved guards and leads should not be allowed to trail in a manner likely to cause persons to trip over them or pull an item over. Do not place electric fires or fans in a precarious position or where long hair can become entangled or ignited.

Do not use waste-paper baskets as ashtrays.

When carrying files, do not carry so many that your vision is obscured.

Filing cabinets should always have enough weight in the bottom drawer to prevent a full and open upper drawer causing the cabinet to tip forward. If possible, filing cabinets of more than three drawers should be anchored to the wall near the top of a cabinet. Filing cabinet drawers should be closed as soon as you have found what is being sought, especially in crowded offices.

NEVER stand on revolving stools or chairs and AVOID using any chair or stool to gain access where steps are provided.

Do not leave stacks of boxes or files on the floor near doorways for people to fall over.

Note that the majority of problems arising from work with VDUs are ergonomic and arise from unsatisfactory siting or seating. It is essential that VDU workstations can be adjusted to accommodate the different body dimensions of those using them. More generally, furniture which is specific to particular technologies has little to commend it and most needs will be better met by a modular system of basic units that can be adjusted to accommodate ergonomic requirements.

For a useful discussion of office furniture, see *Adaptable Facilities in Further Education for Business and Office Studies*, DES, Building Bulletin No. 64, HMSO, 1986 and *Computer Rooms: Making Room for Information Technology*, Scottish Education Department, Edinburgh, 1984. For VDUs, see Health and Safety Executive, *Working with VDUs*, 1986.

**The use of glassware**

Glassware is produced and used in vast quantities and considerable variation in quality occurs. Winchester bottles

should be treated with particular care since, in places, the wall thickness may be less than 1 mm. Many accidents have occurred through lifting full Winchesters by the neck, the weight of the contents being sufficient to shatter the bottle. Winchesters, therefore, should never be lifted by the neck and, if they are to be transported any distance, an appropriate carrier should be used.

Never store containers of liquids on a laboratory floor if there is underfloor heating. This is particularly dangerous where volatile organic solvents are concerned. It is also bad practice to keep bottles of any chemicals, but especially liquids, in direct sunlight. Very sharp increases in the temperature of the contents can take place. Beware also of the 'burning glass' effect of liquids in spherical glass containers. The sun shining through a flask of liquid placed on a ledge can start a fire, the flask acting as a lens.

Care must be taken when handling glassware and any broken glass must be cleared up at once. A piece of plasticine is very useful for collecting small slivers of glass. The broken pieces should be put in a cardboard box or other suitable receptacle clearly marked 'Broken Glass'. A person disposing of broken glass may be cut very badly through thoughtlessness on the part of others. Be particularly careful to ensure the removal of broken glass from sinks.

All glassware should be inspected for flaws. If any that are detected cannot be repaired, the item should be rejected. In general, the use of chipped or cracked glassware should be avoided.

Always ensure that the type of glass used (e.g. borosilicate, soda-glass, Pyrex) is suitable for the task being undertaken.

Always carry glass tubing vertically. When breaking glass, use a cloth or other suitable material to protect the hands. When inserting glass tubing or rod into bungs, use the technique illustrated below. The procedure may be used in reverse to remove a seized tube from a bung.

***A safe technique for threading glass tubing through rubber bungs, corks etc.***

1. Select the appropriate sized stop-cock and bung.

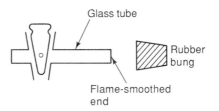

Glass tube

Rubber bung

Flame-smoothed end

2. Choose the correct size cork borer.

3. Lubricate the cork borer, with, for example, glycerol, teepol or soft soap.
4. Bore the hole in the normal manner so that the operation leaves the borer in the bung with the hand-grip on the same side as that from which it is wished to insert the glass stop-cock.

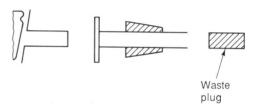

Waste plug

5. Select and lubricate the next largest cork borer and slide it over the first until it has passed through the bung.

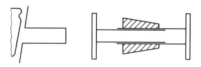

6. Withdraw the smaller cork borer and slide the glass tube into position.

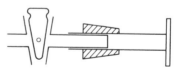

7. Withdraw the cork borer.

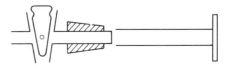

Glass stoppers sometimes 'stick'. This is usually because they fit badly, have been put in a warm bottle that has subsequently cooled or because of some chemical reaction that has cemented the stopper in place. A tight glass stopper in a bottle should be loosened by standing the bottle in a container large enough to contain the contents in the event of spillage and tapping the stopper *gently* with a piece of wood. Providing the contents of the bottle are not volatile or react violently with water, placing the neck of the bottle under a running warm tap sometimes also has the desired effect. In some cases, it is sensible to attempt to loosen a jammed glass stopper only in a fume cupboard and to wear protective gloves. Glass-stoppered bottles should not be used to store alkaline solutions such as sodium hydroxide.

The explosion of gases in glass eudiometers requires particular care. Eye protection and a safety screen are essential. The ASE advises that eudiometers can be used safely in schools for 'exploding small quantities (up to 10 cm$^3$) of hydrogen/oxygen, hydrogen/air, or alkane/air mixtures' but cautions that hydrocarbons other than alkanes and mixtures of hydrocarbons with *oxygen must not* be used.

Glass bell jars are not always as sturdy as they seem. Such jars should not be evacuated unless they have been specified by the manufacturer as suitable for work involving reduced pressure.

**The use of pipettes**

Mouth-operated pipettes are relatively inexpensive to purchase. They are also dangerous if used incorrectly. The principal hazard when pipetting is failure to keep the tip of the pipette fully immersed in the liquid being sampled. Mouth-operated pipettes must NEVER be used to dispense the following:

1. Volatile liquids, e.g. organic solvents, aqueous ammonia.
2. Concentrated acids or caustic alkalis; caustic alkalis also attack glass and should not be used in accurately calibrated glassware.
3. Toxic solutions or liquids.
4. Radioactive materials.

Note also that the DES advises that there should be no mouth pipetting of any solution having a concentration greater than 0.1 M.

Automatic pipettes and rubber pipette fillers are readily available from commercial suppliers and their use in laboratories should be a matter of routine. Pipettes should always be cleaned immediately after use and the practice of storing pipettes in a proper rack be emphasized. Laying a pipette on a laboratory bench can result in the mouthpiece becoming contaminated. Fitting pipette fillers to glass pipettes can be a source of injury if not carried out properly. Pupils should be taught to hold a pipette as near the top as possible to reduce the stress on the glass due to leverage, to ensure that the glass is suitably lubricated and to make use of a protective cloth.

## The use of burettes

When properly held in a clamp, the top of a burette is above the level of the user's head. The burette should be released and brought down below eye level before an attempt is made to fill it using a funnel. Students must not be allowed to climb on stools to fill burettes.

## Cleaning glassware

Glass is not a completely inert material. It should always be cleaned as soon as possible after use. Cleaning should commence with the mildest effective agent and a reagent such as 'chromic acid' should be avoided; modern cleansing agents are safer and more effective. On no account should a 'chromic acid' mixture be stored for occasional use in cleaning glassware.

Laboratory glassware must NEVER be used as drinking vessels.

## Glassblowing

Gas supplies to glassblowing benches should be fitted with non-return valves that are approved by local Gas Board officials. This is particularly important if compressed air or oxygen is to be used.

Glassblowing torches should be selected in accordance with the nature of the gas to be used, e.g. North Sea gas, propane. Different gases have different flame characteristics and practice in their use is essential.

Glassblowing benches should be fitted with extract ventilation to remove combustion products which may include toxic oxides of nitrogen when North Sea gas/oxygen flames are being used.

## Laboratory sinks

Particular hazards are associated with the use of laboratory sinks made of polythene or polypropylene. Although such sinks have an excellent resistance to most acids, they may be distorted by organic solvents or even by dilute mineral acids at temperatures in excess of 70°C. Many plastic sinks are flammable and easy to ignite. Where polythene and polypropylene sinks have been fitted in laboratories, suitable adjacent notices should be posted warning that they constitute a fire hazard if hot, burning or flammable materials are discarded in them.

For a summary of the relative merits of plastic, ceramic and stainless-steel sinks, see *Education in Science*, Bulletin No. 65, 1975, p. 32.

**Substances hazardous to health**

The use of substances hazardous to health is governed by the *Control of Substances Hazardous to Health Regulations, 1988.* These *Regulations* came into force on 1 October 1989 (SI 1988 No. 1657) and practical guidance is given in *Approved Codes of Practice* (HMSO, 1988). The *Regulations* apply to substances that have already been classified as very toxic, toxic, harmful, corrosive or irritant under the *Classification, Packaging and Labelling of Dangerous Substances Regulations 1984* and to those substances that have maximum exposure limits or occupational exposure standards. The COSHH *Regulations* also cover materials that have chronic or delayed effects, notably substances that are carcinogenic, mutagenic or teratogenic (see page 17).

A substance is to be regarded as posing a hazard to health if it is hazardous in the form in which it occurs and/or in the way in which it is used in the activity in the workplace, whether or not 'its mode of causing injury to health is known, and whether or not the active constituent has been identified'. Note that the term 'substance hazardous to health' includes not only individual chemicals but also mixtures, micro-organisms, allergens, dusts, etc. The COSHH *Regulations*, therefore, apply to virtually all substances hazardous to health likely to be encountered in schools, except asbestos, lead, and materials producing ionizing radiations which are governed by separate legislation. Failure to comply with COSHH *Regulations* not only exposes teachers, students and others to one or more harmful substances, it constitutes an offence under the *Health and Safety at Work Act 1974*.

The COSHH *Regulations* require an employer (LEA, school governors):

1. to assess risks to health arising from the way a substance is used in a school or college,
2. to consider whether it is possible to prevent anyone being exposed to that substance.

If (2) is not possible, then an employer must:

(i) determine how exposure to the risk can be controlled so as to reduce the level of associated risk;
(ii) establish effective controls;
(iii) ensure adequate training and provide appropriate information for teachers and other employees; and
(iv) where necessary, monitor employees' exposure to hazardous substances and provide health surveillance. Such surveillance will not normally be required in a school environment.

The employer's assessment of the level of risk is likely to be based on questions such as the following.

1. What substances are present and in what form?
2. Where, in what ways, and by whom are the substances actually used or handled?
3. How likely is it that those at risk will be exposed to a hazardous substance and what are the consequences of such exposure?

Control of a hazardous substance may involve ceasing to use that substance, using it in a different form, replacing it by a less hazardous substance or using it under strictly controlled conditions designed to contain the hazard. Note, however, that it remains the employer's responsibility to ensure that any control measures introduced to comply with the COSHH *Regulations* are properly applied.

As far as teachers and other employees are concerned, knowledge of the hazards presented by a substance is a necessary, but not a sufficient, condition of compliance with the *Regulations*. It is also necessary to understand

(i) the particular risks of using that substance in the course of their normal duties (e.g. demonstrating an experiment to a class of 11-year-old pupils, conducting a laboratory class with sixth-form students, preparing reagents for class use);
(ii) how the risks referred to in (i) are controlled; and
(iii) the precautions that must be taken.

Sources of information about the hazardous properties of substances are listed in the bibliography and an appropriate selection of these should be available in a school science department. Provision should also be made to keep information about hazards up to date and to ensure that information about new or changed hazards is brought to the attention of *all* those who might be affected, including, as appropriate, students, laboratory technicians and cleaning staff.

Many Local Education Authorities have their own lists of prohibited and restricted chemicals for use in schools. Such lists reflect not only the requirements laid down by law and Statutory Instruments but also what an Authority regards as best practice. The advice given by The Association for Science Education identifies the following categories of restriction.

1. Chemicals that are prohibited, e.g. naphthalen-2-amine, 4-aminobiphenyl and its salts, benzidine.
2. Chemicals that give rise to such a degree of risk that their use in schools cannot be justified, e.g. 1,2-dibromoethane, chloric(VII) acid.

3. Chemicals that should not normally be held or stored, e.g. cyanides, colchicine.
4. Chemicals that should be available only in small quantities for observation or exhibition, e.g. anthracene, tellurium metal.
5. Chemicals that are suitable for use only by particular categories of user such as teachers, senior pupils (i.e. post-GCSE or Standard Grade), pupils in the early years of secondary schooling under close supervision.
6. Chemicals that are suitable for use only in special circumstances, e.g. in a fume cupboard.
7. Chemicals with a short safe shelf-life, e.g. white phosphorus, sodium peroxide.

Fuller details of the chemicals in these various categories are given in ASE, *Topics in Safety*, 1988, Chapter 8. In responding to the advice given by the ASE, the following points are important.

1. There is room for a teacher to exercise his/her professional judgement in the choice and mode of use of materials. Schools vary significantly in the facilities and resources they have for science teaching and science is taught in a variety of locations which differ greatly in the means available to dispose of, or contain, hazardous chemicals, e.g. fume cupboards. Teachers, too, differ in their experience and training. In addition, there may be particular circumstances such as a senior school project in which it is appropriate, with necessary safeguards, to use a substance categorized by the ASE as 'not recommended for school use'.
2. The professional judgement of a teacher in the choice and mode of use of materials is limited in a number of ways, notably by any relevant statutory controls, including the requirement under *The Health and Safety at Work Act 1974* to comply with any safety instructions issued by his or her employer.
3. Science teachers may use their individual or collective professional judgement to influence an employer in drawing up advice or instruction to them about the safe conduct of their profession, subject to the overriding provisions of health and safety legislation and regulations.
4. The absence of advice or information about any material excluded from a list such as that produced by the ASE cannot be taken as implying anything about its safety. New information about possible hazards associated with a substance and/or procedure often takes considerable time

to appear in the literature and to be accommodated in practice.

The ASE also offers advice and recommendations about the suitability of many familiar chemical experiments for use in schools. (ASE, *Topics in Safety*, 1988, Chapter 7.) The suggested categories here are as follows.

1. Experiments inappropriate for use in schools, e.g. the oxidation of ammonia using oxygen in an enclosed apparatus.
2. Experiments suitable for teacher demonstration only, e.g. heating a mixture of ammonium chloride and sodium nitrate.
3. Experiments suitable for supervised senior pupils, e.g. reactions involving acyl or aryl halides.
4. Experiments considered safe for class use in the last two or three years of a GCSE, Standard grade or other similar course, e.g. cooling curve determinations involving octadecan-1-ol or octadecanoic acid.
5. Experiments considered safe in the first two years of secondary education with close supervision, e.g. heating potassium manganate(VII).
6. Experiments in which the use of a fume cupboard is recommended, e.g. organic nitrations.

As with the categorization of hazardous chemicals, there is some room for professional judgement by the science teacher in allocating an experiment to one or other of these categories, subject, once again, to the constraints referred to above.

For further advice on the level of risk associated with substances and procedures used in school science, see Appendix A, the *Hazcards* produced by the Consortium of Local Education Authorities for the Provision of Science Services (CLEAPSS) and the publications of the Scottish Schools Equipment Research Centre (SSERC). Note also that suppliers of chemicals are required to provide hazard data by suitably labelling the chemicals that they supply. For a brief introduction to COSHH and schools, see Health and Safety Commission, *COSHH: Guidance for Schools*, HMSO, 1989. See also, page 127.

**Toxic chemicals**

There are a number of different measures of the toxicity of a given chemical. The Health and Safety Executive publishes annually tables of Occupational Exposure Limits and for any substance that has been assigned such a limit, exposure to that substance by inhalation should be reduced to at least that standard. In schools, it is unlikely that pupils will be exposed to toxic chemicals for the length of time anticipated when drawing up the Occupational Exposure Limits. However, it should be remembered that pupils may be more vulnerable than adults and that the level of risk for teachers, pupils and technical staff alike will be greater in badly ventilated rooms. Some substances are assigned short or long-term maximum exposure limits (MEL). The MEL is the maximum concentration of an airborne substance, averaged over a reference period, to which employees may be exposed by inhalation under any circumstances. For details, see Health and Safety Executive, *Control of Substances Hazardous to Health Regulations 1988, Approved Codes of Practice*, 1988 and *Guidance Note, EH40, Occupational Exposure Limits*, HMSO. The latter is up-dated annually and carries a suffix indicating the year of issue, e.g. EH40/89.

Another measure of toxicity ($LD_{50}$) relates to mortality rates in test animals when a toxic substance is administered by a variety of different means. The toxicity is expressed in terms of unit body weight. Although there are ethical difficulties with such a measure and its validity is questionable, $LD_{50}$ values constitute the only available data for some materials. The lowest known fatal dose for humans or $LD_{LO}$, also expressed in terms of unit body weight, is a much more useful measure of toxicity but, not surprisingly, values are known for relatively few chemicals.

Comparison of the various toxicity measures of a number of well-known laboratory chemicals leads to the following conclusions.

1. Under appropriate conditions, some familiar laboratory substances have a toxicity at least as great as that of other substances that are generally and commonly regarded as very poisonous (e.g. cyanides).
2. The hazard arising from the use of a toxic material is related to the manner in which it is stored and used, e.g. solutions are usually easier to contain and, therefore, to control, than gases or dusts.
3. A chemical element can display significantly different degrees of toxicity in its different compounds, e.g. mercury(I) chloride is about sixty times less toxic than the corresponding mercury(II) salt, partly because of the lower solubility in water of the mercury(I) compound.

Toxicity and other data, together with safety advice, relating to a number of substances commonly found in schools, are given in Appendix A. See also the Health and Safety Executive publication *Toxicity Review* (various volumes listed on page 122).

The number of chemicals that are poisonous, corrosive or otherwise objectionable is large. Many people who enter school laboratories, e.g. caretakers, cleaners, pupils, have an inadequate training to appreciate this fully. For your own safety and that of others, ensure that all toxic or corrosive materials are suitably labelled and kept under safe conditions.

## The spillage of chemicals

Emphasis must be placed on preventing chemicals in any form coming into contact with extraneous matter. Neatness and cleanliness in the laboratory are essential. If acid or strong alkali is spilt, the cleaning-up should be carried out immediately under appropriate supervision and care taken to deal with the spillage in an appropriate way, e.g. never mop up concentrated nitric acid or other oxidizing acids with a dry cloth or seek to contain their spillage by sprinkling sawdust on them.

Water-soluble liquids can be diluted with water and then soaked up with paper, cloth or mop. Concentrated acids should be treated with a solid neutralizing agent, such as anhydrous sodium carbonate before being mopped up. Beware of the heat that can be produced by diluting significant quantities of concentrated sulphuric acid with water.

Liquids that are not miscible with water should be treated with sand or powdered clay before being mopped up or scraped into a plastic bucket or other suitable container.

Where appropriate, provision should be made for containing chemicals in the event of a breakage or spillage, e.g. apparatus containing mercury should be placed in a tray (from the point of view of both economy and safety). Mercury from a broken thermometer may be recovered by means of a teat pipette or using a capillary tube attached to a filter flask and pump. Mercury which cannot be recovered from crevices or cracks should be sprinkled with sulphur. It is sometimes convenient to treat spilt mercury with a mixture of solid carbon dioxide ('dry ice') and propanone and then sweep up the solid metal. Proprietary packs for dealing with mercury spillages are available at modest cost. There is much to commend the provision of a simple and easily accessible kit for dealing with the spillage of materials used frequently in school science laboratories. Such a kit might contain the following items.

- Eye protection
- Floor cloths, paper towels
- Heavy-duty rubber gloves
- Heavy gauge polythene bags
- Polythene bottle
- Small paint brush

- Wooden spatulas
- Plastic bucket
- Small plastic spoon
- Teat pipettes
- Anhydrous sodium carbonate
- Mineral absorbent (e.g. powdered clay)
- Disinfectant
- Liquid detergent
- Mixture of powdered sulphur and calcium hydroxide
- 2 M hydrochloric acid
- Powdered copper
- A solid, weak acid such as 2-hydroxypropane-1,2,3-tricarboxylic acid (citric acid)

Waste disposal must accord with the *Control of Pollution Act 1974* or subsequent legislation e.g. *Environmental Protection Act 1990*.

## Carcinogenic materials

The carcinogenic effects, if any, of a substance are often extremely difficult to establish. A potential carcinogen may have no obvious short- or long-term toxicity and there may be a long period of exposure before any carcinogenic consequences arise. Different forms of the same substance (e.g. dust, vapour or solid) may also present very different levels of risk and a combined or sequential exposure to a variety of substances may have additive or synergistic effects.

In considering the risk associated with a hazardous material, it is important to acknowledge that a school is a very different working environment from a chemical plant or most of manufacturing industry. Typically, in a school, a range of hazardous materials is used in small quantities on an irregular basis. However, it is equally important to recognize that most of those working with hazardous materials in schools are young people towards whom teachers owe a general duty of care and that part of their scientific education involves learning to work safely with materials that can present a hazard to their health and safety. Note, however, that some hazards may present a greater risk to young pupils than to the members of the teaching or technical staff.

The use of carcinogens in schools is governed by the *Control of Substances Hazardous to Health Regulations 1988* (SI 1657, 1988) and the approved codes of practice, *Control of Substances Hazardous to Health (General ACoP) and Control of Carcinogenic Substances (Carcinogens ACoP) 1988*. The latter Code of Practice applies whenever 'persons are exposed, or are liable to be exposed, to substances which have been assigned the "risk phrase" *R45: May cause cancer* under the *Classification, Pack-*

*aging and Labelling of Dangerous Substances Regulations 1984* (as amended)' and are listed in Part IA1 of the approved list. It also applies to any substance or substances in Appendix 1 of the Code and any substance or substances arising from a process listed in that Appendix. The two Codes of Practice are to be regarded as complementary. Attention is also drawn to (i) *The Use of Carcinogenic Substances in Educational Establishments* (SED, Circular No. 825 and DENI, Circular 1972/97), (ii) *Carcinogenic Aromatic Amines in Schools and Other Educational Establishments* (DES, Administrative Memorandum No. 3/70) and (iii) the regulations governing the use of ionizing radiations in schools (see page 20).

The following substances must not be kept or used in schools.

1. Naphthalen-1-amine[†] or naphthalen-2-amine.
2. Biphenyl substituted by:
   (i) at least one nitro or primary amino group, or by at least one nitro and primary amino group,
   (ii) in addition to substitutions as in 2(i) above, further substitution by halogens, methyl or methoxy groups, but not by other groups.

   Compounds whose presence in schools is forbidden under this provision include biphenyl-4,4$^1$-diamine (benzidine), 4-aminobiphenyl (xenylamine), 3,3$^1$-dimethylbiphenyl-4,4$^1$-diamine (*o*-tolidine) and 3,3$^1$-dimethoxybiphenyl-4,4$^1$-diamine (*o*-dianisidine).
3. Nitrosamines. Pupils should under no circumstances prepare N-nitroso compounds from amines.
4. Nitrosophenols, except for 4-nitrosophenol which is not thought to be carcinogenic.
5. Nitronaphthalenes.
6. Chloroethene (vinyl chloride monomer).

Similar restrictions apply to the salts (where formed) of the above and to preparations in which the substances or their salts are likely to be present.

Exposure to the following[†] should also be avoided in schools.

[†] At the time of writing, draft amendments have been proposed to Schedule 1 of the COSHH Regulations 1988 and the associated Codes of Practice. The amendments, if accepted, would *inter alia*:
   (i) assign to benzene a MEL of 5 ppm 8 h TWA;
   (ii) assign to methylbenzene (toluene) MELs of 100 ppm 8 h TWA and 200 ppm 10 min reference period;
   (iii) delete *pure* naphthalen-1-amine from the list of carcinogens;
   (iv) replace the current controls on insoluble chromium(VI) compounds by a specific reference to the manufacture of dichromate(VI) from chromite ore. But see also page 139.

benzene
calcium chromate(VI)
1,2-dibromoethane (ethylene dibromide)
dioxan
hydrazine
propenenitrile (acrylonitrile)
strontium chromate(VI)
tetrachloromethane (carbon tetrachloride)
trichloromethane (chloroform)
trichloroethene (trichloroethylene)
zinc chromate(VI)

Attention is also drawn to the following.

1. The small-scale and properly-conducted distillation of 'crude oil' should raise no significant carcinogenic hazards. The 'crude oil' supplied to schools is generally prepared for educational purposes. However, it is good practice to avoid skin contact, and to wear gloves and eye protection, particularly when cleaning the apparatus that has been used for the distillation.

2. Methanal (formaldehyde) and hydrogen chloride react rapidly in air to form an appreciable concentration of *bis*-chloromethylether, a potent carcinogen. This substance may also be formed in aqueous and non-aqueous media and in Friedel–Crafts reactions using methanal and a variety of metal chlorides. Hence, the possibility of its formation must be considered whenever methanal and hydrogen chloride come into contact. When concentrated hydrochloric acid is specified in preparations of condensation polymers involving methanal, it is usually possible to use 10 M (*ca.* 50% aqueous) sulphuric acid instead. The ASE advises that concentrated hydrochloric acid should not be stored in biology laboratories or preparation rooms and that methanal should not be stored in chemistry laboratories or preparation rooms. As far as possible, the use of these reagents in these rooms should also be avoided. Glassware that has contained aqueous methanal (e.g. 'formalin') must not be cleaned using hydrochloric acid.

3. Not all azo-dyes are carcinogenic but school preparations of azo dyes should be restricted to those that are water soluble, e.g. methyl orange. Azo dyes which have structures similar to those of known carcinogenic aromatic amines, or can be metabolized to produce such amines, should not be prepared. Examples are trypan blue and congo red. In preparing a soluble azo dye it is important to ensure that diazotization is complete before proceeding to the next stage of the preparation. This overcomes the risk

arising of a coupling reaction between any undiazotized amine and the diazonium salt.

Note that some commercially available azo dyes, e.g. congo red, basic fuchsin, although not thought to constitute a hazard themselves, may contain a small proportion of impurities, some of which may be carcinogenic. All azo dyes, therefore, should be handled with care.

4. Although exposure on a large scale to insoluble nickel compounds in the form of dusts is a well-established cause of occupational cancer, there seems little risk from the work with nickel and its compounds normally carried out in schools. However, nickel salts are moderately toxic and, even in relatively low concentrations, can cause allergic reactions. Precautions designed to prevent skin contact are, therefore, appropriate.

5. Compounds of chromium(VI) are toxic but there seems to be no good evidence that insoluble chromium(VI) compounds in general are carcinogenic to humans. The implementation of a draft amendment to the *Control of Carcinogenic Substances Regulations* would replace the entry 'Insoluble chromium(VI) compounds' by a reference to a specific industrial process involving chromite ore. However, calcium chromate(VI), strontium chromate(VI) and zinc chromates (including zinc potassium chromate(VI)) are classified as 'substances which may cause cancer' under the EC Directive 67/548/EEC. Work with these compounds, therefore, is covered by the Approved Code of Practice for work with carcinogens and these substances should not be used in schools. In the absence of reliable data about other insoluble chromium(VI) compounds, it is good practice to prevent or minimize exposure to them, e.g. insoluble chromates(VI) such as barium chromate(VI) precipitated from aqueous solution should not be isolated. It is also good practice to prevent aqueous solutions containing chromium(VI) from coming into contact with the skin.

6. The use of asbestos in schools is governed by DES Memorandum 3/86 and SED Circular 1113. See page 25. The so-called 'blue asbestos' or crocidolite is a potent carcinogen but is unlikely to be encountered in schools.

7. There are stringent controls on work with ionizing radiations in schools. See below.

## Radioactivity and ionizing radiations

The acquisition, storage and disposal of radioactive materials are governed by the *Radioactive Substances Act 1960* and by various Exemption Orders made under the Act. Work with ionizing radiation is regulated by the *Protection of Persons against Ionising Radiation Arising from any Work Activity, The Ionising Radiations Regulations 1985* made under the *Health and Safety at Work Act.* Educational establishments are also the subject of arrangements set out in *Procedures for the Use of Ionising Radiations in Educational Establishments* (SED, Circular 1166) and the corresponding †DES Memorandum. The Circular and Memorandum update the provisions made for the protection of users of ionizing radiations in accordance with revised international standards. Circular 1166 or the AM, as appropriate, must be read by any teacher before undertaking any work that involves ionizing radiation. The essential points (derived from Circular 1166) are as follows.

1. In all cases, any exposure of pupils or staff to ionizing radiation must be justifiable on educational grounds. Any such exposure should be the minimum necessary to achieve the educational objectives and the total dose received must in no case exceed the specified dose limits. Note that these limits are subject to periodic review.

2. When a class includes pupils under 16 years of age, the use of sources of ionizing radiations must be confined to demonstrations conducted by teachers. Pupils must not be allowed to use sources or equipment themselves and must not be present in laboratories where older pupils are conducting experiments with ionizing radiations except where specifically approved sealed sources of activity not exceeding 370 kilobecquerels are being used.

3. Annual dose limits are specified for individual pupils, students and teachers and these must not be exceeded:

   **Pupils and students**
   Whole body dose limit: 500 microsieverts p.a.
   Dose limit of a single organ or tissue: 5 millisieverts p.a.

   **Teachers and technicians**
   Whole body dose limit: 5 millisieverts p.a.
   Dose limit of a single organ or tissue: 50 millisieverts p.a.
   Dose limit for the lens of the eye: 15 millisieverts p.a.

4. Responsibility for ensuring that work with ionizing radiations is safe and complies with the regulations lies ultimately with the employer. In the discharge of this responsibility, the duties of an employer include:
   (i) the appointment of radiation protection supervisors and of a radiation protection adviser as defined in *The Ionising Radiation Regulations 1985*;
   (ii) ensuring that every teacher who uses ionizing radiations is suitably qualified and trained;

† AM2/76 is now seriously out of date and, at the time of writing, a new Memorandum is imminent.

(iii) ensuring that each school maintains and updates regularly its stock list of radioactive substances; and

(iv) making an application for a school to work in a specified category (see below) or to amend an application previously approved.

5. Regulation 11 of *The Ionising Radiation Regulations 1985* requires that local rules be drawn up, in writing, setting out the general principles and description of the means of complying with the *Regulations*. A set of 'model rules' has been prepared by the Scottish Schools Science Equipment Research Centre (SSSERC) with particular reference to Category C approval (see below).

6. Work with ionizing radiation requires approval in accordance with the procedures set out in the relevant Circular or Memorandum.

7. There are three categories of approval. In each case, both general and specific conditions must be met before approval can be granted. For example, for work in *Category C*, Section 8.1 of the procedures appended to SED Circular 1166 specifies the following:

### Sealed sources

8.1.1. the total activity of all sealed radioactive sources to be kept will not exceed 1.1 megabecquerels.

8.1.2. no single sealed source will exceed 370 kilobecquerels.

8.1.3. only sealed sources of approved kinds will be used. The only exceptions to this rule are:

8.1.3.1. approved sources for half-life experiments (see Explanatory Notes).

8.1.3.2. use of certain low level radioactive artefacts designed specifically for educational use such as a spinthariscope or cloud chamber sources or instruments containing radio-luminescent paint:

8.1.3.3. use of geological specimens.

8.1.3.4. Uranium compounds, such as are required for the preparation of approved sources for half-life experiments (see para. 8.1.3.1. above). No more than 0.1 kg of uranium compound should be held.

(NB: Thorium compounds should not be held. There is no restriction on potassium compounds consisting of a naturally occurring mixture of isotopes.)

### General conditions

8.1.4. the requirements of this Circular are met.

8.1.5. local rules are prepared and applied in accordance with the *Ionising Radiations Regulations 1985* (see Explanatory Notes).

8.1.6. storage arrangements must comply with the *Ionising Radiations Regulations 1985*. (See Explanatory Notes.)

Note that thoron generators may not be held or used in schools in Scotland. For the position in England and

Wales, see the relevant Administrative Memorandum.

For work in *Category C*, the qualifications required of teachers for appointment to the permanent teaching staff of a school will normally be adequate. Note that *The Ionising Radiations Regulations 1985* require the appointment in each school of a radiation protection supervisor. Special additional training is not necessary for the supervision of Category C work.

*Category B* work allows a greater total mass of uranium compounds (up to 2 kg) and a total maximum activity of open sources not exceeding 74 megabecquerels. An estimate of the dose received from every experiment must be made and there must be strict adherence to the specified dosage limits (see above). Any sealed source must be of an approved design and the total activity of all sealed sources, together with that of any open source, must not exceed 150 megabecquerels.

There are also detailed requirements about the design and use of, and the dose associated with, equipment specifically designed to demonstrate the properties of cathode rays or X-rays. Any X-ray equipment must be specifically designed for educational purposes.

For Category B work, the radiation protection supervisor should be a qualified teacher who has received special instruction in radiation protection, although this may have formed part of the programme of study and training leading to initial qualification as a science teacher. This special instruction, which must have included work with at least one open source, is a requirement of every teacher undertaking work that falls within Category B.

*Category A* work provides the highest degree of risk and is unlikely to be undertaken in schools.

8. Full records must be kept of the receipt, relocation and disposal of any radioactive materials.

9. Provided that:
    (i) the prior consent of an employer and headteacher is obtained,
    (ii) the sources or equipment to be used are used only for demonstration purposes and are such as could be approved under the provisions of Category B,
    (iii) no radiation source, including waste is left behind, and
    (iv) all surfaces subject to contamination are monitored,
    then a school which is not approved for work with ionizing radiations may arrange for radioactive sources and/or X-ray equipment to be used by a visiting lecturer.

10. Teachers on teaching practice may use only sealed sources relevant to Category C unless the trainee teacher satisfies the criteria for work at a higher level. Any X-ray equipment must be designed specifically for teaching purposes. The consent of the head of the school is required before any work with ionizing radiations is undertaken by a student on teaching practice and the head of the student's training institution should be informed. A member of the school's science staff must be present where radioactive sources or X-ray equipment are being used by a teacher in training. Any sources or equipment for work with ionizing radiations must not be brought to a school without prior approval for such work being obtained.

Attention is drawn to the fact that there are strict regulations governing the transport of radioactive substances by road. Advice is available from the National Radiological Protection Board.

The disposal of radioactive material is subject to stringent controls and advice should be sought from the employer before any arrangements are made.

The following guidelines are suggested for working with materials of low activity in a school laboratory.

1. The normal laboratory rules (no eating, smoking, etc.) must be rigorously followed.
2. A laboratory coat or other suitable protective clothing should always be worn. If possible, it should be kept for work with radioactive material but in any case must be monitored at the end of each working session. It should be kept in the laboratory.
3. Hands must be scrupulously washed and monitored after each practical class. Disposable towels should be used.
4. The radioactive sources must not be allowed to come into contact with the skin.
5. Mouth operations (pipetting, licking labels, etc.) are forbidden.
6. Protective gloves (disposable polythene are convenient) should be worn.
7. If possible, a working area should be set aside for exclusive use with radioactive sources. The most practical procedure is often to confine such work to a series of large plastic trays lined with paper towels.
8. Glassware for use with radioactive sources should be kept solely for such use and stored separately.
9. It is essential to check the quantity of radioactive materials, whether these are stored or being disposed of, at the end of a practical class.

10. It is advisable to label bottles, etc. containing radioactive material with an appropriate warning notice. The recognized symbol for radiation is a black trefoil on a yellow background. Rolls of adhesive tape bearing this symbol and the legend 'radioactive' are readily purchased from the usual laboratory suppliers.

**Asbestos**

Inhalation of asbestos is known to lead to the possibility of a number of conditions, including fibrosis of the lung tissue (asbestosis), cancer of the lung and malignant tumours of the pleura and peritoneum (mesothelioma). This last condition is specially associated with blue asbestos (crocidolite) and even low concentrations of this substance constitute a major hazard. The level of carcinogenic risk associated with white asbestos is lower but, since all forms of asbestos are dangerous, the use of asbestos and asbestos products should be avoided. A range of products is available to replace laboratory items made of asbestos. *Soft asbestos mats* may be replaced by ceramic tiles or by pieces of oil-tempered hardboard. Ceramic-centred, iron wire *tripod gauzes* can be used instead of the still-available asbestos-centred variety. Ceramic fibre wool or a mineral wool such as Rocksill offer alternatives to *asbestos wool*. Note, however, that Rocksill is made from blast furnace slag and, therefore, has a variable composition. It may contain oxidizable impurities and minor explosions have been reported on heating the mineral wool with a strong oxidizing agent such as potassium manganate(VII). Portions of a new stock of Rocksill, therefore, should be roasted strongly before being brought into general laboratory use. Ceramic fibre wool is resistant to most chemicals but is attacked by concentrated alkalis. It is available in a platinized form for use as a catalyst. Asbestos *fire blankets* should be replaced by fibre glass equivalents and, for almost all school purposes, thick, heat-resisting leather *gloves* obviate the need for gloves made of, or containing, asbestos.

In some experiments, *asbestos paper* can be replaced by ceramic paper but there seems to be no generally satisfactory substitute. Depending upon the nature of the experiment, it may be possible to heat material on a combustion spoon or a tin lid (*not* an aluminium milk bottle top) rather than on a piece of asbestos tape.

The use of asbestos in schools in England and Wales is governed by the DES Memorandum 3/86, *The Use of Asbestos in Educational Establishments* (1986). For Scotland, see SED Circular 1113, (1984).

**The labelling of chemicals**

*The Classification, Packaging and Labelling of Dangerous Substances Regulations*, together with the various Amendments and associated Statutory Instruments, require commercial suppliers to label, in a specified manner, containers used for the handling or storage of the substances prescribed by the *Regulations*. The particulars shown on a label include a maximum of two of the following hazard warning symbols.

| Harmful substances | Corrosive substances | Explosive substances | Oxidizing substances | Flammable substances | Toxic substances |

Radioactive substances are governed by other *Regulations*. Teachers, technicians, pupils and all others with legitimate access to a laboratory should be familiar with these symbols and with their significance.

Note, however, that:

1. The *Regulations* apply to commercial suppliers, not users. Those using hazardous chemicals in laboratories, therefore, are not required by law to label such chemicals in accordance with the *Regulations*. See, however, page 114.
2. The *Regulations* were not devised with educational establishments particularly in mind.
3. Suppliers are sometimes required to display different symbols or advice on containers of solutions of a substance present in different concentrations.
4. The absence of a hazard symbol or statement from a label of a container does not necessarily mean that there are no hazards associated with the contents.

In these circumstances, it seems sensible for a school to adopt a consistent labelling policy. As part of such a policy, chemicals should be clearly and appropriately labelled at all times except when they have been taken from the container for immediate use. Hazard symbols may be purchased from the usual laboratory suppliers as adhesive labels or as tape. The appropriate hazard symbol to affix to a container of a solid reagent can usually be found from a supplier's catalogue.

In the case of solutions prepared as laboratory stock solutions/bench reagents, e.g. 0.1 M sodium hydroxide, 2 M sulphuric acid or Fehling's solution, the most appropriate hazard symbol may depend upon the concentration. The suggestions of the Association for Science Education are given in Table 2.1.

**Table 2.1** ASE suggestions for hazard symbols

| Substance | Concentration[1] | Symbol[2] |
| --- | --- | --- |
| Ammonia solution | 35% or '880' | CORROSIVE |
| | 5 M or more, including 25% | IRRITANT |
| Barium salts | 0.05 M or more | HARMFUL |
| Ethanoic (acetic) | 5 M or more | CORROSIVE |
| acid | 2 M or more but less than 5 M | IRRITANT |
| Fehling's solution B | as formula | CORROSIVE |
| Hydrochloric acid | concentrated (32% or 36%) | CORROSIVE |
| | diluted but more than 4 M | IRRITANT |
| Hydrogen peroxide | 20% or more (> 70 volume) | CORROSIVE |
| Lead salts | 0.03 M or more | HARMFUL |
| Methanal | 30% or more | CORROSIVE |
| (formaldehyde) | 5% or more but less than 30% | IRRITANT |
| Nitric acid | 4 M or more | CORROSIVE |
| | 1 M or more but less than 4 M | IRRITANT |
| Potassium or | 0.25 M or more | IRRITANT |
| sodium chromate or | | |
| dichromate | | |
| Potassium hydroxide | 1 M or more | CORROSIVE |
| | 0.2 M or more but less than 1 M | IRRITANT |
| Sodium chlorate (I) | 10% or more available chlorine | CORROSIVE |
| | 5% or more but less than 10% | IRRITANT |
| | available chlorine | |
| Sodium hydroxide | 1 M or more | CORROSIVE |
| | 0.2 M or more but less than 1 M | IRRITANT |
| Sulphuric acid | 2 M or more | CORROSIVE |
| | 0.5 M or more but less than 2 M | IRRITANT |

1. The percentages given in the regulations are weight for weight. The corresponding concentrations (mol dm$^{-3}$, abbreviated here as M) are rounded up or down as appropriate.
2. i.e. the wording to be displayed on the bottle together with the appropriate hazard symbol(s).

## Plastics and polymers

The number of plastic and polymeric materials available to, and used in, schools has grown rapidly in recent years. The following points should be noted.

1. Only small quantities of plastic materials should be heated for test purposes. Polystyrene produces toxic styrene vapour on heating and PVC yields hydrogen chloride. Strong heating of acetal resins leads to the evolution of methanal and acrylic materials decompose to give methyl methacrylate (2-methylpropenoate).
2. Expanded polystyrene should be cut by a hot wire which is not sufficiently hot to cause the liberation of the toxic monomer.
3. Protective gloves must be worn whenever hot plastics, resins or adhesives are handled in the laboratory.
4. When polymerization reactions are catalyzed by peroxides, di(dodecanoyl) peroxide (lauroyl peroxide) should be used in preference to di(benzoyl peroxide) (benzoyl peroxide).

5. A number of organic reagents, e.g. trichloromethane, 1,2-dichloroethane, glacial ethanoic (acetic) acid, are commonly used to bond acrylic materials. The hazards associated with these substances are well known and appropriate precautions should be observed. Solutions of acrylic materials in ethanoic acid cause severe blistering of the skin.

6. Friction welding of acrylic materials should not be undertaken in school science workshops or laboratories.

7. Polytetrafluoroethene, PTFE, should not be overheated as this may lead to the influenza-like symptoms of 'polymer-fume fever'.

8. Methyl ethyl ketone peroxide, MEKP, is often used in conjunction with an accelerator of cobalt naphthenate to catalyze the setting of resins. MEKP and cobalt naphthenate constitute an explosive mixture. Hence, it is advisable to use resins that incorporate the accelerator and require only the addition of the MEKP catalyst.

9. The DES advises that polyurethanes should not be prepared in schools. On no account should polyvinyls be synthesized in a school laboratory.

10. The machine working of some plastics sometimes produces long filaments that can easily become entangled with the moving parts of the machine. Such filaments, therefore, must be removed before they constitute a significant hazard.

For a brief survey of the hazards of working with plastics, together with relevant advice on precautions and first aid, see Plastic and Rubber Institute, *Plastics in Schools: Safety and hazards*.

**Cracking reactions**

Some school texts suggest a procedure for converting naphtha into a fuel gas by means of a cracking reaction. In some instances, the catalyst suggested is pyrophoric. Note also that the procedure is hazardous unless all air is removed from the apparatus.

**Violent reactions**

The following list, by no means exhaustive, indicates a number of hazardous materials or mixtures which can react suddenly and violently with little or no warning.

- Strong or concentrated acids with strong or concentrated bases
- Oxidizing agents with (i) metal powders, (ii) reducing agents
- Alkali metals and/or alkali earth metals with water, acids or chlorinated solvents; consequently, neither sodium nor

potassium may be used for drying such solvents as trichloromethane (chloroform) or tetrachloromethane (carbon tetrachloride). Note that explosions have occurred when small pieces of lithium have been heated in air, particularly in conditions of high humidity

- Metal hydrides
- Hydrocarbons with halogens, 'chromic acid' or sodium peroxide
- Concentrated nitric acid–alcohol mixture (reacts only after a latent period)
- Liquid bromine

For a comprehensive, indexed guide to published data, see L. Bretherick, *Handbook of Reactive Chemical Hazards*, Butterworths, 4th edition, 1990. Also useful is The Royal Society of Chemistry, *Safe Practices in Chemical Laboratories*, RSC, 1989. Although not concerned specifically with education, Croner's *Dangerous Substances* and *Substances Hazardous to Health* (Croner publications), are both loose-leaf publications designed to incorporate monthly and quarterly updates respectively. A succinct summary is available via the *Hazcards* produced by CLEAPSS (1989 edition). Many suppliers of chemicals will provide 'hazard data' upon request.

The Health and Safety Executive Library and Information Services include public enquiry points at the Executive Offices in Sheffield, Bootle and London and via the Prestel network. For details of these and other services relevant to school science teaching, see Health and Safety Executive, *Education, A list of HSC/E Publications Relevant to Educational Establishments, 1987*.

## Solid peroxides and concentrated solutions

If peroxides enter the eyes, the probability of severe damage is so great that eye protection MUST be worn whenever peroxides are used or handled.

Strict cleanliness of equipment should be observed, great care being taken to avoid contamination by other peroxides or incompatible materials. Unused peroxides must not be returned to a stock bottle and stock must not be allowed to accumulate in store cupboards. Peroxides must not be kept in direct sunlight or near sources of heat such as radiators, fires or steampipes. In polymerization experiments, di(benzoyl peroxide) (benzoyl peroxide) should be replaced by di(dodecanoyl) peroxide (lauroyl peroxide) which is less hazardous to store and handle.

Most peroxides are decomposed by aqueous sodium hydroxide. Thus, di(dodecanoyl) peroxide may be disposed of by adding it carefully, a little at a time, to ten times its own weight of 10% aqueous sodium hydroxide. The reverse procedure should not be undertaken.

**Fume cupboards**     A fume cupboard is a container designed to prevent contamination of a laboratory, so that under all normal conditions, air should flow into the container and not out of it. In a badly designed and/or sited fume cupboard, this may not be the case.

Even when a suitable fume cupboard is available, it remains important that the quantities of hazardous reactants and products in a chemical reaction are kept to the minimum necessary for the purpose in hand.

A fume cupboard must be used whenever failure to do so would lead to a significant exposure to gases, vapours, fumes or dust that are hazardous to health. An indication of the level of risk can usually be obtained from data published annually by the Health and Safety Executive (*Maximum Exposure Limits and Occupational Exposure Standards*), although it is unlikely that those working in school science laboratories will be exposed to hazardous materials for the lengths of time to which most of the data relate. As always, good practice dictates that any exposure to hazardous materials be reduced to the minimum practicable.

The COSHH regulations require employers (i) to introduce appropriate measures to prevent or control risks to health arising from the work of their employees, and (ii) to ensure that control measures are used and that the relevant equipment is properly maintained. These requirements seem likely to focus greater attention than hitherto on the provision, use and servicing of fume cupboards in school science laboratories. Schools will need to maintain a record of the inspection, maintenance, testing and repair of fume cupboards. Testing must be done at least once every 14 months.

It is not the case that fume cupboards are needed only for work with more senior pupils. A fume cupboard is likely to be useful at some time with any science class within a secondary school, if only for demonstration experiments. Technical staff will need access to a fume cupboard, preferably in a preparation room, for preparing and disposing of noxious materials. A laboratory used for the practical teaching of chemistry at sixth-form level is likely to need at least two fume cupboards, one of which should be suitable for demonstration purposes. A fume cupboard should not be used for the long-term storage of hazardous materials. These should be kept in purpose-designed secure stores, access to which is restricted to authorized staff.

Advice on the design standards of fume cupboards is available in the DES, Architects and Building Group, *Design Note 29: Fume Cupboards in Schools* (DES, 1982) and in the relevant British Standard for Laboratory Fume Cupboards (BS 7258, 1990). The following features are of particular importance.

1. *Face air velocity.* The velocity of the air flow into a fume cupboard must be sufficient to overcome the normal flow (and its disturbance) in the laboratory in which the fume cupboard is sited. When the sash is fully raised, the minimum air velocity into the space below it should not be less than $0.3$ ms$^{-1}$ and the variation in velocity should not be greater than 30%. If this percentage is exceeded, there is a significantly increased risk that the disturbed air flow will cause hazardous material that should be contained within the fume cupboard to enter the atmosphere. Note that as the sash of a fume cupboard is lowered, there is a tendency for the air velocity to increase. This increased rate of flow can cause Bunsen flames to be extinguished. This problem is overcome by ensuring that the fume cupboard has a secondary air intake or by-pass. This operates as the sash is lowered, commonly by opening a vent at the top of the fume cupboard.

   Given the importance of the extent to which the sash is opened, it is convenient to 'stop' or lock the sash at a height that is the maximum for normal use in chemical operations. Further opening of the sash for other purposes, e.g. cleaning, then requires the unstopping or unlocking of the sash. *Design Note 29* specifies a maximum sash opening of at least 400 mm. This is likely to provide sufficient room for most operations carried out in the fume cupboard while allowing it to operate efficiently and offer an acceptable degree of protection to the operator. Another stop or lock, defining the lower limit of opening the sash, is also desirable. This prevents complete closure of the fume cupboard. In fixing this lower limit, it is necessary to ensure that operating the fume cupboard at this limit does not affect the flame of a Bunsen burner used in the cupboard. In the rare event of a failure of the extraction fan of a fume cupboard when that cupboard is in use, the appropriate course of action may be to evacuate the laboratory, rather than attempt to close the fume cupboard completely.

2. *Noise.* Noise is a much under-estimated hazard. *DES Design Note 29* advises a maximum noise level of 55 dBA. This is likely to be significantly lower than that generated by most fume cupboards currently in use in school science laboratories. Note that the axial extraction fans commonly found in school fume cupboards are much noisier than

remote centrifugal fans, and that it is often possible to reduce the noise of operation by incorporating wider ducting. See also page 48.

3. *Construction*. A fume cupboard is a container in which hazardous operations are carried out. Combustible construction materials, therefore, should be kept to a minimum and the internal surfaces of the cupboard must be resistant to heat and chemical action. The range of corrosive, toxic substances used in school science teaching is, of course, relatively restricted but the selection of the appropriate material for the working top is important. Some fume cupboards have interchangeable working surfaces but the additional expense of this feature is unlikely to be justified in a school.

Suitable materials for use in a school fume cupboard are slate, lead, glazed brick, formica, melamine resin plastics, and tiles fixed with acid-resistant cement. Of these, melamine appears the most commonly used in fume cupboards installed in recent years. The working top of a fume cupboard is normally subject to hard wear and spillages. As a result, stains quickly appear. The appearance of the working top is generally more easily maintained if the surface is coloured black or some other dark colour.

4. *Installation. Design Note 29* contains a number of recommendations about the installation of fume cupboards and these should be followed whenever a new fume cupboard is being installed. Particular attention should be given to ensuring adequate ventilation from the cupboard and a commensurate flow of air into the laboratory via a suitably-designed and appropriately-located intake.

5. *Double-sashed fume cupboards*. These seem to have little to commend them from the safety point of view. If the sashes are fitted properly with stops to prevent their complete closure, the risk of cross-flows causing hazardous materials to escape from the confines of the fume cupboard is considerable. In addition, when fitted between two rooms, e.g. between two laboratories or between a laboratory and a preparation room, a double-sashed fume cupboard enhances the risk of a fire in one room spreading to the other.

The sash mechanism, air flow and service controls of all fume cupboards should be checked regularly. Frequent cleaning of fume cupboards, both the working surfaces and the glass, is also important.

Some schools have movable fume cupboards designed to be brought into a laboratory as required. Such fume cupboards are often used for demonstration experiments carried out by the teacher, with the pupils arranged around three of the sides. The castors should be fitted with effective brakes and it should not be possible to accidentally disconnect any gas or water supplies. Venting of the fume cupboard should be via flexible ducting to a fixed outlet.

Recirculatory fume cupboards rely upon filtration and absorption to contain hazardous materials rather than upon extraction using fans and ducting. They are, therefore, much cheaper to install. However, they may not be as robust as their more familiar and conventional counterparts and not all types of recirculatory fume cupboards meet the standards suggested in *Design Note 29*. All recirculatory fume cupboards require a close and regular attention to maintenance. The 'life' of the filters will depend upon usage but might reasonably be expected to be of the order of 3–4 years in most school laboratories.

It seems likely that many fume cupboards in use in schools fall short of the desired standards. In these cases, attention should be given to improving the fume cupboards to meet the minimum face air velocity (e.g. by servicing the fan, fitting stops to the sash, cleaning the ducting system) and to 'strengthening' the glass components. This latter can be done by replacing inadequate glass with suitable protective glazing or by covering it with an appropriate safety film. Note that, when using a fume cupboard, eye protection should still be worn as long as there is any risk to the eyes. Also, a fume cupboard must not be used (i) to carry out reactions in which there is a risk of an explosion or (ii) as an enclosed sink for the disposal of undiluted hazardous liquids.

## Gas cylinders

Hazards associated with gas cylinders are of two types: (i) the physical hazards associated with the structure of the cylinders themselves, and (ii) hazards associated with their contents.

Gas cylinders vary in size from the small canisters of fuel for camping stoves to the industrial or commercial sort. The very high pressure gas cylinders may have round or flat ends and the temptation to store the latter vertically without support must be resisted. Gas cylinders must always be clamped in position or laid horizontally on the floor and wedged to prevent them rolling.

The weight of a gas cylinder may give a misleading impression of its strength. The 'weak' point of an industrial gas cylinder is the base of the valve stem and great care must be taken to ensure that the valve does not forcibly strike a hard surface. If the valve is in some way sheared off, e.g. by dropping or knocking over a cylinder, the cylinder becomes a jet-propelled missile. Particular care is needed when taking cylinders up or down stairs or steps.

Before use, the valve of every cylinder should be inspected and checked. Any loose dirt should be blown out of the seating before fitting the regulator. It is most important that the valve can be opened smoothly.

Do not allow familiarity with gas cylinders to breed contempt and so permit unwarranted liberties with them, especially with regard to the regulating valves. Most accidents with gas cylinders are due to maltreatment.

Stiff valves should be treated cautiously. It should be possible to open the valve by hand pressure using the standard key. Do not use hammers or excessive leverage, e.g. a Stilson wrench. Cylinders with stiff valves should be made safe and returned unused to the supplier with an explanatory note.

A gentle tap with a piece of wood is permissible on the wing nut which screws the pressure regulator into the cylinder head. Cylinder valves should always be tested in the open or in a well-ventilated area before being taken into a laboratory. Always blow foreign matter from the outlet before putting on the regulator valve.

Cylinders, valves, pressure reducers, gauges, etc. for combustible gases have outlets and fittings screwed with a left-hand thread. Those for non-combustible gases are screwed with a right-hand thread. All connections should be made secure by the use of such items as 'Jubilee' clips.

Never empty a cylinder completely, but leave it with a slight positive pressure (say, 2 atmospheres = 200 kPa) and the valve closed to prevent diffusion of air into the cylinder. This is especially important with flammable gases. When a cylinder is empty, mark it clearly and unambiguously. All gas cylinders should be tested periodically and, whether empty or not, returned to the supplier on a regular basis (12–18 months). In all installations the cylinder key should be made captive to the cylinder to facilitate rapid cut-off in an emergency.

Explosions have been caused by the too rapid opening of a valve resulting in compression heating in the regulator. Oxygen cylinders are prone to this type of accident. Never use grease or oil on oxygen cylinders or lines—they cause explosions. Types of cylinder gases[†] include:

(a) 'Permanent' gases, e.g. oxygen, nitrogen, carbon monoxide.

---

[†] As 'transportable gas containers', gas cylinders are subject to the *Pressure Systems and Transportable Gas Containers Regulations 1989* and the associated *Approved Code of Practice*, COP38. *Guidance on the Regulations* HSCR/30 is also available.

(b) Liquefied gases, e.g. carbon dioxide, sulphur dioxide, chlorine, nitrous oxide (dinitrogen oxide).
(c) Dissolved gases. The only example likely to be encountered is acetylene dissolved in propanone (acetone).

**Identification of gas cylinders**

The only legally recognized means of identifying a gas cylinder is the written word—colours are merely a secondary guide. Cylinders of gas for medical use are painted differently from those for industrial use. Where American cylinders are in use especial care is needed as the US colour code is completely different from the British. See also BS 5045, Part 2, 1989.

## Acetylene (Ethyne)

Only approved regulating valves may be used and no pipe fitting of copper or alloy of copper containing more than 70% copper may be used for dry acetylene, to avoid the danger of metal acetylides forming.

With moist acetylene, explosive corrosion products can result where even low copper alloys are used and traces of mineral acid enhance the formation of explosive acetylides. The pressure in any piped acetylene system should not exceed 0.62 bar g ($\equiv$62 $kNm^{-2}$) above atmospheric pressure. The system must be fitted with a flame arrester and, if other gases are involved, non-return valves must be used. Anyone wishing to use acetylene at a pressure between 0.62 and 1.5 bar g should obtain a Certificate of Exemption from the Health and Safety Executive.

The explosive limits for acetylene are:

in air          2–82%
in oxygen       2–93%

N.B. A heavy blow on an acetylene cylinder can ignite the contents as a result of adiabatic compression.

## Hydrogen

The combustion limits are:

in air          4–75%
in oxygen       4–94%

N.B. Too rapid opening of a valve can cause ignition due to static electricity.

Hydrogen is involved in a large proportion of school laboratory accidents. When lighting a jet of hydrogen, a sample must always be selected and tested to see that it is free from air before the jet is ignited. A similar testing procedure is necessary when town gas, rather than hydrogen, is used to reduce a metallic oxide. Where natural gas is supplied to laboratories, it may be necessary to use a hydrogen cylinder although some schools have adopted the practice of bubbling the natural gas through methanol or ethanol to increase the reducing property of the gas flow. In these circumstances, it is essential that all air is removed from an apparatus before attempting to ignite the gas mixture.

For a summary of safeguards in the laboratory preparation of hydrogen, see *Education in Science*, 1974, Bulletin No. 60, p. 33.

### Hydrogen sulphide

Hydrogen sulphide is an extremely toxic gas: 0.77 ppm has a faint but readily perceptible odour. The maximum permissible concentration is 20 ppm; 100 ppm paralyses the olfactory nerve so the gas can no longer be smelled; 700–900 ppm rapidly produces unconsciousness; 5000 ppm produces immediate unconsciousness due to paralysis of the respiratory centre.

Work on plants handling tonnage quantities has shown that alcohol in the system (consumed in the previous 16–24 hours) increases the susceptibility to hydrogen sulphide.

A person with a perforated eardrum should not work in areas of potentially toxic concentrations of hydrogen sulphide. Ear plugs do not give effective protection.

### Oxygen

More than half the accidents due to compressed gases are caused by oxygen. Oxygen-enriched atmospheres increase the fire risk enormously, e.g. if the oxygen content of the atmosphere is increased from 21 to 24%, clothing burns rapidly instead of smouldering.

### Propane

The explosive limits of the gas, which is denser than air, are:

| | |
|---|---|
| in air | 2–10% |
| in oxygen | 2–93% |

Cylinders of liquefied or dissolved gases must be used in a vertical position in an approved stand, or chained or clamped to the wall or bench. It is also good practice to use cylinders of 'permanent' gases in a vertical holder—they take up less floor space and the valves are less likely to be kicked.

With 'permanent' gases, the pressure indicates the quantity of gas remaining in the cylinder but with liquefied or dissolved gases the enormous variation of pressure with temperature makes weighing the best guide. The withdrawal of dissolved gases, e.g. acetylene, at more than 20% of the cylinder content per hour, entails the risk of contamination of the gas with solvent vapour.

***Aerosols***   Some laboratory reagents are now available in aerosol form, e.g. ninhydrin. Many of the substances used in aerosols are potentially hazardous. To prevent inhalation or skin absorption of these substances, aerosols should be used only in a fume cupboard or an alternative procedure, e.g. 'dipping', adopted. Aerosols should be stored in a cool place and any detailed instructions accompanying an aerosol be scrupulously observed.

***Compressed air***   Compressed air supplies in workshops and laboratories should be treated with respect—compressed air jets when misused can cause serious injuries. Compressed air can kill as swiftly as electricity. Cleaning swarf or dust from a machine should not be done with the compressed air line—use a brush or vacuum cleaner. A jet of compressed air playing on the body can introduce air into the bloodstream, especially if there are small scratches or punctures of the skin. Do not dry solvents from the skin with compressed air; both air and solvent can enter the bloodstream. Compressed air supplies to which students have access should carry a warning such as the following.

---

**WARNING**

Never direct a jet of compressed air against another person (or yourself).

Practical jokes with compressed air have caused horrifying injuries and death.

---

***Vacuum systems***   Much vacuum apparatus is constructed of glass, although more equipment made of plastics is now available, including vacuum desiccators. Glass vacuum desiccators should conform with the specifications of BS 3423, *Recommendations for the Design of Glass Vacuum Desiccators.*

When assembling vacuum apparatus examine the equipment for stresses and strains, both before and after filling the equipment. A kilogram of reagents (approximately 75 cm$^3$ mercury) can introduce severe strains in a glass apparatus. Use metal or plastic (PVC) tubing wherever possible and include flexible items in the apparatus, e.g. bellows couplings. When using ground-glass unions, ball-and-socket joints are preferred to cone-and-socket joints.

If a piece of glassware is placed between two crossed polaroid sheets in front of a lamp, areas of strain in the glass will appear darker than the rest, indicating that further annealing is necessary.

As far as possible, vacuum apparatus should be screened. Wide-bore tubing, bulbs and items up to about one-litre capacity should be strapped with cloth, adhesive tape or cellophane tape, be covered with cloth mesh and varnished (or sprayed) with PVC. Larger items should be encased in a stout gauge wire screen. Safety goggles must be used when operating with glass vacuum apparatus.

Always ensure that rubber bungs are large enough to resist being sucked into a vacuum vessel.

Ensure that stop-cocks are properly lubricated and never try to force one.

Always operate stop-cocks slowly.

## Cryogenics

Extreme cold is the principal hazard involved in the use of cryogenic systems and liquefied gases, e.g. solid $CO_2$ or liquid air. Prolonged contact with the skin may cause burns similar to those resulting from contact with extreme heat. Eye protection should be worn when handling these materials. A pad used as a pot holder is preferable to gloves.

## Mechanical hazards

The principal hazards include injuries caused by moving parts, failure of equipment, incorrect or careless use of hand tools, faulty or damaged tools, inadequate discipline, etc. Many accidents in this category can be avoided merely by the correct use of equipment that is well maintained and inspected.

All machines, whether hand- or power-operated, should be fitted with appropriate guards or other safety devices. These should always be used. Correct protective clothing and other apparel appropriate to the work should be worn. Long hair should be protected by suitably fitting head-gear, e.g. hair-nets.

### Centrifuges

These can very easily be damaged and are a source of danger when improperly used. It is good practice to secure a centrifuge to a firm base whenever it is in use.

Do not try to stop a centrifuge with the hand. The periphery of a 10-cm radius rotor at 5000 r.p.m. is travelling at over $180 \text{ km h}^{-1}$ (110 m.p.h.).

Always balance the load on the centrifuge accurately before switching on to avoid putting undue stress on the bearings.

Keep the centrifuge clean. Corrosion can seriously weaken the rotor.

Laboratory centrifuges should comply with BS 4402 (1982) and should be used only in a manner prescribed or approved by the manufacturer. Older models that do not meet this standard should be gradually replaced. For servicing purposes, a record should be kept of the amount of use a machine receives. Heads and accessories should be inspected regularly for signs of cracks or corrosion and on no account should the specified maximum load for the centrifuge be exceeded.

### Guillotines

All guillotines should be fitted with an appropriate guard.

### Wires under tension

Eye protection should always be worn when working with wires under tension.

### Air rifles

A mounted air rifle or pistol is sometimes used in experiments concerned with momentum or velocity. On no account should the alignment of the rifle or pistol be altered. The apparatus should be clamped firmly to the laboratory bench and both teacher and pupils kept behind the rifle or pistol when it is fired. Teachers should familiarize themselves thoroughly with the apparatus before using it in front of a class.

### Model steam engines

Only those with a safety valve fitted to the boiler should be used. Before use, it is essential to check that this safety valve is functioning properly.

**Protective clothing**

Appropriate protective clothing should be worn in laboratories and workshops by both pupils and teachers. To wear protective clothing is to recognize that a hazard exists. It is not an excuse for careless work. Dirty overalls or coats should not be tolerated, being in themselves a source of hazard.

Laboratory coats should be worn buttoned up. When unbuttoned and billowing about the wearer they are not only useless but a danger. These and similar items of clothing should not be allowed to hang freely, but be secured to prevent them trailing loosely over apparatus or machinery. Care should be taken in the choice of materials. Most synthetic fibres are not absorbent and, in some circumstances, compare unfavourably with cotton as a protective medium. Also, a substantial static charge can accumulate on a synthetic fibre garment. White coats are neither status symbols nor magic talismans. Leave them and their contamination in the laboratory. A range of gloves should be available for use as required in a school. Disposable gloves are appropriate for work with radioactive materials. A technician is likely to require heavy-duty gloves from time to time. For most routine washing-up procedures, domestic-quality rubber gloves are adequate.

## Eye protection

Accidents involving the eyes are the most commonly reported type of accident in school science teaching. Most, but not all of these accidents lead to no permanent damage but the case for greater vigilance in the use of eye protection is overwhelming.

Eye protection must be worn whenever there is any risk to the eyes. Pupils may be exposed to such risk as a result not only of their own practical work but also that of others, including demonstrations conducted by a teacher. As always, experimental procedures should be designed or adapted to minimize the hazards involved.

Attention is drawn to the relevant British Standard, BS 2092, (1987) and to *The Protection of Eyes Regulations*, 1974 (SI 1974/1681).

Safety spectacles and goggles should conform to BS 2092. In addition, goggles should offer resistance to chemical splashes, indicated by a letter C marked on the goggles themselves. Likewise face shields/visors should also bear the legend BS 2092 or BS 2092 C.

Safety spectacles do not provide all-round eye protection but they are perhaps more comfortable to use and easier to store than goggles or face shields. However, the spectacle lenses readily become scratched and not all types can be worn over prescription spectacles. The greater degree of protection offered by goggles, their adjustability for size and greater durability are offset by the problem of misting up and the discomfort of wearing them. Although goggles usually last longer than safety spectacles, they are usually more expensive and are a greater nuisance to wash and sterilize. The protection offered by a face shield extends beyond the eyes and such protection is easily worn over prescription spectacles. However, face shields are relatively expensive, awkward to store and need careful adjustment if they are to fit securely.

In some instances, employers have provided guidance or instruction for science teachers on the use of eye protection. In the absence of such guidance or instruction, note should be taken of the advice from the National Industry Group of the Health and Safety Executive that

(i) for most operations, safety spectacles conforming to BS 2092 are suitable,

(ii) goggles (BS 2092C) should be worn whenever there is a particular risk (e.g. working with bromine, acid chlorides, acid anhydrides, concentrated acids or alkalis), and

(iii) a face shield is appropriate whenever large quantities of chemicals are being handled, e.g. moving, opening or dispensing storage quantities of reagents such as '0.880' aqueous ammonia or concentrated sulphuric acid.

It is important that a school science department has a clear policy on the wearing of eye protection, and that this policy is understood and followed by all those (principally teachers, technicians and pupils) whom it is meant to protect. For eye protection and ultra-violet/laser radiation see page 46.

**Electrical hazards**  Electrical safety in schools is the subject of a detailed Guidance Note (GS23) issued in 1990 by the Health and Safety Executive. Attention is drawn also to the *Memorandum of guidance on the Electricity at Work Regulations* (HMSO, 1989).

Two of the worst electrical hazards are careless or unskilled workmanship and faulty or worn out equipment. Neither of these hazards needs arise.

## Plugs

Plugs should be wired as follows:

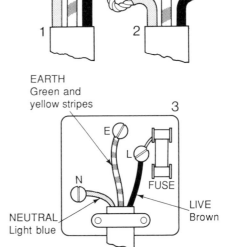

1. Trim the wires and insulation to the correct length.
2. Twist the bare ends of the wire into a clockwise loop.
3. Wrap the trimmed wires round the appropriate terminals and screw down firmly. Check that the wires are firmly gripped.
4. Fix the flex firmly by the strap so that no strain can be placed on the terminals in the plug.
5. Make sure that there are no loose strands of wire to cause short-circuits within the plug.
6. Replace the plug top.

EARTH
Green and
yellow stripes

NEUTRAL
Light blue

LIVE
Brown

Note that (i) since 1 July 1970, Great Britain and most other European countries have the following colour code, (ii) standard 13A plugs and sockets are not proof against the ingress of dirt or moisture.

*Earth*:      green and yellow     (stripes)
*Live*:       brown            (dark)
*Neutral*:    blue              (light)

This code has the advantage of being distinguishable by persons who are red/green colour blind. Electrical equipment wired using the earlier colour code is likely to be obsolete or obsolescent. If this is not the case, it should be inspected thoroughly and, if appropriate, rewired.

## High voltages

1. The electrostatic machines such as van der Graaf generators and Wimshurst machines used in schools usually generate only low currents. However, care is necessary when such machines are used in conjunction with capacitors (see below).
2. Induction coils for use in schools should not be capable of producing a current in excess of 5 mA.
3. H.T. units, capable of delivering up to 400 V d.c. may produce a current in excess of 5 mA and their use in schools should be restricted to competent staff. All leads in circuits incorporating such units should be fitted with shrouded 4 mm plugs. E. H.T. units, capable of delivering up to 5 or 6 kV must have a maximum current output below 5 mA. Equipment that does not meet this condition must not be used in schools.

    Some demonstrations require the use of high-voltage alternating current. These include the electrical conductivity of glass, striking an electric arc using mains electricty and a demonstration of a.c. transmission along model power lines using transformers. In 1987, the Health and Safety Executive drew the attention of LEAs to the risks associated with high voltages and advised that a.c. power-line demonstrations could continue if one of the following precautions, or any others of equal effectiveness, is taken.
    (a) the voltage of the transmission line is limited to 50 V a.c. r.m.s. or 120 V d.c.;
    (b) the demonstration as a whole is located within an enclosure constructed, for example, in clear polycarbonate so that live conductors operating above 50 V a.c. r.m.s. or 120 V d.c. cannot be touched; or
    (c) all conductors and terminations, etc. operating above 50 V a.c. r.m.s. or 120 V d.c. are fully insulated so that live conductors cannot be touched.

For more recent advice, see GS23 and ASE, *Topics in Safety* 1988, pp. 18–23.

Demountable transformers for use by pupils must be properly insulated and earthed. In addition, the secondary coil must be incapable of producing over 25 V at 5 mA or more.

Defective mains-operated equipment must not be repaired by pupils, and teachers should do so only if technically competent and authorized by their employer. Before any repair is undertaken, the equipment must be disconnected from the mains supply. On completion of the repair, the insulation and earth bonding of the equipment must be tested by a competent person using an appropriate testing instrument.

## *Capacitors*

All high-grade capacitors and, in particular, large energy storage capacitors as used in pulsed capacitor banks, will recover a considerable proportion of the original charging energy if left on open circuit after discharge. This phenomenon is known as the 'residual effect', 'dielectric hysteresis' or 'dielectric absorption' effect and a capacitor is said to have an 'absorptive capacity'.

Experience has shown that recovery may be as much as 10% of the original voltage, and a 30 kV capacitor may build up to 2 or 3 kV in 10 min. Further, dangerous voltages can build up on open-circuited high-voltage capacitors over a period of many months after discharge.

It has been found that a discharge of energy exceeding 10 joules into the human body can be hazardous to life, while 0.25 joule gives a heavy shock; 10 joules would be obtained by complete discharge of a capacitor charged as follows:

| Capacity ($\mu$F): | 0.002 | 0.2 | 20 | 80 | 320 | 2000 |
|---|---|---|---|---|---|---|
| Charged to (kV): | 100 | 10 | 1 | 0.5 | 0.25 | 0.1 |

It is essential that each spare or disconnected capacitor should be kept individually short-circuited by a robust connection when not in use.

It should also be remembered that 'new' capacitors have already been energized for test purposes, and should also be kept short-circuited when stored. Capacitors built into equipment which is not in use must similarly be short-circuited individually, otherwise hazard may exist when they are connected in series or if there is a circuit fault when in parallel.

It is recommended that all such capacitors should carry a label adjacent to their terminals, e.g.

---

**WARNING**
Keep short-circuited
when not in use.

---

## Mains electricity

Any teacher using mains electrical equipment in school science teaching must be aware of how to disconnect the mains power supply. Where residual current devices (RCD) or other fail-safe mechanisms are fitted, these should be tested weekly. This normally involves no more than pressing the relevant button marked 'test', 'test monthly' or 'test weekly'.

Commercially available 'test plugs' are useful in detecting a number of faults in the wiring of electrical sockets but note that they will not reveal a reversal of neutral and earth connections. On no account should teachers attempt to carry out repairs to the mains supply. Guidance Note GS 23 advises that change to fixed electrical installations should be only with the 'consent and approval of a competent person who is in overall control of the installation'.

Any item of equipment connected to a mains supply of electricity must have an appropriate earth linkage and be fitted with a suitable fuse or electromagnetic circuit breaker. Like a conventional fuse, the latter device breaks the circuit when the current exceeds the rated value but it has the advantage that it can be reset quickly. The appropriate fuse for an item of equipment connected to a 240 V mains supply is given by the following relationship.

$$\text{fuse rating (amps)} = \frac{\text{power rating} \quad \text{(watts)}}{240 \qquad \text{(volts)}}$$

Hence, for items of equipment with a power rating not exceeding 720 W, a 3 A fuse is appropriate. Fuses with a higher rating are likely to be required for such items of electrical equipment as incubators, ovens, hot plates, VDUs, slide and cine projectors and colour television sets. For any item with a power rating over 2.4 kW, a 13 A fuse must be used.

Aquaria fitted with electrical accessories (heaters, light units) present particular problems of insulation and maintenance. Good electrical wiring and connections are of the utmost importance. In lighting units, fluorescent tubes should be preferred to incandescent bulbs. Any items made of metal associated with an electrically controlled aquarium (e.g. lamp holders, aquarium hood) must be earthed. Aerators must be so placed as to prevent syphoning back or splashing of water from the aquarium. Attention is also drawn to the need to ensure (i) that an aquarium is adequately supported (when full of water, even a small aquarium is heavy), and (ii) that sheet glass used to cover an aquarium has smooth edges.

For further safety advice on aquaria in schools, see CLEAPSS, L124, *Aquaria-Electrical Safety* (1984).

### Portable electrical equipment

Portable electrical equipment, such as microscope lamps and low-voltage power supplies, is subject to considerable wear and tear. Such equipment should be tested and inspected not less than once a term. A more thorough inspection and testing, with particular reference to the earth linkage and insulation should be carried out yearly. Test sets are available from commercial suppliers but note that these sets themselves require periodic testing in accordance with the manufacturer's instructions.

Equipment bearing the following legend ▣

is sometimes referred to as 'double insulated'. It does not require an earth linkage and incorporates a double layer of insulation between the casing and any live components. In such cases, it is usually possible to do no more than check visually that the insulation has not been impaired in any way.

### Electric shock and burns

The smallest current which can be detected through the skin ('threshold of perception') is generally considered to be approximately 1 mA r.m.s. at 50 Hz a.c. and 5 mA d.c. (The tongue is considerably more sensitive.) On increasing the current a stage is reached at which severe muscular contractions make it difficult for the casualty to release his or her hold. This 'threshold of muscular decontrol' is about 15 mA at 50 Hz a.c. and 70 mA d.c.; in the lower frequency ranges the effect increases with frequency, e.g. at 60 Hz the threshold current is 7 mA. Very high frequencies do not produce this effect. Increase in current beyond about 20 mA 50 Hz a.c. or 80 mA d.c. brings danger to life. The next stage is irregular contractions of the heart, leading to cessation of the pumping action. This occurs at about 100 mA for both a.c. and d.c. and is almost certain to be fatal. If the current through the body rises as high as 1 A, severe burning results. The electrical resistance of the body can vary enormously from person to person and in the same person at different times and under different conditions. This resistance can be as high as 10 000 ohms or as low as a few hundred, depending largely on whether the skin is dry or moist. Even with a resistance of 10 000 ohms the 230 V a.c. supply will result in a current of more than 20 mA, which could be lethal.

In fact, much lower voltages can be dangerous and death has been recorded from only 60 V.

It will be appreciated that the above remarks apply essentially to current passing through the body, e.g. from hand to hand, or hand to foot. It is possible for part of the body, e.g. a finger, to short-circuit two conductors of differing potential or a charged capacitor. This will not necessarily result in electric shock as described above but it can inflict severe burns which will require medical treatment.

## Ultraviolet radiation

Ultraviolet radiation lies in the band of wavelength between 10 and 400 nm. The action of such radiation on the eye can be acute, being absorbed by the outer layers, the cornea and conjunctiva. Conjunctivitis results 4–8 days after the exposure and lasts for several days.

Ultraviolet lamps should always be properly shielded and eye protection worn if the source is exposed. No source should be viewed directly. Although ordinary glass spectacles offer protection against ultraviolet radiation of not more than 315 nm from ultraviolet lamps with clear quartz envelopes, experiments should be designed so that there is no risk of such radiation reaching the eye.

Note that an electric arc produces a large amount of ultraviolet light and is as dangerous as an open source.

## Lasers

The name 'laser' is derived from the term Light Amplification by Stimulated Emission of Radiation. Lasers are being used to an increasing extent in rapidly widening fields of application.

The very short concentrated pulse of light can cause very severe eye damage, e.g. irradiation of the cornea first kills the outer surface epithelial cells, which slough off after a few hours giving rise to an excruciatingly painful eye condition. When a light pulse from a laser system enters the lens of the eye, it is concentrated on the retina where tissue may be destroyed to give a permanent blind spot.

Animal experiments show that retinal damage begins at about $10^{-2}$ joule $cm^{-2}$ received on the retina. The focusing of parallel light by the eye lens can result in the intensity of the light incident on the retina being $10^6$ times greater than that received on the pupil. Thus, unless other special factors are operating, the maximum laser energy density at the pupil of the eye should not exceed $10^{-9}$ joule $cm^{-2}$ ($\equiv 10$ $\mu J$ $m^{-2}$, including a safety factor of 10).

Remember:

1. Any light reflecting surface will reflect laser pulses.
2. Work with lasers should be carried out in brightly lit rooms to avoid enlarging the pupils of the eyes.

3. Warning notices should be posted where lasers are being used.
4. Personnel in the area should stand behind the laser and at right angles to the proposed path of the beam before firing.
5. The danger area should be 'fenced off' and a warning notice set up.
6. All workers regularly associated with laser systems are recommended to have a periodic ophthalmological examination.
7. The laser source should be rigidly fixed so that the direction of the beam cannot be inadvertently altered.

The use of lasers in schools in England and Wales is governed by Administrative Memorandum 7/70, *The Use of Lasers in Schools*, and in Scotland by Circular 766, (1970), *Use of Lasers in Schools, Colleges of Education and Further Education Establishments*. Also relevant are *The Protection of Eyes Regulations 1974*, (SI 1974/1681), and *Radiation Safety of Laser Products and Systems—Specification for Manufacturing Requirements for Laser Products*, 1983 (BS4803, Part 2).

BS4803 provides a classification of lasers such that the use of class II lasers should not require the wearing of special protective goggles. The helium–neon lasers used in schools, having a power output of less than 1 mW, fall into this category. However, the advice of the DES and the SED remains that teachers demonstrating and students using lasers should wear special protective goggles.

Note that the wearing of goggles while working with low-powered lasers may increase, rather than decrease, the level of risk since it may be less easy to see the beam and direct it safely. Again, it is good practice to design experiments involving lasers in such a way that there is no risk of radiation entering the eyes of either students or teachers.

## Photographic darkrooms

Since much of the work done in a photographic darkroom is conducted in complete or semi-darkness, design features are of particular importance. Cupboards should be fitted with sliding rather than swing doors and materials must not be stored on the floor. The floor must be made of non-slip material and be resistant to the chemicals used in photographic processing. Proper precautions must be taken in using these chemicals which can cause skin irritation and dermatitis and many of which are toxic. They must be kept away from the skin and polythene or rubber gloves are recommended. Tongs should be used to handle the photographic material being processed.

Good ventilation, not less than eight changes of air per hour, is essential in a darkroom. Note that some colour-processing techniques require the use of a hooded fume extractor.

Where a large darkroom is to be used simultaneously by more than one worker, broad white lines should be painted on the walls at eye level to provide a guide to change of direction.

Darkrooms are normally fitted with a conventional white light to allow the room to be cleaned. This should be operated via a key switch to prevent accidental illumination of the darkroom. Safety lights should be operated by pull-switches conveniently placed in relation to the working area.

When pupils are allowed to work unsupervised in a photographic darkroom, the teacher must be satisfied that they fully understand what they are required to do, that they are properly prepared and competent to do it, and sufficiently responsible and reliable to work without immediate supervision.

## Noise

Reference has already been made to noise as a much underestimated hazard. It is well known that sudden and loud sounds can cause damage to hearing but it is not generally appreciated that continuous and prolonged exposure to quite low noise levels may produce a similar effect. Because of the gradual and insidious effect of low noise levels, impairment of hearing may be unrecognized for many years.

The effect of noise on hearing depends upon the frequency band in which the sound is being transmitted. However, chronic exposure to sound intensity 85–90 dB above the threshold of hearing on the dB(A) scale may have an adverse effect on hearing. Hence, everything should be done to reduce the level of noise in science laboratories and classrooms, consistent with safety. For example, roaring Bunsen flames should be moderated and excessively noisy fume cupboard motors should receive attention. Attention is drawn to HSE, *The Noise at Work Regulations 1989* and the associated *Noise Guides (No. 1, Legal duties of employers to prevent damage to hearing; No. 2, Legal duties of designers, manufacturers, importers and suppliers to prevent damage to hearing)*, HMSO, 1989. The *Regulations* specify three levels of action, the first two of which relate to a daily personal noise exposure of 85 dB(A) and 90 dB(A) respectively.

# 3 BIOLOGICAL HAZARDS

Work in the biological sciences raises a number of unique safety issues in addition to those associated with the use of laboratory chemicals or electrical apparatus. These include the handling and disposal of micro-organisms, the problems of maintaining and utilizing living material, the risks of cross infection, the organization of field work, and the personal nature of some biological knowledge which can cause distress in individual children.

## Microbiological hazards

Micro-organisms include protozoa, microscopic algae and fungi (yeasts and moulds) as well as bacteria and viruses. Some micro-organisms can grow only on or in other animals or plants but most are free-living.

Work with micro-organisms has become a significant component of many school courses in science and this is likely to remain so under the provisions of the National Curriculum introduced into maintained schools in England and Wales from September 1989. In addition, microbiological activity underlies work in biotechnology and informs many practices in home economics, health education, agriculture, and rural and environmental sciences.

The principal hazards of working with micro-organisms are as follows:

1. Micro-organisms which enter the body may multiply rapidly and to such an extent that the normal defence mechanisms against secondary infection become inadequate.
2. The metabolism of micro-organisms may produce toxins, some of which are highly dangerous.
3. Some micro-organisms, notably bacteria, are capable of rapid mutation to generate species which may be highly pathogenic. Thus *Staphylococcus aureus* has been shown to mutate to drug-resistant pathogenic varieties and *Serratia marcescens* readily produces strains which are resistant to antibiotics and which are associated with serious illness.
4. Individuals vary widely in their susceptibility to infection so that a particular micro-organism may pose a significant hazard to one person in a class but not to the remainder.
5. The susceptibility of an individual to infection by a particular species will vary from time to time and will be

lower immediately after illness or treatment with some drugs.

6. Some micro-organisms stimulate an allergic reaction which may be manifest by a variety of unpleasant symptoms.

7. Cultures of non-pathogenic organisms may become contaminated with other species. The fungus *Aspergillus* is a common source of such contamination and a species such as *Aspergillus flavus* is dangerously pathogenic.

It follows that all cultures of micro-organisms should be treated as potentially hazardous and that working safely with micro-organisms requires strict observance of correct procedures.

**Levels of practical work involving micro-organisms**

The DES (*Microbiology: An HMI Guide for schools and non-advanced further education*, 1985) has defined three levels of practical work involving micro-organisms. The levels are distinguished by the degree of risk associated with them and by the type of training required *before* teachers embark upon them. Note that the COSHH *Regulations* apply (page 58).

## Level 1

*Level 1* (the lowest) involves work with organisms which have no, or little, known risk. Such work can be carried out by teachers without special training in microbiological work. The organisms involved are likely to be those non-pathogenic yeasts, moulds and algae commonly associated with such everyday phenomena as plant 'rusts', fermentation and mouldy cheese or bread. It is likely that work at this level can be carried out in almost all schools. The DES advises that 'the most appropriate work will be observation and simple culturing in containers which the pupils cannot open'. Note that microbiological work involving pupils aged 5–11 years is strictly confined to this level.

## Level 2

*Level 2* involves work with appropriate culture media and incubation conditions, using organisms cultured from the environment or supplied by a recognized supplier, and involving containers which are sealed before examination. Cultures are not transferred to fresh media and must not be grown using samples taken from environments (e.g. lavatories, drains, body surfaces) likely to harbour organisms harmful to humans. Work at this level will be met in science or biology courses for pupils 11–16 years and can be carried out safely by teachers with appropriate knowledge and experience. It may be necessary to acquire this knowledge and experience at a short in-service course but competence at advanced aseptic techniques is not required. Microbiological work involving pupils aged 11–16 years is strictly confined to levels 1 and 2.

### Level 3

*Level 3* Work at this level requires good aseptic technique from both teachers and pupils and this entails training and practice beyond that provided by the minimal short course appropriate for level 2. Work at level 3 will involve 'inoculation, sub-culturing and dilution procedures using bacteria and fungi from a recognized supplier'. Examples of appropriate work include growth and inhibition studies, and the use of culture methods as an isolation technique.

**Sterilization of equipment and materials**

Proper sterilization of equipment is essential for microbiological work at any level. Some bacteria exist as spores as well as in vegetative form. The latter are killed relatively easily by heating to about 60°C for 30 minutes and are destroyed much more rapidly by boiling water. Although almost all bacteria supplied for use in schools do not normally form spores, cultures can become contaminated with spore-forming organisms, some of which may be pathogenic. Spores are much more resistant to destruction by heat or chemical agents and the conditions required for sterilization are correspondingly more severe. Commonly, these conditions involve the use of *steam* under increased pressure and at temperatures significantly in excess of 100°C. Because of the variability within species or strains, it is essential to incorporate a substantial safety margin when determining the relationship between the time, temperature and pressure required for effective sterilization using steam. The shorter the time, the higher both the temperature and the pressure required and equipment used in schools (autoclaves, pressure cookers) must be capable of meeting at least the minimum conditions of 121°C and 103 kPa, when the time needed for sterilization is 15 minutes. Note that domestic pressure cookers severely limit the amount of equipment, culture or media that can be sterilized on a single occasion. On no account should a pressure cooker used for microbiological work be used for any other purposes. Autoclaves and pressure cookers require regular inspection and proper maintenance. Particular attention should be paid to the following:

(i) *Rubber seals and gaskets.* These perish, become worn with use and may be damaged by attempts to fit a lid in the wrong position. The seating of sealing rings should also be checked.

(ii) *Safety valves.* These are designed to prevent the build-up of dangerously high pressures. They should be inspected for signs of damage.

(iii) *Corrosion.* This is likely to be a problem only with old equipment. When the interior of an autoclave or pressure cooker shows significant signs of corrosion, it should be replaced.

(iv) *The performance of the equipment.* This may be done biologically using spore strips of *Bacillus stearothermophilus* but this requires the incubation of samples and is, therefore, time consuming. A speedier and more convenient method of testing the performance of an autoclave, pressure cooker or oven uses thermal indicators. These are relatively inexpensive and rely upon a change in colour to indicate conditions. Different types of indicators are available for different items of sterilizing equipment, e.g. steam autoclaves, 'dry' ovens. Note that so-called autoclave indicator tape is not suitable as a means of assessing performance. It is intended to differentiate processed from unprocessed items in an autoclave.

When using an autoclave or pressure cooker for steam sterilization, the following are important:

(i) *The volume of water used.* This must be sufficient to prevent the autoclave/or pressure cooker from boiling dry and adequate to sustain an atmosphere of steam under the conditions required.

(ii) *The amount of material to be sterilized.* The equipment must not be overloaded and its contents must be so arranged as to permit the total displacement of air by steam.

(iii) *The displacement of air.* Steam must be allowed to escape for 2–3 minutes before the equipment is closed to the atmosphere. The timing of the sterilization process should not start until all the air has been displaced. It should not be necessary to adjust the pressure once the equipment is in use.

(iv) *A pressure cooker should not be depressurized by cooling it rapidly under running water.* It should be allowed to stand until the pressure inside the cooker has returned to atmospheric level. In the case of an autoclave, the return to atmospheric pressure can be hastened by placing it over a sink and cautiously opening the escape valve. This allows the release of the hot steam under pressure. The valve should then be closed until the autoclave is fully cooled. Attention is drawn to the *Pressure Systems and Transportable Gas Containers Regulations*, HMSO 1990.

Pipettes and other items of glassware are best sterilized by '*dry*' *heat* in an oven. The contents of the oven need to be at a temperature of 160°C for at least an hour to ensure effective sterilization. The whole process, therefore, will take much longer than this, because of the time required to warm up both the oven and its contents to the sterilizing temperature. The pipettes should be wrapped in paper or aluminium foil and placed in a suitable pipette canister.

*Chemical sterilization* offers a convenient means of dealing with spillages and contaminated equipment and of treating some cultures (e.g. yeast used for fermentation and some yoghurt bacteria) prior to disposal. It is important to use a clear phenolic disinfectant (e.g. Clearsol, Sudol) as many other 'cloudy' phenol- or cresol-based derivatives are often corrosive and toxic and may be ineffective against spores. The manufacturer's instructions should be used to determine an appropriate dilution. Chlorine-based disinfectants have the disadvantage that the chlorine concentration decreases with storage. For this reason, clear phenolic agents are to be preferred. In making up any sterilizing solution, it is advisable to wear gloves and other protective clothing. Chemical sterilization should not be used in preparing equipment for micro-biological work.

*Ultra-violet radiation* should not be used in an attempt to sterilize glassware or other items of equipment.

**Techniques and precautions**

Correct technique is of paramount importance when working with micro-organisms. The following general precautions should be strictly observed.

1. Hands must be washed before any work is undertaken, before leaving the laboratory while the work is in progress, and when the work has been completed. Warm water and soap are generally adequate for this purpose. All exposed grazes or cuts must be protected by sterile, waterproof dressings.
2. All 'hand-to-mouth' operations are prohibited, including the moistening of labels with the tongue and the use of mouth-operated pipettes. Cultures can be labelled using self-adhesive labels, spirit-based pens or wax pencils.
3. Wherever possible, cultures should be incubated at ambient temperature rather than at 37°C which tends to encourage the selection of organisms adapted to human body temperature. The organisms listed on page 57 will grow satisfactorily at 25°C or below. The DES advises that 30°C 'should be the upper limit for school work'.
4. Laboratory benches should be swabbed with a clear phenolic disinfectant before being used for micro-biological

work. Such work should not be carried out close to a source of draughts, e.g. windows, doors, Bunsen flames. Personal belongings must be kept off all working surfaces.

5. Culture media designed to encourage the growth of pathogenic organisms should not be used in microbiology. Examples are McConkey's agar, blood agar and the corresponding broths. Most microbiological work in schools is likely to use media of relatively high acidity or salinity or which lack organic supplements.

6. A laboratory coat or other appropriate form of protective clothing should always be worn when preparing and handling media. All such clothing should be left in the laboratory at the end of a microbiology class and appropriate arrangements made for proper storage and systematic laundering.

7. Microbiological materials must not be placed in a refrigerator used for storing food.

8. Cultures of particular organisms must always be obtained from a reputable supplier. Culturing from the environment brings added risks and these must be contained when carrying out work at levels 2 and 3. On no account should an attempt be made to culture organisms from such sources as drains, lavatories, animal cages, blood or faecal matter.

9. Where stock cultures are maintained, a sub-culture must be plated out and examined for signs of contamination before the rest of the stock is used for further work. If there are signs of mixed growth in the sub-culture, the stock must be sterilized, discarded and replaced by fresh material. Very few schools are likely to have the facilities required to maintain and store cultures adequately on a long-term basis.

10. The inspection of cultures by pupils working at levels 1 or 2 is confined to closed containers that have been sealed before examination. The examination of appropriate micro-organisms (see below) by routine sub-culturing and microscopic techniques may be carried out only by students working at level 3.

11. Aerosols are perhaps the commonest means of contamination in micro-biological work and their formation can be prevented only by proper aseptic procedures. If a culture is to be centrifuged, plastic centrifuge tubes are to be preferred to glass and these must be capped. Loops or wires used for inoculation must be sterilized before use by heating in a hot Bunsen flame. The spluttering of an inoculating loop during flame sterilization may be avoided by dipping the loop into 70% aqueous ethanol and drain-

ing it against the side of the container before inserting into the flame. The mouths of McCartney bottles, culture tubes, etc. must be flamed when removing and replacing plugs or caps. Such plugs or caps must be kept off all unsterilized surfaces. Care is also needed to prevent aerosol formation when disposing of any condensation in a Petri-dish culture by pouring it into a suitable disinfectant.

12. After inoculation, all plates must be sealed with tape and clearly labelled to indicate the date and identity of the inoculum. The base and lid of a Petri dish should be taped diametrically but a complete seal must be avoided since this would generate anaerobic conditions and encourage the growth of pathogenic organisms. Note that the DES advises that 'The microbiology carried out in schools should not require the use of a transfer cabinet provided that good aseptic technique is practised.'

13. After inoculation, Petri dishes should be incubated in an inverted position to prevent any condensation from collecting upon the micro-organisms. Condensation problems suggest that the medium was too hot when poured. If the agar is cooled to 50–55°C before pouring and the paired plates are incubated overnight before use, condensation problems are likely to be minimal.

14. All contaminated material must be sterilized before disposal or, where appropriate, re-use. The safest procedure involves autoclavable plastic bags. Non-disposal glassware, with any caps loosened or removed, can be placed in one bag and disposable items, such as plastic Petri dishes, in another. The bags must not be tightly sealed before being placed in the autoclave. A loose wire tie is adequate. This is then tightened before the sterilized bag and contents are disposed of. This may be done by incineration or, less satisfactorily, via the normal system for refuse collection. The sterilized contents of Petri dishes must not be washed down a laboratory sink. Sterilized glassware should be washed before being stored. It will require renewed sterilization before being re-used for microbiological work.

15. The spillage of a culture on to a laboratory bench or floor may lead to the formation of a contaminated aerosol. To minimize the hazard, the spillage should be covered with a cloth or paper towel freshly soaked in a suitable disinfectant (see above). The disinfectant should be allowed to remain in contact with the spillage for at least 10 minutes before all the material is gathered into a suitable container, using disposal gloves and swabs. The container

and the contaminated material should be autoclaved or placed in a suitable disinfectant for 24 hours before being disposed of. Spillage on clothing can be treated with a clear phenolic disinfectant of the appropriate concentration. Seriously contaminated laboratory clothing must be disinfected before it is cleaned by conventional methods.

All spillages should be reported to, and dealt with by, teachers and it is good practice to keep a record of all such incidents.

16. No experiments which involve the deliberate contamination of a pupil should be performed. (The DES permits an exception to this rule, namely the handshaking experiments using *Saccharomyces cerevisiae*.)

## The choice of micro-organisms

A number of micro-organisms suggested for use in recent school projects are now considered unsuitable for use. The following species, together with any non-indigenous plant pathogens, must not be used in school microbiology.

*Aspergillus nidulans*
*Aspergillus niger*
*Chromobacterium violaceum*
*Clostridium perfringens (welchii)*
*Penicillium chrysogenum*
*Penicillium notatum*
*Pseudomonas aeruginosa*
*Pseudomonas solanacearum*
*Pseudomonas tabacci*
*Serratia marescens*
*Staphylococcus aureus*
*Xanthomonas phaseoli*

The following is a list of selected micro-organisms 'drawn from recent science teaching projects which present minimum risk given good practice'. It is taken from DES, *Microbiology: An HMI Guide for schools and non-advanced further education* (HMSO, 1985). Note (i) that it is not a definitive list so that other organisms may be used if appropriate advice is taken, (ii) that strains of the species of fungi referred to can differ physiologically and, therefore, may not give the expected results and, (iii) that the DES publication includes a large number of suggested topics for school microbiology courses.

### Bacteria
*Acetobacter aceti*
*Agrobacterium tumefaciens*
*Bacillus subtilis*

*Chromobacterium lividum*★
*Chromatium* species
*Erwinia carotovora* (=*E. atroseptica*)
*Escherichia coli*[†]
*Lactobacillus* species
*Micrococcus luteus* (=*Sarcina lutea*)
*Photobacterium phosphoreum*
*Pseudomonas fluorescens*★★
*Rhizobium leguminosarum*
*Rhodopseudomonas palustris*
*Spirillum serpens*
*Staphylococcus albus (epidermidis)*★★
*Streptococcus lactis*
*Streptomyces griseus*
*Vibrio natriegens* (=*Beneckea natriegens*)

## Viruses

*Bacteriophage* (T type) (host *E. coli*)
Cucumber Mosaic Virus
Potato Virus X
Potato Virus Y (not the virulent strain)
Tobacco Mosaic Virus
Turnip Mosaic Virus

## Fungi

*Agaricus bisporus*
*Armillaria mellea*
*Botrytis cinerea*
*Botrytis fabae*
*Chaetomium globosum*
*Coprinus lagopus*
*Fusarium solani*
*Fusarium oxysporum*
*Helminthosporium avenae*
*Mucor hiemalis*
*Mucor mucedo*
*Myrothecium verucaria*
*Penicillium roqueforti*
*Phycomyces blakesleanus*
*Physalospora obtusata*
*Phytophthora infestans*

★This species replaces *Chromobacterium violaceum* and *Serratia marcescens*.
†Some strains have been associated with health hazards. Reputable suppliers will ensure that acceptable strains are provided.
★★These organisms have been known to infect debilitated individuals and those taking immunosuppressive drugs.

*Pythium debaryanum*
*Rhizopus sexualis*
*Rhizopus stolonifer*
*Rhytisma acerinum*
*Saccharomyces cerevisiae*
*Saccharomyces ellipsoides*
*Saprolegnia litoralis*
*Schizosaccharomyces pombe*
*Sclerotinia fructigena*
*Sordaria fimicola*
*Sporobolomyces* species

## Algae, Protozoa, Lichens, Slime moulds

Though some protozoa are known to be pathogenic, the species quoted for experimental work in the recent science projects, together with the species of algae, lichens and slime moulds quoted, are acceptable for use in schools.

---

*The importance of seeking advice about the use of micro-organisms other than those included in the above list cannot be over-emphasised.* Apart from minimizing any risks, the list perhaps excludes some micro-organisms that are safe to use and which teachers would wish to use in their courses. Advice can be obtained from the Microbiology in Schools Advisory Committee (MISAC).

**The assessment of risk**

The *Control of Substances Hazardous to Health Regulations* apply to the use of micro-organisms in schools. It is necessary, therefore, for teachers to assess the degree of risk presented by such organisms as used in schools. However, the range of work involving micro-organisms in schools is likely to be wide so that straightforward 'rules' governing risk assessment are of limited use.

The HMI guide to *Microbiology* (HMSO, 1985) indicates types of microbiological work appropriate to pupils at different stages of their education. The various practical activities are linked to the various levels of work (1 to 3) to which reference has already been made above. (Note that these three levels of work are not the same as the 'categories of hazard and containment' identified in the first report of The Advisory Committee on Dangerous Pathogens.) For almost all the routine microbiological work undertaken in schools, the associated risks can be assessed by reference to the HMI guide. In other cases, as when innovative practical work, perhaps involving unfamiliar procedures and/or micro-organisms is being contemplated, a more formal and systematized assessment of risk is appropriate. For significant changes in the practical teaching of microbiology in schools, this risk assessment may involve seeking expert, external microbiological advice, perhaps with the assistance of an LEA adviser. In all cases, the determination of the level of risk will depend upon answers to questions such as the following.

(i) Which micro-organism(s) are to be used? Are they among the species categorized as 'appropriate' in the HMI guide? If not, is it necessary to seek expert advice? Are the micro-organisms to be taken directly from the environment? If so, what is the nature of that environment and what is the advice available?

(ii) What is the source of micro-organisms to be used? Is it a recognized supplier? Is it the environment? (If so, see comments under (i).)

(iii) What culture medium or media are to be used, e.g. a common foodstuff such as bread, a simple nutrient agar, a liquid medium? What are the risks associated with the proposed medium or media and what advice is available?

(iv) At what temperature is incubation to take place, given the advice available about incubation at temperatures of 37°C or above?

(v) What is the likelihood of contamination arising from the proposed procedures?

(vi) What is the scale (e.g. Petri dish, test tube, McCartney bottle, jam jar, small scale pilot fermenter) of the proposed microbiological work?

(vii) Where is the proposed work to be carried out and, more particularly, what does this imply for the containment of any hazard? Also, will the work involve, for example, cultures with removable lids, cultures that will be sealed throughout until disposal or cultures that will be closed after inoculation and sealed after incubation?

(viii) What are the levels of knowledge, experience and competence of all those associated with the proposed work (i.e. teachers, pupils, technicians)? Are these levels appropriate for the proposed work?

For an elaboration of risk assessment along these lines see ASE, *Topics in Safety*, Association for Science Education, 1988, Chapter 5a.

**Biotechnology**

Most of the risks arising from the development of biotechnology in schools are those associated with the longer established teaching of physics, chemistry and biology. It follows, therefore, that legislation, regulation, advice, prohibition and precautions relevant to the latter are likely to apply to the teaching of school biotechnology. Thus, in assessing the risks associ-

ated with any proposed biotechnological activity, it is appropriate to refer to the relevant HMI advice about the use of micro-organisms in schools. Information is also available from The National Centre for School Biotechnology, at the University of Reading, Reading RG1 5AQ. See also *Education in Science*, January 1988.

However, biotechnology may involve the growth of micro-organisms on a relatively large scale, e.g. in a fermenter. As always, micro-organisms must be obtained from a reputable supplier, and proper procedures and aseptic techniques adhered to in preparing, inoculating and culturing micro-organisms and in the subsequent treatment/disposal of cultures/ferments and equipment. Attention is also drawn to the following:

(i) Fermentation vessels must be properly vented to allow the gaseous product(s) of the fermentation to escape. In some cases, e.g. the fermentation of silage, the gas produced (mainly methane) is flammable.

(ii) When inoculating a fermentation medium, the volume of the live inoculum should be a significant proportion (10–15%) of the volume of the medium. This ensures that any contaminant introduced during the inoculation will have to compete for survival with an already established organism.

(iii) Some fermentation vessels have mains and other electrical connections. These must be kept away from water and inspected regularly for signs of wear.

(iv) Equipment should not be left running out of school time unless it is designed for continuous use and incorporates an appropriate fail-safe device. It is good practice to attach a suitable notice, similar to that which may be reproduced from Education Service Advisory Committee, *Educational Establishments—Unattended Operation of Experimental Apparatus Outside Normal Working Hours* (Health and Safety Commission, 1986).

(v) When a spillage of micro-organisms occurs on a large scale, with a correspondingly large risk of aerosol formation, the laboratory should be evacuated immediately. Steps can then be taken to contain, sterilize and dispose of the spillage.

(vi) Because of possible allergic reactions, antibiotic-producing organisms should not be cultured in schools.

Among other hazards associated with school work in biotechnology are the following:

(i) *Enzymes.* Enzymes can cause severe irritation of the eyes or skin and produce distressing allergic reactions. They should be handled carefully and precautions taken to prevent aerosol formation and skin contact.

(ii) *Plant 'hormones'*. These are more correctly referred to as plant growth substances and are normally used in low concentrations. However, many such substances are toxic and their use requires appropriate precautions.

**Genetic modification**

The regulations governing work involving genetic modification require, among much else, registration, notification and the establishment of a local safety advisory committee (Health and Safety Commission, *Genetic Manipulation Regulations 1989: Guidance on Regulations*, HMSO, 1989). In addition, HMI advise that 'No attempt should be made in schools and colleges to practise the techniques of genetic engineering and induction of bacterial mutation.' Although genetic 'engineering' can be distinguished from genetic 'modification', it is clear that schools should not undertake laboratory work involving those techniques referred to by HM Inspectorate. The advice, however, does not seem to preclude some familiar practical activities which illustrate some of the basic genetic, biochemical or microbiological principles of 'genetic engineering', provided that these do not involve (i) bacterial mutation or (ii) the transfer of nucleic acid and the transmission of the new characteristics from one generation to another.

**School laboratory animals**

Over one hundred diseases of animals are known to be transmissible to man so that the maintenance of living animals in a school poses a health hazard as well as considerable organizational problems such as cleaning and feeding during the school holidays.

Animals must be kept in hygienic cages or aquaria which are of the correct design and size. School stocks of animals must be obtained from a reliable source. Animals kept in schools should not be 'boarded out' to domestic premises during the school holidays.

Although the importance of zoonoses must not be over-emphasized in the school context, it is important to remember that animals are liable to infection which could be passed on to pupils by bites, scratches, ectoparasites or the inhalation of contaminated aerosols, dust or droplets.

The most common diseases which can be contracted are probably salmonellosis (*Salmonella typhimurium* and *S. enteriditis*), staphylococcal infections and ringworm (*Trichophyton* sp.). Wild animals, dead or alive, must not be used for school work since they may well harbour zoonoses. This is especially true of rats, which may harbour, for example, ratbite fever (*Spirillum* sp.), Weil's disease (*Leptospira* sp.) and *Salmonella* sp., of rodents in general and of pigeons and hedgehogs. Many birds are susceptible to ornithosis (psittacosis), a disease which is transmissible to humans and often fatal. Abattoir material also needs to be used with care because of the possibility of infection with *Salmonella*.

The following, therefore, *must not* be kept in schools:

 (i) all native wild mammals, especially hedgehogs and rodents;
 (ii) all imported wild mammals, especially primates such as monkeys;
 (iii) all species of native wild bird;
 (iv) all members of the parrot family (e.g. parakeets, macaws, love-birds, budgerigars and parrots);
 (v) all crocodiles, alligators, terrapins and tortoises and poisonous reptiles;
 (vi) all species of mammalian parasite.

Attention is also drawn to the risk of infection of humans, especially children, by *Toxocara canis* and *Toxocara cati*, nematode parasites found in the faeces of infected dogs and cats, respectively. Human toxocariasis is difficult to treat satisfactorily so that hygiene and preventive control measures are of particular importance. Untreated milk carries the risk of brucellosis. Ticks on deer can transmit Lyme disease.

Animals kept in schools must not be housed in a room used for microbiological work. Note that animals can also be infected by humans, e.g. the mumps virus is transmissible from humans to dogs and cats.

For advice on handling and maintaining animals in schools see DES (1971), Schools Council (1974), UFAW (1978, 1987) and W. F. Archenhold, E. W. Jenkins and C. Wood-Robinson, (1978). A list of accredited breeders and suppliers is available from the Laboratory Animals Breeders Association, c/o Bantin and Kingman, Grimston, Aldborough, NU11 4QE, or from The Universities Federation for Animal Welfare, 18 Hamilton Close, South Mimms, Herts. EN6 3QD.

On no account should animals kept as pets be used for dissection nor should animals bred for dissection in a school be allowed to become pets. All animals, or parts of animals, used for dissection must be free from disease and the number to be dissected should be the minimum consistent with the achievement of the educational aims. In most instances of work with pupils up to the age of 16 years, dissection by the teacher, rather than by the pupils, is likely to be adequate and consideration should always be given to the use of specimens, models and other aids to supplement, or as a partial substitute for, dissection. A list of suggested alternatives to dissection is available from The Royal Society for the Protection of Cruelty to Animals (RSPCA, 1984).

When dissection of whole animals is undertaken, pupils and teachers must be fully aware of the hazards presented. It is also good practice to encourage discussion of the ethical, aesthetic, educational and scientific implications of such work. In general, recently killed or freshly-frozen animals are to be preferred to animal cadavers that have been chemically preserved.

For a helpful statement on the place of animals in education, issued jointly by The Association for Science Education, The Institute of Biology and The Universities Federation for Animal Welfare, see *Biologist*, Vol. 33, No. 5, 1986, pp. 275–8. See also Dixon, 1988.

Note that schools cannot be designated appropriate places in which licensed persons may carry out work covered by the *Animals (Scientific Procedures) Act 1986*, which came into force in January 1987. The Act, which applies to animals in the wild as well as those in captivity, regulates procedures applied to a vertebrate that 'may have the effect of causing that animal pain, suffering, distress or lasting harm'. The Act, therefore, forbids such activities in schools as pithing a frog (or other vertebrate) or work with embryonic or larval stages of mammals, birds and reptiles once half the normal gestation or incubation period has elapsed. This latter protection is extended to 'any other case' (fish and amphibia) once an embryo or larva has become capable of independent feeding. Under the Act, therefore, work with chick embryos beyond the stage of mid-development is forbidden in schools. Codes of practice and other advice arising from the Act will provide further guidance for schools. See also *SSR*, 71, 255, 1989, pp. 74–5.

The provisions of the more general *Protection of Animals Act 1911* remain in force.

**Field work and educational visits**
The organization of field work poses a number of problems for the teacher. Clearly, different problems arise if the work is to be conducted at a centre some distance from the school and over a period of several days. But whatever the nature and duration of the work, it is essential to know the individual capabilities of the pupils involved, especially those with special educational needs, and to be fully aware of all the hazards that the field environment, in the broadest sense of the term, presents. A preliminary visit by the teacher to the site of any field work allows note to be taken of any natural or other hazards and, if appropriate, to estimate the significance of any likely changes in the weather. Such a preliminary visit should be given a high priority.

Any field trip or visit should be recognized as an official school function, and approved in accordance with any procedures and regulations laid down by a local authority or governing body. The necessary approval is likely to depend upon satisfactory answers to such questions as the following about aspects of the proposed out of school activity:

(i) Its location, duration and educational purpose
(ii) The likely major hazards associated with the activity
(iii) The arrangements for transport, finance and insurance
(iv) The size and composition of the groups of pupils involved, including details of pupils with special educational needs, disabilities or requiring regular medication
(v) The qualifications and relevant experience of the staff involved, and the responsibilities of the leader
(vi) The staff–pupil ratio
(vii) The emergency procedures, including contact address(es)
(viii) The procedures for obtaining informed parental consent

Note that from 1 April 1989 charges may be made by maintained schools for some strictly defined out-of-school activities, mainly those which are optional and take place outside school hours. Even when charges may not be made for school-time activities, parents or others can be invited to make voluntary contributions towards school funds or in support of a specific project. For details, see DES Circular 2/89. Note also that in some cases, the costs of insurance may be delegated as part of a statutory scheme of local management of maintained schools. In all cases, it is good practice to examine carefully the extent of the insurance cover provided, and, in particular, to note any exclusion clauses.

For most outdoor activities, a 'recall procedure' is essential and the recall signal must be fully understood and obeyed promptly by all members of a group. Precise and unambiguous instructions for a rendezvous are also necessary and each member of a group must be told, in advance, what to do if he or she becomes separated from the main party and 'lost'. Adequate first-aid equipment is essential. However, note that a trivial accident on a lonely moorland or mountain site causes much greater disruption than a similar incident in the classroom or laboratory; and, in these circumstances, a teacher is unlikely to have access to expert medical help should this be required. Some Local Authorities require teachers in charge of out-of-school visits to hold a recognized first-aid qualification but every teacher in charge of a group of pupils must possess basic first-aid skills. These include the care of wounds and the control of bleeding, a technique for artificial respiration, the treatment of shock and the transport of an injured or sick person to a place where professional medical help is available. For advice on first aid, see Chapter 5.

Teachers contemplating out-of-school activities are strongly urged to consult the publication by the DES, in association with the Scottish Education Department, the Welsh Office Education Department and the Department of Education, Northern Ireland, *Safety in Outdoor Education*, HMSO, 1989.

Attention is drawn below to some common situations in which personal injury may be sustained if proper precautions are not taken.

### *The exploration of rough country and steep slopes*

Upland and mountain terrain should be treated with respect. What appears an innocuous slope in warm sunshine can, within an hour, be converted by a sudden weather change into a death trap for the unprepared.

Before setting out, ensure that *everyone* is fit enough to undertake the exercise, is properly equipped, has a reserve of warm clothing and some emergency rations and that someone in the party has a map, compass and first-aid kit.

Do not risk being benighted on a mountain, and have a whistle or an electric torch (with fresh batteries) to signal with in case you miscalculate distances or time. In general young persons are physiologically and psychologically less resilient than healthy adults and a suitable safety margin must be allowed. A particular pitfall to avoid is the confusion of muscular development with physical fitness for a particular exercise. Suitable preparation might include simulation or practice exercises.

People living in lowland or urban conditions must be taught that torrent-tracked streams can rise very rapidly in level, bringing down rock as a result of heavy rain in the upper catchment areas. Camping sites should take account of this fact.

Beware of falling rocks and try to avoid dislodging stones: there may be someone below you. A small stone has a lethal momentum after it has fallen a few hundred feet.

Glaciers, rock faces, mines, caves, open water etc. should be attempted ONLY under an experienced leader and after suitable training exercises.

For detailed advice on the preparation for, and conduct of, such activities, see DES *et al.*, *Safety in Outdoor Education*, HMSO, 1989.

### Seaside locations

Marshland and tidal saltings should be traversed only after taking local advice. The tide comes in over many salt marshes almost as fast as an adult can run.

### Living in tents and caravans

Ensure that fire buckets are filled and placed at strategic points and that sanitary arrangements conform to the highest possible standards of hygiene. In particular, attention must be given to the siting of latrines and the disposal of waste and rubbish.

### Forest and heath areas

In forest and heath areas and where agricultural crops are ripening, take particular care to avoid starting fires, e.g. by carelessly discarded cigarette ends, inefficiently extinguished camp fires, etc.

### Walking in narrow lanes

In narrow country lanes, do not straggle in the roadway: the motorist is not expecting you or your pupils near the crown of the road. If walking on the roads at night or at dusk cannot be avoided, the leader and rearguard of the party should wear distinctive clothing and carry appropriate lights.

### Industrial visits

Many schools now arrange for their pupils industrial visits of a day or half-day's duration. In addition, it is increasingly common to find pupils, individually, or in small groups, spending much longer periods of time in industry as part of a programme of 'work experience' or a schools industry link scheme. In all these situations, it is essential to determine and agree, in advance, the allocation of responsibility for the supervision of pupils at all times and to ensure that everyone involved is fully aware of the hazards presented by the industrial environment and of the safety rules devised to contain them. Note that there are legal restrictions on the employment in industry of pupils below the statutory school leaving age and that it may be necessary to arrange special insurance cover to protect such pupils participating in work-experience schemes.

### Urban fieldwork

The risks associated with outdoor activities in cities and towns should not be underestimated. Apart from the hazards associated with road traffic, risks to safety are present in many urban locations, e.g. canals, rivers, construction sites, derelict or disused buildings and railway lines. Pupils must be made aware of the hazards they might encounter before undertaking field work in any urban setting. They should also be warned how to deal with any approach from a stranger. Adequate arrangements must be made to monitor the group and to cater for any emergency, including pupils getting lost in an unfamiliar part of a city or town.

***The personal nature of biological knowledge***

In the biological sciences, some teaching situations can cause emotional distress to individual pupils. It is the teacher's responsibility to prevent such situations from arising. Stressful incidents include distress (even fainting) at the dissection of a freshly killed animal and the individual upset of a child discovering that he or she is adopted or illegitimate as a result of class studies of inheritance of eye colour.

Many physiological experiments will actually involve the pupils themselves and great discretion is needed in publicly discussing individual variations within a class. The use of pupils as the subjects of experiments raises complex legal, as well as moral and educational, issues. Where such experiments involve procedures beyond the normal everyday experience of pupils, teachers must explain fully the precautions to be taken and must ensure pupils understand the reasons for them. The following guidelines should be observed.

1. No pressure must be brought to bear upon a pupil to urge him/her to become the subject of an experiment.
2. No chemical should be swallowed.
3. The advice of a School Medical Officer should be sought before conducting any experiment which involves the tasting of any substance other than conventional foodstuffs or a common substance, e.g. sodium chloride, known to be safe in the quantities to be used. Note that the tasting of phenylthiourea (phenylthiocarbamide) or PTC involves a number of hazards. Paper strips, containing no more than 0.1 mg of PTC, should be used and no pupil should be allowed to taste more than two strips. The strips must not be taken out of the laboratory and pupils must not have access to the solid or a stock solution which should be kept in a locked poisons cupboard.
4. Medical advice should also be sought before undertaking any experiment involving an unusual degree of physical or physiological stress. Particular attention should be given to the needs of epileptic or asthmatic pupils. The ASE advises that

   Any pupil who is medically excused normal school P.E. activities should not take part in investigations on the effect of exercise on respiration, pulse rate, the operation of the temperature-regulating activities of the body etc.

Care should be taken in the method of taking breath samples for analysis: teachers should be aware of the possible consequences of forced breathing and holding of breath and should know of the first-aid measures required. Care should always be taken to avoid situations in which competition between members of a group may have unfortunate consequences.

Note that rhythmical impulses of sound or light from electronic or stroboscopic experiments can be dangerous, especially for epileptics.

5. Because of the spread of AIDS, the DES has strongly advised that blood and cheek cells must not be taken from pupils (or teachers) in schools. This advice should not be ignored, although the Institute of Biology has suggested that cheek cell sampling, using cotton buds and taking proper precautions, can still be undertaken without significant risk.

Cells scraped from the tracheal lining of pigs and lambs, offer an acceptable alternative to human cheek cells. They can be stained in the usual way using methylene blue. A piece of clear sellotape pressed on to a clean wrist may also yield cells that are convenient for microscopic examination.

Fresh animal blood from an abattoir is a satisfactory, if less convenient, source of blood cells than human blood, and offers no risk of transmitting the HIV virus held responsible for AIDS. 'Expired' human blood, obtained from the Blood Transfusion Service will have been screened both for the HIV virus and for the virus responsible for serum hepatitis.

Any blood used in school science teaching, whether obtained from an abattoir or from the blood transfusion service, should be handled using an appropriate sterile procedure. As a minimum, this will ensure that there is no risk of the blood coming into contact with the skin, and will require strict hygiene and the sterilization of all contaminated equipment after use by means of a clear phenolic disinfectant.

6. Prior parental consent is generally advisable for all experiments involving pupils as the subjects of experiment. However, it should be recognized that a pupil is unlikely to become involved in such an experiment with a full knowledge of the possible hazards and the DES comments that 'teachers may consider it advisable to avoid all such experiments with pupils below the age of 16 years'.

7. On no account should an experiment be performed which involves the deliberate contamination of a pupil with micro-organisms.

8. On no account should any experiments be conducted or demonstrated in which drugs or other means are used to influence the mental state of a pupil or teacher and teachers are strongly advised not to perform experiments involving the use of an electroencephalograph to study 'biological feedback'.

9. Although the HIV virus has been isolated from human saliva, there is no evidence that the virus can be transmitted in this way. However, it is obviously good practice to ensure that, in the course of science teaching, teachers, pupils and technicians do not come into contact with saliva other than their own. Pupils, therefore, should clean their own glassware after use. Technicians engaged in a subsequent washing of the glassware should wear gloves.

## Abnormal susceptibilities of individuals

### Haemophilia

Teachers must be informed, at the earliest opportunity, of any pupil who suffers from haemophilia.

### Colour blindness

All persons working in a school should ensure that they are aware of any abnormality in their colour vision. If any abnormality exists, it should be reported to the teacher who may need to take steps to overcome resulting difficulties.

### Epilepsy

Teachers or pupils in their charge who suffer from epilepsy are not barred from working in laboratories and, with proper treatment, most lead a full and normal life. It is, however, essential that the teacher be aware of any such disabilities and knows how to deal with an attack suffered by one of his/her pupils.

Note that an epileptic attack can be induced by the use of stroboscopic lighting of a critical frequency. The phenomenon is imperfectly understood but teachers must be aware of this hazard and take appropriate precautions where necessary.

A major fit can be frightening in appearance, especially to anyone seeing an attack of epilepsy for the first time. Keep calm and remember that the first requirement is to prevent the victim from self-injury. Do not restrain convulsive movements but gently guide the victim away from hard objects on which he/she could suffer injury. Loosen the tie, collar or other tight clothing and cradle the patient's head in the arms. If an opportunity arises, gently insert the corner of a clean, folded handkerchief between the victim's teeth so as to prevent the tongue and lips from being bitten.

There are approximately 100 000 children in Britain who have epileptic disorders. Of these, some 60 000 attend ordinary schools and are more likely to suffer minor rather than major attacks of epilepsy. These minor attacks are of three types, although a child can have more than one type of epilepsy.

*Minor motor seizures.* These are characterized by involuntary movements of any part of the body, e.g. an arm, finger or an entire side. These seizures may last for a few seconds only but may also develop into a major epileptic fit ('grand mal').

*Petit mal.* These attacks are often very difficult to detect in the classroom or laboratory situation. A pupil may have a vacant or blank stare, may stumble, have a brief 'black-out' lasting for a second or so or simply be unable to hear what is being said to him/her. Petit mal attacks may occur many times during the course of a school day.

*Psychomotor attacks.* These are manifest by behaviour which is suddenly irrational or inappropriate to the circumstances, e.g. a pupil may smack his/her lips repeatedly or get up and run around the laboratory. When the attack has passed, the individual will not know what has happened during the seizure.

Further information and advice is obtainable from the British Epilepsy Association (3–6 Alfred Place, London WC1E 7ED), which publishes a helpful leaflet entitled *A Teachers' Guide to Epilepsy.*

## Allergy and hypersensitivity

The skin may be adversely affected by contact with chemical reagents which cause an allergic reaction. Although only a small proportion of the school population will be susceptible to any particular allergen, individual instances are none the less distressing. Allergic reactions are often associated with biological materials. The coats of laboratory animals, *Primula* and *Pelargonium* sp., grasses and some fungi have all been cited as sources of allergens. The giant hogweed, *Heracleum mantegazzianum,* has sap containing a substance which in contact with the skin and in sunlight causes exaggerated sunburn reaction. The stem, leaves, flower heads and sap of daffodils, hyacinths, jonquils, narcissi and tulips may act as irritants causing painful lesions on the fingers. The cowslip, *Primula veris,* has been known to cause dermatitis and the common houseplant *Primula obconica* has pollen and glandular hairs which contain an irritant poison. Many members of the ivy family, especially the poison ivy, *Rhus toxicodendron*, are known to contain an irritant sap.

Advice on animal allergens is given in HSC, *What you should know about allergy to laboratory animals*, HMSO, 1990. Note that the COSHH *Regulations* apply to allergens.

An individual may be hypersensitive to substances in the vapour, liquid or solid state and a number of compounds can cause dermatitis if brought into contact with some skins. The compounds which are most frequently responsible for dermatitis belong to the following groups: hydrocarbons, chlorinated hydrocarbons, nitrochlorohydrocarbons and phenols. Such individuals must take special precautions, e.g. wear protective gloves or use suitable barrier creams.

Note that exposure to a substance of biological or chemical origin, even in a dose as low as $10^{-9}$g, may cause serious damage to body proteins. Such a small, initial 'sensitizing' dose may produce no observable effects but subsequent exposure to an even smaller 'challenging' dose can cause a virulent reaction and severe tissue damage. 'Cross-sensitization' of the skin is also possible, i.e. exposure to one substance may render the skin susceptible to challenging doses of a larger number of chemically-related materials.

1-Bromo-2,4-dinitrobenzene is a powerful contact sensitizer sometimes used in school science teaching and, as with the corresponding chloro- and fluoro-derivatives, precautions against skin contact, inhalation and ingestion are essential. In general, however, the use of such substances in schools should be avoided. See page 142. Attention is drawn to the recommendation of the DES that

teachers should not use chemicals with which they are unfamiliar, especially biochemicals, unless they have been given authoritative advice about them. Such advice can be obtained from the Regional Medical Services Adviser of the Department of Employment.

## Pesticides

Insecticides, fungicides and weedkillers are three classes of substance likely to be found in school biology laboratories, in greenhouses or in sheds associated with the teaching of agriculture, horticulture, rural science or environmental science. Many of these substances are very toxic in higher than recommended concentrations and, for some, e.g. paraquat, there is no known antidote. All such substances, therefore, must be securely stored, adequately labelled and properly used.

Until recently, almost all pesticides supplied for sale within the United Kingdom were approved under the Pesticides Safety Precautions Scheme, a voluntary agreement between the agrochemical industry and the government. This scheme has now been replaced by the statutory *Control of Pesticides*

*Regulations 1986.* Those Regulations (SI 1986/1510) govern the storage, sale and use of all pesticides. Approval under the *Regulations* involves specification of where and when a pesticide may be used, the maximim quantity to be applied, the time that must elapse between treating and harvesting a crop, and the protective clothing that must be worn during the application. The *Regulations* also provide that this information must appear on product labels, and require that the user follows the stated instructions.

Some pesticides, or a given pesticide in a particular concentration, may be used only by those working in the agriculture, horticulture, forestry or related industries. On no account should these materials, intended for industrial use, be used by science teachers or others in ordinary schools. Work with pesticides in schools should be confined to products prepared and sold specifically for domestic, rather than commercial, use and, therefore, readily available from, for example, garden centres. Details of most of the products sold within the UK are available in the *Directory of Garden Chemicals*, available from The British Agrochemicals Association, (4 Lincoln Court, Lincoln Road, Peterborough, PE1 2RP). Note that (i) a particular pesticide may be the essential ingredient of several different formulations, sold under different trade names, (ii) some insecticides contain anticholinesterase reagents and that some people may be medically advised not to risk exposure to compounds of this type and (iii) some local authorities have banned the use of particular pesticides in schools.

To ensure that the conditions governing the use of pesticides are strictly observed, these substances in schools should be used only by teachers or other adults, or, in appropriate circumstances, by mature students under strict supervision. (It should be noted that in the agricultural contexts, the relevant Code of Practice (*Preventing Accidents to Children in Agriculture*) provides that a person under the statutory school leaving age 'should not be permitted to handle, use or be exposed to any pesticide or any toxic, corrosive or flammable substance'.)

Pesticides must not be stored alongside seeds or other types of garden chemicals, such as fertilizers. Clear labelling, including hazard information, is of particular importance. Diluted solutions prepared from stock should not be stored but made up, in appropriate quantities, as required. On no account should pesticide solutions be transferred to soft drinks bottles. Pesticides in aerosol form may be disposed of via the normal refuse arrangements. No attempt must be made to puncture or incinerate aerosol containers. *Small* quantities of 'domestic' pesticides may be disposed of after dilution by pouring down an outside drain. When the quantity to be disposed of is not small, or the school is not connected to a mains drainage system, advice should be sought from the Local Education Authority before undertaking disposal.

Seeds supplied to schools are occasionally dressed with a protective coating of fungicide/insecticide. Such seeds should not be handled unnecessarily by teachers, technicians or pupils and, wherever possible, untreated seed (e.g. from a Health Food shop) should be used. If it is essential to work with treated seed, much of the coating can be removed by thorough washing before and after an overnight soaking in water. Treated seeds must never be used for animal or human consumption. Hands and other exposed skin must be washed after handling any treated seeds.

Note that plants or other material collected 'in the field' may contain or be coated with toxic pesticide or other material. Even though the risk of significant contamination is small for most of the year, appropriate precautions should be taken in handling material collected from the field. Fumigation of greenhouses or animal houses must be carried out in strict accordance with the manufacturer's instructions. Fumigants intended for professional use are generally inappropriate for school use and should be avoided. Note that the COSHH *Regulations* apply to the use of fumigants.

**Poisonous plants**   Poisoning by plant material is usually associated with younger pupils, although cases of older children being poisoned in this way have been reported.

The range of toxic plant material is much greater than is commonly realized although, in some cases, only part of a plant may be dangerous, and the hazards associated with some garden plants are not as widely recognized as they should be. Table 3.1, on page 74, lists some of the more common toxic species of plant material.

**Table 3.1** Common toxic plant species*

| Common name | Botanical name | Poisonous parts |
|---|---|---|
| **Garden flowers** | | |
| Aconite (winter) | *Eranthis hyemalis* | All |
| Christmas Rose | *Helleborus niger* | All |
| Foxglove | *Digitalis purpurea* | All |
| Iris (Blue Flag) | *Iris versicolor* | All |
| Larkspur | *Delphinium ajacis* | Foliage and seeds |
| Lily of the Valley | *Convallaria majalis* | All |
| Lupin | *Lupinus* sp. | All |
| Monkshood | *Aconitum anglicum* | All |
| Narcissus (Daffodil, Jonquil) | *Narcissus* sp. | Bulbs |
| **Garden vegetables** | | |
| Potato | *Solanum tuberosum* | Green sprouting tubers and leaves |
| Rhubarb | *Rheum rhaponticum* | Leaves |
| **Shrubs and trees** | | |
| Broom | *Cytisus (Sarothamnus) scoparius* | Seeds |
| Cherry laurel | *Prunus laurocerasus* | All |
| Laburnum (Golden Rain) | *Laburnum anagyroides* | All |
| Rhododendron | Species: *Azalea* (American laurel, Mountain laurel) | Leaves and flowers |
| Yew | *Taxus baccata* | All; seeds lethal |
| Snowberry | *Symphoricarpus albus* | Fruits |
| **Hedgerow plants** | | |
| Black Nightshade | *Solanum nigrum* | All |
| Buttercups | *Ranunculus* sp. | Sap |
| Deadly Nightshade | *Atropa belladonna* | All |
| Privet | *Ligustrum vulgaris* | Berries |
| Thorn Apple | *Datura stramonium* | All |
| **Marshland plants** | | |
| Hemlock | *Conium maculatum* | All |
| Hemlock, Water Dropwort | *Oenanthe crocata* | All |
| Kingcup, Marsh Marigold | *Caltha palustris* | Sap |
| **House plants** | | |
| Castor Oil Plant | *Ricinus communis* | Seeds |
| Dumb Cane | *Dieffenbachia* sp. | All |
| Hyacinth | *Hyacinthus* sp. | Bulbs |
| Poinsettia | *Euphorbia pulcherrima* | Leaves and flowers |
| **Woodland plants** | | |
| Cuckoo Pint (Wild Arum) | *Arum maculatum* | All |
| Mistletoe | *Viscum album* | Fruits |
| Oak | *Quercus* sp. | Fruits and leaves |
| Poison ivy | *Rhus toxicodendron* | All |
| Toadstools | *Amanita muscaria* *A. pantherina* *A. phalloides* | All |

* For fuller details, see: Altmann, 1980; Forsyth, 1980; Nonis, 1982; Woodward, 1985.

# 4 FIRE

There are three essential factors, sometimes called 'the fire triangle', which must be present before a fire can break out: remove one of these three factors and the fire will go out. The control of these three essentials is the basis of all fire prevention and control. The three essential factors are:

1. A source of *fuel*.
2. *Oxygen*, usually from the air but also from certain chemicals, to act as a *support medium*.
3. *Heat* sufficient to bring the fuel to a temperature at which sustained combustion can be initiated (the ignition temperature).

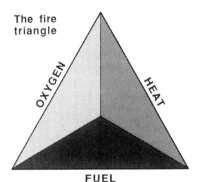

The fire triangle

OXYGEN   HEAT

FUEL

Fire is a self-sustaining combustion process which takes place in the vapour phase, producing heat and smoke or incandescence or all three. If the heat generated raises the temperature sufficiently, non-flammable materials may decompose and in doing so produce noxious or toxic decomposition products and perhaps lead to structural collapse. Solids usually need to be heated to a point at which they give off flammable vapour before they will ignite but many organic solvents are sufficiently volatile to give off flammable vapours and be a fire hazard well below normal air temperatures (see notes on refrigerator fires, page 76 and page 86).

Below the self-ignition temperature of a combustible mixture a source of ignition is normally necessary to initiate combustion. The nature of the chemical processes involved is such that ignition may result from an extremely short burst of energy, e.g. an electric spark.

**General precautions against the outbreak of fire**

1. *Control the potential fuel supply*
This may be done by the selection for use of non-flammable materials, materials of low combustibility, fire-proofed materials, etc. or by limiting the amount of flammable materials in any specific location which has not been designed and designated for their storage.

2. *Limit the supply of oxygen (air)*
Positive limitation of oxygen as a means of fire prevention is normally available only in industrial or laboratory situations. The exclusion of the oxygen support medium is, however, an important fire-extinguishing method. Keep fire stop doors closed. Do not leave them fixed open. Fire stop doors limit the flow of air to a fire.

3. *Heat limitation*
Care in preventing the overheating of combustible materials is a fundamental fire precaution. Any form of intense radiant heat whether direct or as a result of the focusing effect of an intermediate transparent object should be avoided. Overloading of electrical circuits leads to overheating and fire risk as does the careless use of smoking materials.

**Laboratory fire-risk reduction**

Solvent supplies in laboratories should be kept to a minimum, preferably not more than will be needed during the current working day. Not more than 500 cm$^3$ of any one volatile, flammable liquid should be kept in bottles on laboratory benches or shelves and all such bottles must be clearly labelled 'Highly Flammable'. Solvent bottles should never be left unstoppered.

Solvents not required during the current working day should be kept in the departmental solvent store.

Solvents not in immediate use should be kept in a specially designed solvent storage cupboard.

Used solvents should be placed in the waste solvent container(s) for recovery or disposal. These solvents should be collected and put in a safe place daily.

Solvents must not be put down the drain. A leaflet *Storage and Use of Highly Flammable Liquids in Educational Establishments* is available from the Health and Safety Executive.

### Refrigerator fires

Solvents must not be placed in refrigerators in open containers. Explosive concentrations of vapour/air mixtures can form from very small amounts of solvent, which may be ignited by sparks from micro switches and thermostats. New refrigerators for laboratory use should have all spark sources placed outside the cold chamber.

**Types of fire fighting equipment**

Fire fighting equipment must be sited so as to be immediately available at all times and must not be moved to less accessible positions or be obstructed or hidden.

### Water extinguishers
### Colour code: red

This group extinguish by the cooling action of the water. Hose reels are normally connected to the mains supply, which is turned on as the hose reel is unwound.

In an automatic hose reel there are three water control valves:

(i) a main stop-cock which is normally locked in the open position by means of a leather strap;
(ii) a main control valve, within the axle of the hose reel, which opens when the hose is unreeled, and
(iii) a manual control valve on the nozzle.

*Important.* After use, the hose should be rewound by turning the reel until the main valve is closed. This may leave some hose still unreeled. Wind this on by hand. DO NOT FORCE THE REEL or permanent damage to the expensive main control valve will result.

*Soda acid.* These extinguishers have now been withdrawn from use in the United Kingdom.

*Carbon-dioxide expelled water.* These extinguishers usually contain 2 gallons of water expelled in a jet when a built-in cylinder of carbon dioxide is punctured. (This jet cannot be turned off.)

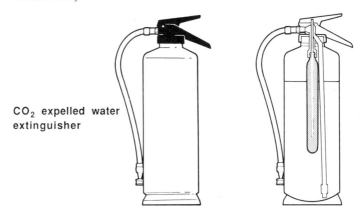

$CO_2$ expelled water extinguisher

### Foam extinguishers
### Colour coded: yellow

Foam extinguishers contain aqueous solutions of foaming agents which mix and react to produce large amounts of stable

 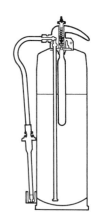

Foam extinguisher

foam. A 2-gallon (9 litre) extinguisher produces about 14–16 gallons (130–140 litres) of foam. (They cannot be turned off.) This group acts mainly by excluding air from the fuel and there is some slight cooling effect. Foam extinguishers are being replaced by AFFF equipment (aqueous film forming foam).

### *Carbon dioxide extinguishers*
### Colour code: black

This type acts by excluding oxygen. Being denser than air a blanket of carbon dioxide ($CO_2$) gas forms over the fuel. There is no cooling effect.

Carbon dioxide extinguishers consist of a cylinder containing carbon dioxide at high pressure. The cylinder is fitted with a plastic horn to direct the jet of gas. Note that the hand *must not* be in contact with the horn when in use. The jet of gas is extremely cold and freezes water vapour in the air causing ice to form on the horn. (The white cloud formed consists of ice crystals and solid carbon dioxide.) This type has a very short duration of action and is trigger operated.

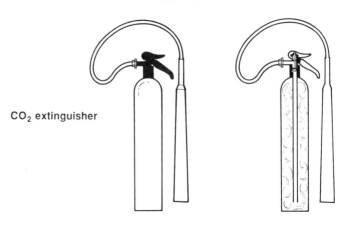

$CO_2$ extinguisher

Note that in a draughty location, a carbon dioxide 'cover' can be blown away with a resulting danger of re-gnition.

### *Vaporizing liquid extinguishers*
### Colour code: green

This type of extinguisher acts in a similar manner to the carbon dioxide type but is more effective due to the higher density of the vapour. It is not recommended for use indoors.

The contents of this type of extinguisher are released by a trigger mechanism. The vapour is inert but can decompose at high temperature, particularly when catalyzed by contact with certain metals, to give highly irritant and corrosive fumes. The most common liquid is BCF (bromochlorodifluoromethane), one of the halogenated hydrocarbons implicated in the damage to the ozone layer.

### *Powder extinguishers*
### Colour code: blue

This type of extinguisher acts mainly by covering a fire in a layer of inert powder and thereby excluding the support medium. A wide range of powders is available, designed for specific types of fire.

*Dry sand.* This can be applied by shovel from a sand bucket.
*Dry chemical.* The powder is expelled from the extinguisher by carbon dioxide (as with a carbon dioxide–water extinguisher).
*ICI–Monnex powder.* This acts not only by covering the fire but by adsorbing free radicals and thereby interrupting the chain reactions sustaining the fire.
*Ternary eutectic mixtures (TEC).* These are formulations for use on metal fires and are designed to form fused crusts over the metal.

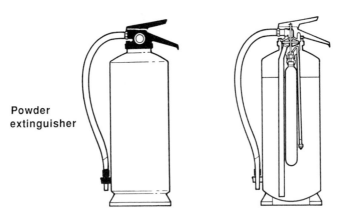

Powder
extinguisher

### Blankets

Non-combustible blankets can be used to smother small fires mechanically, usually in association with a carbon dioxide extinguisher. The most common material is woven fibre glass which is light in weight, flexible and allows the blanket to be cleaned after use. Less common materials are fire-proofed wool or leather.

**Classification of fires**

The appropriate method of fighting a fire depends upon the class to which the fire belongs. The wrong choice of extinguisher can intensify a fire and/or endanger the fire fighter, e.g. by producing highly toxic fumes or causing the fire to flare up.

Fires are classified (BS.EN 2:1972) as follows:

*Class A* Fires involving solid materials, normally of an organic nature, in which combustion generally occurs with the formation of glowing embers.
*Class B* Fires involving liquids or liquefiable solids.
*Class C* Fires involving gases or liquefied gases in the form of a liquid spillage, or a liquid or gas leak.
*Class D* Fires involving metals.

Note that electrical fires do not constitute a class since any fire involving, or started by, electrical equipment must be a fire of Class A, B, C or D. For advice on dealing with electrical fires, see page 83.

**Choice of extinguisher**

### Class A fires (Paper, wood etc.)

Water is the best extinguishing agent, from either a hose-reel or a carbon-dioxide expelled water extinguisher. The hose-reel is to be preferred as the supply can be controlled.

Soda acid extinguishers are an effective if obsolete altern-ative but can do damage to property by staining and corrosion due to the effect of the acidic residue. However, any of the other types of extinguisher may be used if a water extinguisher is not available.

### Class B fires
### (Fats, oils, solvents etc.)

Depending on the size and location of the fire the following extinguishers may be used:

(a) a fire blanket;

(b) a carbon dioxide extinguisher or, if appropriate, a vaporizing liquid extinguisher (BCF);

(c) a combination of (a) and (b);

(d) a foam extinguisher, directing the jet to the back of the fire and working forward towards the operator;

(e) a powder extinguisher, working from the periphery to the centre of the fire.

**WARNING**: DO NOT USE ANY WATER EXTIN-GUISHER ON CLASS B FIRES. If a water extinguisher is used the burning liquid will float on the water and spread out, thus intensifying the fire as a result of the increase in surface exposed to the air. Flash evaporation of the water may cause the fire to erupt violently.

### Class C fires
### (Gases, liquefied gases)

A foam or dry chemical powder extinguisher can be used to control fires involving shallow liquid spills. If gas cylinders are at risk from the heat of a fire, they may be cooled by spraying with water. Rubber tubing to gas burners should be inspected each term for signs of deterioration and particular care must be taken to ensure that all connections are secure and leakproof.

### Class D fires
### (Metal)

A metal fire is a strongly exothermic reaction, usually with oxygen, but also with any suitably reactive gas, in which the heat of reaction raises the temperature of the metal to incandescence. The more finely-divided the metal, i.e. the greater the surface-to-mass ratio, or the more reactive the metal, the greater the fire risk. Many metals which are of commercial use in the massive state are a hazard when in the powdered or finely-divided form. Also many metals at high temperatures can react, explosively sometimes, with halogenated hydrocarbons, nitrogen, carbon dioxide or steam, thus limiting severely the available means of combating metal fires.

There are two basic methods of dealing with a metal fire:

(i) treating the reacting metal as a heat sink and controlling the subsequent fires due to ignition of other flammable materials, allowing the metal reaction to go to completion;
(ii) blocking the chemical reaction at the metal surface by cutting off the supply of support reactant, e.g. oxygen, using a suitable powder extinguisher.

Conventional extinguishers should not be used against metal fires. An appropriate dry powder should be kept available with a suitable means of application. Powdered talc, soda ash, limestone and dry sand are normally suitable for Class D fires. Special fusing powders are available for fires involving some metals, especially those which are radioactive.

N.B. Some metals when burning emit very dazzling light and coloured goggles should be kept at hand. Others, notably cadmium and mercury, produce highly toxic vapours when heated.

## Electrical fires

First of all, switch off the power (the source of heat). Then, if necessary, use a carbon dioxide or vaporizing liquid extinguisher (BCF). Do not use water or foam because of their electrical conductivity. Remember that even if electrical equipment, e.g. TV set or refrigerator motor, is switched off, an electrical condenser can still administer a dangerous shock.

Powder extinguishers should only be used as a last resort; it is almost impossible to remove the finest powder from complicated equipment, e.g. switches and relays, during salvage operations.

REMEMBER: Although the primary task is to extinguish the fire, the planning of fire precautions should always take into account salvage of the damaged items. A residue-free, non-corrosive extinguishing agent is always to be preferred, particularly where delicate apparatus or materials may be present.

## Action on discovering a fire

Circumstances must dictate whether attacking a fire with portable first-aid fire-fighting equipment should take priority over summoning the fire brigade, raising the alarm, etc. Clearly it is undesirable to allow a small fire to obtain a hold through summoning outside help but on the other hand it is dangerous to delay calling for assistance in dealing with any outbreak which may not be quickly extinguished by immediate personal action. Any fire which threatens to block an exit from a laboratory is to be regarded as very serious.

A fire should be attacked as soon as possible, provided that there is no personal danger in doing so. If attempts to extinguish the fire cannot be continued without danger, or if they are clearly failing to keep the fire in check, the fire-fighter(s) should withdraw immediately and await the assistance of the fire brigade, having first checked that no-one is trapped. Any doors and windows that can be closed should be closed.

**WARNING.** Asphyxiant, irritant and toxic gases, smoke and fumes are a greater hazard to life than heat burns, especially in laboratories. Many plastic materials and cleansing fluids when heated give off highly noxious fumes. Carbon monoxide may be present when dealing with a fire in a confined space. Beware also of the danger of re-ignition, especially of Class B fires. Carbon dioxide or BCF vapours have little cooling effect and, if the blanket of inert vapour is displaced by air, re-ignition of the hot vapour may occur. In the case of foam or powder blankets, a similar hazard may also arise due to disturbance of the layer but this is less likely than with vapours.

### Raising the alarm

This may be done verbally or by operating the installed system. In the case of a minor fire it may only be necessary to warn people in the immediate vicinity. The school fire alarm should only be sounded as a signal that the premises are to be evacuated, i.e. if the fire is spreading rapidly, if smoke is spreading in substantial amounts, or if stairways and other escape routes are threatened.

### Action on hearing the alarm

When the alarm sounds, everyone should WALK quickly from the building via the nearest available exit and then go to the agreed assembly point. Most schools clearly indicate the fire exit routes from each of the rooms in the buildings.

At the assembly point, a teacher is responsible for ensuring that no-one in his/her charge is left in the building. It is not sufficient merely to call a roll, since this would not necessarily account for visitors, persons temporarily absent from the school or those pupils who had not yet arrived at the class from another lesson. It is up to every teacher to satisfy him/herself that none of his/her immediate colleagues, pupils or visitors are unaccounted for.

DO NOT USE LIFTS AFTER AN ALARM HAS SOUNDED: Lift shafts can act as chimneys or become smoke-logged. A power failure would result in the lift occupants being trapped.

## General fire hazards

### Reactive chemicals

Highly reactive chemicals, particularly strong oxidizing agents, should not be placed in waste bins where enough heat can be generated to bring about combustion. Fires due to a spontaneous combustion in waste bins are more common than is generally realized and, as they may occur during the night, are particularly dangerous.

Burns and scalds can be received from a variety of sources, e.g. burners that have blown back, non-luminous flames, hot glass, tripods, solvent fires, clothing set alight, overheated electrical equipment and electrical flash. All burns should receive medical or first-aid treatment.

Burners should be in a physically stable position, protected from draughts and remote from flammable materials, especially organic solvents. Rubber tubing should be in good condition and protected from radiant heat.

NEVER HEAT FLAMMABLE LIQUIDS WITH A NAKED FLAME.

### Electrical equipment

Faulty electrical equipment, including the failure of electrical cut-outs, thermostats, etc. is one of the most important causes of major fires in laboratories. See Guidance Note GS23 (p. 41).

Electrical and electronic apparatus can initiate fires due to the overheating of cable and components or by arc or spark discharges. Electric heaters and soldering irons can be a source of danger. Overheating is generally caused by allowing a component to pass a higher current than that for which it is rated. Ensure that circuits are correctly fused. In more permanent installations cut-outs are to be preferred.

If an electric motor is stopped mechanically with the current flowing overheating will occur. Fires can result from the inadvertent obstruction of fan blades. Voltage dropping resistors require adequate ventilation to prevent overheating and the danger of ignition of flammable gases and vapours by sparking should not be overlooked.

Static electricity can ignite flammable atmospheres. Charges can accumulate on metal drums from which non-conducting liquids, e.g. organic solvents are being drawn. A spark of considerable energy can be generated. The danger can be avoided by earthing the bare metal surface of the drum.

The most important precaution in avoiding electrical fires is ensuring high standards of craftsmanship when wiring up circuits and apparatus. Never use temporary expedients.

### Flammable liquids

*The Classification, Packaging and Labelling of Dangerous Substances Regulations* (1986, 1988) define a flammable liquid as one with a flashpoint between 21°C and 55°C. The flashpoint is defined as the minimum temperature at which the vapour of a liquid gives rise to an explosive mixture with air. A liquid with a flashpoint below 21°C is categorized as highly flammable. This latter definition differs from that in *The Highly Flammable Liquids and Liquefied Petroleum Gases Regulations* (1972) which define a highly flammable liquid as having a flashpoint below 32°C. In addition *The Petroleum (Consolidation) Act 1928* is based upon a flashpoint of 22°C in respect of hydrocarbons derived from petroleum.

As far as schools are concerned, it seems sensible to store any liquid supplied with either the label 'Flammable' or 'Highly Flammable' as though it belonged to the latter category as defined in *The Highly Flammable Liquids and Liquefied Petroleum Gases Regulations*.

A number of commonly used organic solvents possess characteristics which combine to produce a high degree of fire hazard. Depending on the contents, a Winchester bottle of flammable solvent if overheated to bursting point can produce a fire-ball 4–6 feet in diameter with a surface temperature in the range 700–900°C. It is for this reason that bottles of solvents should be kept in suitable storage cabinets.

Flammable solvents should not be placed in refrigerators unless they are in vapour tight containers. Refrigerators which have not been specially modified contain several sources of ignition, e.g. a thermostat, a light or a micro-switch to operate the light.

The flashpoints of some common organic liquids are given in Table 4.1.

Vapour–air mixtures are easily ignited. A 200 μJ spark from a static discharge or a small dry battery short-circuit can be

**Table 4.1**   The flashpoints of some common organic liquids

| | | | |
|---|---|---|---|
| Benzene | −11°C | Ethoxyethane | −45°C |
| Bromoethane | −20°C | Ethyl ethanoate | −5°C |
| Butanal | −7°C | Heptane | −1°C |
| Butanone | −6°C | Hexane | −28°C |
| Carbon disulphide | −30°C | Hex-1-ene | < −20°C |
| Cyclohexane | −20°C | Methanol | +10°C |
| Cyclohexene | −60°C | Pentane | −48°C |
| Diethylamine | −18°C | Petroleum, crude | <32°C |
| Ethanal | −38°C | Petroleum ether (40/60) | −51°C |
| Ethanol | +13°C | Propanone | −18°C |

sufficient. Many solvent vapours can be ignited by hot surfaces. Carbon disulphide is especially dangerous since its
vapour can be ignited by contact with the surface of a steam
pipe or a hot electric light bulb. Ethoxyethane (diethyl ether)
has a self-ignition temperature of only 179°C. Note that
high-density vapours can creep along floors and benches for
several metres generating a flammable and/or explosive train.

When keeping solvent vapours in confined spaces, e.g.
refrigerators, the following points should be borne in mind:

1. The small percentage of vapour required to render an
   air–vapour mixture explosive: for ethanol, propanone, ethoxyethane and carbon disulphide, the required percentages
   are 2.3%, 2.1%, 1.2% and 1.0%, respectively.
2. The small quantity of liquid which can produce enough
   vapour to form an explosive mixture even in a large en-
   closure. The evaporation of 5 cm$^3$ of benzene can produce
   an explosive atmosphere in a chamber 3 ft$^3$ ($8 \times 10^4$ cm$^3$) in
   volume, e.g. a drying oven or refrigerator.

Spark-free refrigerators should be specified for laboratory use.
Refrigerators should be modified, when purchased, to remove
spark sources from the cold chamber.

## Piped gases

It is important to ensure that gas taps on the mains supply are
always turned off properly when not in use. Make sure that
pilot lights are not inadvertently extinguished whilst being
supplied with gas.

## Cylinder gases

Where cylinders can safely and conveniently be kept out-of-
doors, a proper cylinder store should be constructed. The
station/store should be secure, well ventilated and protected
from the worst of the weather.

If only short pipe runs are needed it is preferable to keep
cylinders in the open air and pipe the gases to the point of use.
Great care is needed to ensure that the correct materials only
are used, e.g. acetylene must not be piped through copper or
over silver-soldered joints. Clear and accurate labels must be
provided on the pipe runs.

Only cylinders in immediate use should be kept in laboratories. Before introducing any gas cylinder into a laboratory or
workshop the valve should be tested.

Great care is needed when using propane, butane, LPG and
other heavier than air flammable gases. Any leaks from faulty
valves or joints fall to the floor and can travel long distances

undetected. Many severe explosions have resulted from leaks of heavier than air gases. For relevant *Regulations*, see page 34.

### Oxygen-enriched atmospheres

All fire hazards are considerably increased in oxygen-enriched atmospheres. Apart from leaking oxygen cylinders the use of cryogenic liquids can result in the build up of oxygen in atmospheres around Dewar vessels. If liquid oxygen is being used the atmosphere around the Dewar may become oxygen enriched. Liquid nitrogen, although non-flammable, can condense oxygen from the atmosphere. When liquid nitrogen traps have been in continuous use, care should be taken when the residual liquid evaporates from the Dewar. The nitrogen will evaporate first leaving any oxygen behind.

### Solvent storage and handling

Solvent cupboards must be air-tight, lockable and made of fire-resisting material which is a poor conductor of heat. Arrangements for the storage of flammable liquids in maintained schools are usually established by the Local Education Authority. Note that the *Petroleum (Consolidation) Act 1928* was not designed with schools in mind and is applicable only when 13.6 litres (3 gallons) of hydrocarbons derived from petroleum are to be stored.

The dispensing of a flammable solvent from a stock bottle should be carried out away from the solvent store and over a metal tray large enough to contain any spillage. Stock bottles of 1 litre or more capacity should be carried using a bottle carrier. For guidance on storage, see *Storage and Use of Highly Flammable Liquids in Educational Establishments*, (Health and Safety Executive.)

Before treating any spillage, ensure that there are no sources of ignition and provide adequate ventilation. Small spillages are conveniently dealt with by absorption in a suitable 'inert' powder (e.g. expanded vermiculite), followed by transference, using a dustpan and brush, to a large quantity of water in a bucket. In some instances, it is necessary to treat the spillage with an appropriate quantity of a suitable detergent before adding the absorbent powder.

**Action**

1. Make yourself THOROUGHLY familiar with the detailed fire orders exhibited in your particular work place. It is too late to start reading instructions when a fire has broken out.
2. At all times know the location of the nearest fire appliances, breathing sets and respirators APPROPRIATE to the materials with which you are working.

## *Fire fighting*

Discretion is essential in deciding the lengths to which first-aid fire-fighting is carried. Portable fire-fighting equipment is not designed to cope with extensive fires and it is important that first-aid fire-fighting should cease and the location should be evacuated as soon as the fire threatens the means of escape or the building structure, or gets out of control. Although further action might reduce material losses, no such saving can compare in importance with human safety.

When fighting a fire remember:

1. Use the correct fire extinguisher. In a laboratory the wrong choice can turn a minor incident into a major disaster.
2. Do not use vaporizing liquid (e.g. BCF) or similar extinguishers where there is poor ventilation unless you are wearing breathing apparatus. The vapours are toxic.
3. Carbon dioxide extinguishers should be used with care. They can reduce the oxygen content of the atmosphere in a confined space to a dangerously low level.
4. A fire needs oxygen to burn but YOU need oxygen to breathe.
5. A respirator is only effective when fitted properly and only absorbs limited amounts of toxic vapours. It DOES NOT supply oxygen and is not suitable for use in high smoke areas.

# 5 FIRST AID

The statutory requirements in respect of the provision of first aid by employers are consolidated as *The Health and Safety (First Aid) Regulations 1981* (SI 917, 1981) and the associated *Code of Practice* and *Guidance*. The essential features of this provision are discussed on pages 98–9.

The *Regulations* relate to all those employed in schools and colleges. Although pupils and students are not normally so employed, employers (Local Education Authorities, governors) have a continuing duty to provide for them and for any visitors.

## The purpose of first aid

The purpose of first aid is to:

- preserve life
- prevent the condition of the casualty from deteriorating
- promote recovery

THERE IS NO SUBSTITUTE FOR PROPER TRAINING

The aim is to achieve these objectives with the minimum of interference with the patient. All first-aid procedures must comply with any local regulations. Medical aid must be obtained in every case of serious injury, whenever an injury involves the eyes, and whenever there is any doubt about whether an injury is serious or not.

The objectives are most likely to be met if the first aider is properly trained.

## First-aid procedure

Effective first-aid treatment of any accident requires the following:

- ASSESSMENT of the situation which involves finding out what has happened, who is injured and the nature of any injury. If there is more than one casualty, or the casualty has more than one injury, the first aider must decide which is the most serious and treat each as appropriate.
- PREVENTION of further injury, including injury to the first aider, the casualty and other pupils or students.
- TREATMENT using appropriate first-aid procedures (see below). Severe bleeding or absence of breathing requires *immediate* attention.
- CARE for the injured person until the formal transfer

of that person to other care or his/her return to normal activities, depending upon the seriousness of the injury.
- REPORTING the accident in accordance with the school's normal procedure.

All accidents, however slight, should be recorded in the approved format which is likely to specify the name of the injured, the date, time and place of the accident, the location of the injury and the treatment given. Note that the reporting of serious accidents is governed by *The Reporting of Injuries, Diseases and Dangerous Occurrences Regulations 1985* (SI 2023, 1985) which came into effect on 1 April 1986. These regulations require that

where any person as a result of an accident arising out of or in connection with work, dies or suffers any of the injuries or conditions specified . . . or where there is a dangerous occurrence, the responsible person shall . . .

(a) forthwith notify the enforcing authority thereof by the quickest practicable means; and

(b) within seven days send a report thereof to the enforcing authority on a form approved for the purposes of this Regulation.

A notifiable accident, injury or condition under these *Regulations* is defined in booklets published by The Health and Safety Executive. For details, see *A Guide to the Reporting of Injuries, Diseases and Dangerous Occurrences Regulations 1985*, HS(R) 23, HMSO, 1986. Note that a serious injury must be reported whether the injured person is an employee (e.g. a teacher, laboratory technician, secretary), a pupil or a visitor. The following are examples of injuries that must be reported to the Health and Safety Executive.

- electric shock causing burns, loss of consciousness or other injury
- acute illness arising from the absorption of any substance by ingestion, inhalation or absorption through the skin
- any burning of, or penetrating injury to, the eye, the loss of sight in an eye
- any injury that causes the injured person to be admitted immediately to hospital for more than 24 hours

In addition, a report is required if an *employee* is incapacitated for more than 3 days as a result of an accident at work or if he/she contracts one of a number of Notifiable Diseases.

In the course of school science teaching, there are likely to be numerous less serious, although still distressing, accidents that are not covered by *The Health and Safety Regulations* on reporting. In these circumstances, any requirements for reporting laid down by an employer (Local Education Authority, governing body, school proprietor) remain in force. The

Health and Safety Commission Education Service Advisory Committee also operates a voluntary scheme intended to collect information about accidents that fall outside the scope of SI 2023, 1985, and which involve injuries to either teachers or pupils causing a minimum of three days absence.

## Eye injuries

Chemicals in the eye must be washed out using a large quantity of gently running water. A piece of rubber tubing fitted to a laboratory tap is helpful in directing the jet of water to where it is needed. Note (i) that the pain of the injury may make it difficult for the casualty to cooperate, (ii) that water running out of an injured eye must not be allowed to enter the other eye. It is essential to ensure that both surfaces of the eyelids are properly washed. On no account allow a casualty to rub an injured eye.

In the case of inert foreign bodies in the eye, keep the injured person as still as possible and prevent rubbing of the eye. If a foreign body is on the coloured part of the eye, or embedded in or stuck to the eye, the casualty must be removed to hospital as soon as possible. If there is also chemical contamination of the eye, this must be treated immediately as above.

If the foreign body is not on the coloured part of the eye, or embedded or stuck, it can be removed either by washing with water, by using the corner of a clean handkerchief or by gently pulling the upper eyelid over the lower.

All eye injuries arising from laboratory accidents should be seen by a qualified Medical Officer.

## Burns and scalds

The emergency first aid for heat burns and scalds rests on the facts that heat damages tissue and that further damage is minimized by cooling the injured area as quickly as possible.

Burn injuries are accompanied by a loss of fluid (plasma) from the blood into the tissues (causing swelling), which, by oozing from the wound, causes the injured area to rapidly become red, swollen, blistered and painful. Shock may be expected to a degree related to the severity of the burn. Minor burns, e.g. to a small part of a finger that has come into contact with a hot tripod, should be treated by holding the affected part under cold, running water for about 10 minutes. It may then be covered with a dry sterile lint or gauze dressing.

No burn, serious or otherwise, must be treated with an antiseptic oil or ointment. Blisters must never be broken and no attempt must ever be made to remove burnt or loose skin. If the clothing is on fire, it is imperative that the victim gets, or is forced, into a horizontal position immediately, to limit the spread of the injury. The casualty must not be rolled on the

10 min

ground since this could cause the flames to spread. If a large quantity of cold water is available *immediately*, this should be used, but speed is of the utmost importance. In the absence of an immediate supply of cold water to extinguish the flames, the casualty should be wrapped in a fire-resistant blanket or coat. Any charred material, which will be sterile, should be left *in situ* by the first aider. Having extinguished the flames, the first aid treatment should aim to:

(a) reduce the effects of heat and alleviate the pain,
(b) reduce discomfort and swelling,
(c) limit the risk of contamination and infection,
(d) reassure the patient and lessen the shock,
(e) ensure that the patient takes sufficient fluid.

Watches, rings, bangles, boots or other items of a constricting nature should be removed before swelling begins and the injury cooled as rapidly as possible by irrigation with cold water or by the application of ice packs. After cooling, a dry, sterile dressing should be applied. If a limb is badly burnt, it should be immobilized. If the patient is conscious, he/she can be given *sips* of cold water at frequent intervals. Any burn larger than about the size of a ten pence piece should be regarded as serious and requiring hospital treatment.

Chemical burns, caused by chemicals on the skin, should be treated with large quantities of running water to dilute and remove the chemical. Contaminated clothing must be removed or cut away and when all chemical contamination has been removed from the skin, the affected area should be covered with a dry, sterile dressing. Chemical burns must not be treated by carrying out 'neutralizing' reactions on the skin. Burns involving phosphorus, bromine or alkali metals and all other serious chemical burns require professional medical attention.

Electrical burns may seem much less serious than is actually the case. Before attempting any first aid, disconnection of the injured person from the electrical supply is imperative. A wooden chair may be used to do this. Note that apart from burns, an electric shock can cause the heart to stop beating. In these circumstances, mouth-to-mouth resuscitation and external chest compression will be necessary immediately the injured person has been disconnected from the electrical supply.

**Cuts and bleeding** Small cuts, causing external bleeding, should be thoroughly washed with running water and treated with a dry, sterile dressing. If the cut contains a relatively large piece of metal or glass, this should only be removed at a hospital. In the meantime, bleeding can be reduced by bringing the sides of the wound together, using sterile dressings, before bandaging around the foreign object. In the case of cuts on a limb, bleeding can also be reduced by raising that limb (provided it is not fractured).

Loss of blood can cause fainting and shock. In appropriate circumstances therefore, an injured person should be required to sit or lie down as treatment is administered.

In the case of arterial bleeding, urgent medical help is needed. First aid involves laying the person down and applying pressure over the wound with a thick, sterile dressing. Further dressings should be added as required and pressure on the wound maintained by hand. If possible, raise the wound, e.g. by raising an injured limb.

**Respiratory injury** Get the patient into the fresh air. If necessary, apply mouth-to-mouth ventilation (artificial respiration). The patient should be seen by a medical practitioner as soon as possible and any known exposure to corrosive, irritant or toxic gases should be reported.

When a victim is not breathing, mouth-to-mouth ventilation must be started *immediately*. The first minutes are vital.

1. Pull the victim clear of immediate danger of further injury. If electrical shock is the cause of unconsciousness, either switch off the current or use an insulating material to pull the victim away from the conductor.
2. Lay the victim on his/her back and remove any obstructions from the mouth and throat, e.g. plant material ingested during drowning, loose dentures.
3. Put one hand under the neck and the other on the forehead of the patient and tilt the head back, raising up the chin. This prevents the tongue blocking the air passage in the throat.
4. Seal the patient's nostrils either by pinching with the fingers or by resting the cheek against the nostrils.
5. Breathe in deeply, seal your lips around the patient's mouth and blow into the patient's lungs until they are filled, watching the chest rise as you do so.
6. Remove your mouth, taking another breath as you watch the chest of the patient fall.
7. Repeat this process, giving the first few breaths quite quickly. After that, continue at a rate of 15/16 breaths per minute, the normal rate for an adult.
8. If, for any reason, e.g. injury, the rescuer cannot seal his/her mouth over that of the patient, close the latter and blow through the patient's nose, using the same technique as for mouth-to-mouth ventilation.

Note that a manual method of artificial ventilation of the lungs of an unconscious person (the Holger Nielsen method) can be used when a casualty is trapped face down or has severe facial injuries.

The lungs of children have a smaller capacity than those of adults. In addition, children's faces are smaller. In these cases, therefore, less air needs to be blown into the lungs with each breath, and, with some younger patients, it may be possible to cover both the mouth and nose simultaneously while transferring air to the victim's lungs.

Artificial mouth-to-mouth ventilation should be carried out for at least an hour or until the patient begins to breathe naturally. Once a patient begins to recover, he or she must be placed in the recovery position. This allows the tongue to fall clear of the air passage and prevents any vomit from entering it. To place an injured person in the recovery position, kneel at right angles to, and about one foot away from, the person's chest. Turn the patient's head towards you, tilting it carefully backward to keep the air-passage open. Then arrange the body and limbs as shown below, the arm alongside the body preventing the patient rolling on to his/her back.

If there is a chest injury or bleeding from the airway, the patient must be placed so as to lie on the injured side.

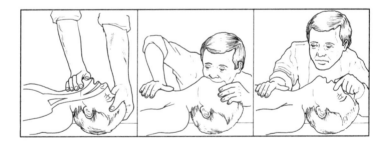

**Unconsciousness**  A patient should be kept under medical observation for 24 hours after resuscitation. In assessing how to deal with a partially conscious or unconscious patient, it is helpful to refer to the following 'levels of responsiveness'.

1. Patient talks normally and answers questions normally.
2. Patient answers direct questions only.
3. Patient's answers to questions are vague.
4. Patient obeys commands.
5. Patient reacts only to pain.
6. Patient does not seem to react in any way at all.

It is also important to remember that unconsciousness can

have several distinct causes including epilepsy, shock, solvent or drug abuse, asphyxia and head injuries. In general, an unconscious person should be moved as little as possible, save to check for any sources of severe bleeding or to apply a resuscitation technique.

If a person is breathing normally but unconscious, loosen tight clothing around the neck and chest, then place the patient in the recovery position. Stay with the patient and arrange for medical help to be summoned.

If an unconscious person is not breathing, it is possible that the tongue may have fallen to the back of the mouth and be blocking the passage to the lungs. In such a case, tilting the head backwards by placing a hand under the neck of the horizontal patient may be sufficient to unblock the air passage and allow the patient to breathe naturally. When a patient does not breathe for him- or herself, mouth-to-mouth ventilation should be tried immediately in accordance with the procedure outlined above.

Where a patient's heart has stopped beating as a result of an accident, external chest compression is necessary. First, check that the heart has stopped pumping by taking a pulse (preferably a carotid pulse). When confronted with a patient who is not breathing and has no pulse, lay the patient on the floor and give four quick breaths using the mouth-to-mouth technique. Then carry out external chest compression as follows:

1. Place the heel of the hand about three-quarters of the way down the breast bone and place the heel of the other hand on top. Interlock the fingers of both hands and press straight down on the heels of the hands. Release the pressure and repeat at a rate of about 80 presses per minute.
2. Fill the lungs of the patient twice using the mouth-to-mouth technique and repeat the cycle.
3. Check the pulse after one minute and, thereafter, every three minutes. If the breathing and heart beat are restored place the patient in the recovery position. If the heart beat, but not the breathing, returns, discontinue the external compression and continue with the mouth-to-mouth ventilation.

Both mouth-to-mouth ventilation and external chest compression are techniques that can be easily learnt. It is *essential* to be trained in such techniques and to have had appropriate practice before using them on real casualties.

Whenever a blow on the head has been sustained, the victim should be seen by a qualified first-aid worker. If there is any possibility of concussion, medical advice must be sought. The patient must not be allowed to take the decision whether or not to consult a doctor: his/her judgement may have been affected if the blow was severe.

**Poisoning**

Poisons in the mouth should be spit out immediately and the mouth washed thoroughly with water.

The swallowing of poisons is always a serious matter. Ingested acids or alkalis should be treated by swallowing large quantities of water, followed by referral of the patient to a hospital. Arsenic, mercury and their compounds, together with the salts of heavy metals, pose serious threats and poisoning by any of these substances requires urgent medical attention. If it is necessary to use a highly toxic material in the course of school science teaching, any appropriate antidote should be to hand before the work is undertaken. In most cases, a less toxic substitute, control of the quantities used, amendment of the experimental procedures and the use of safe techniques will reduce the risk of poisoning to an acceptable level.

**Shock**

Shock is a state of collapse which may be fatal if not brought under control. It may stem from physical or emotional injury, e.g. burns, vomiting, bleeding, fear and pain. It is essentially a weakening of the circulation of the blood which causes the body to give priority to the blood supply to the vital organs at the expense of, for example, the skin. The symptoms of shock include faintness, giddiness, dizziness, complaints of blurred vision, collapse, pallor, clammy or cold skin, anxiety and breaking into sweat. Unless other injuries make it impossible, a person suffering from shock should be laid down and, if possible, the feet raised *higher* than the head. Reassurance of the patient is important and he/she should be covered by a blanket. If circumstances permit, a blanket underneath a patient in shock is also desirable. On no account should drinks be administered. Medical help should be sought as a matter of urgency.

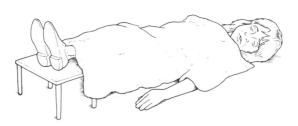

**First-aid kits**

The provision of first-aid facilities for those *employed* in schools is governed by *The Health and Safety (First Aid Regulations) 1981* (SI 917, 1981) and the associated *Approved Code of Practice* and *Guidance*. The revised *Code of Practice* (HMSO, 1990) came into effect on 2 July, 1990.

Local Education Authorities and other employers are required to inform employees of the arrangements made in connection with first aid and to ensure the provision of adequate equipment and facilities. The criteria for deciding the scale and type of first-aid equipment and facilities needed are set out in the *Approved Code of Practice* and *Guidance*. It should be noted that the former emphasis on the 'number of employees' in determining the provision has been much reduced. Attention is drawn to the following.

1. First-aid boxes should contain 'a sufficient quantity of suitable first-aid materials and nothing else', and normally should contain only those items that a first aider has been trained to use.
2. First-aid boxes should be clearly identified by means of a white cross on a green background in accordance with the *Safety Signs Regulations 1980*. They should be so constructed as to protect the contents from dust and damp.
3. In most cases, a first-aid box should contain:
   a guidance card
   twenty individually wrapped sterile adhesive dressings of assorted sizes appropriate to the work environment
   two sterile eye pads with attachments
   six individually wrapped triangular bandages
   six safety pins
   six medium sized individually wrapped sterile wound dressings (approx. 10 cm × 8 cm)
   two large sterile individually wrapped unmedicated wound dressings (approx. 13 cm × 9 cm)
   three extra large sterile individually wrapped unmedicated wound dressings (approx. 28 cm × 17.5 cm)

A suitable copyright-waived 'guidance card' is included as an Annexe to the *Approved Code of Practice* referred to above.

The contents of travelling first-aid kits must be appropriate for the circumstances in which they are likely to be required.

4. The use of antiseptics is not necessary for the first-aid treatment of wounds.
5. Eyebaths/eye cups/refillable containers are not suitable for irrigation of the eye. Eyes should be washed with copious amounts of clean tap water, followed by sterile water or sterile normal saline, stored in sealed sterile containers of not less than 300 cm³ capacity. At least three such containers

should be available. The supply of clean water should be sufficient to allow irrigation to continue for ten minutes.

6. Where a first-aid room is provided, it must be clearly identified and a 'suitable person' made responsible for the room and its contents. A 'suitable person' is a 'first-aider who holds a current first-aid certificate issued by an organisation whose training and qualifications were approved by the Health and Safety Executive for the purposes of the *Regulations*', or 'any other person' whose training and qualification are approved by the Executive for the same purposes. Additional specific training may be necessary when circumstances so dictate. Certificates of qualification are currently valid for three years, after which period a refresher course leading to re-certification is required. For the design/contents of a first-aid room, see the *Approved Code of Practice*.

7. Records should be made and kept of all first-aid treatment. A format for recording such treatment is given as Appendix 2 of the *Approved Code of Practice*.

Since pupils and students are not employees of a Local Education Authority or a governing body, they are not covered by the *First Aid Regulations*. However, the *Regulations* inform the guidance about first-aid available from Local Education Authorities and/or the relevant government department e.g. the Department of Education and Science, and the *Approved Code of Practice* and the guidance notes do not replace or lessen the force of such provisions. Local Education Authorities and governing bodies also have a moral duty to ensure that adequate first-aid arrangements are made for visitors to schools.

**First-aid procedures and AIDS**

Some concern has been expressed about the risk of infection with AIDS or the virus associated with it arising from administering first aid to an infected person. Given what is known about the modes of transmission of the virus, there seem to be no grounds for changes in such first-aid techniques as mouth-to-mouth resuscitation or the procedures for dealing with severe bleeding. However, good hygiene is, as always, important and it is suggested, therefore, that before administering first aid all first aiders should

(i) ensure that any exposed cuts or abrasions on their hands are covered with waterproof dressings, and
(ii) wash their hands thoroughly.

Such washing is always appropriate after administering first aid. As a further precaution, consideration can be given to requiring all first aiders to use disposable gloves when administering first aid.

# THE SCIENCE TEACHER AND THE LAW

**General**

Under the *Education Reform Act 1988*, the governing bodies of county, voluntary-controlled and special agreement schools have considerable power over staff appointments, numbers and dismissals as well as responsibility for the operation of disciplinary and grievance procedures. However, the staff in these schools remain formally employees of the Local Education Authority and governors exercise their staffing responsibilities under the legal framework established by means of the *Education (Modification of Enactments Relating to Employment) Order 1988*, made under S222 of the *Education Reform Act 1988*. This Act does not alter the position of staff in voluntary-aided schools who are already employed by the governors. A governing body is also normally the employer in independent schools.

Employment law provides employees with a range of statutory rights, many of which are associated with a minimum qualifying period of continuous employment. Employment legislation is complex and diverse and subject to interpretation by Industrial and Employment Appeal Tribunals. For an introduction to the legislative framework, and a guide for governors and headteachers responsible for the financial management of schools under The Local Management in Schools Initiative, see *Local Management in Schools, A Practical Guide*, London, 1988.

In addition to statutory provisions derived from employment legislation, the conditions of service of teachers in the maintained sector are determined by arrangements specified under the *Teachers' Pay and Conditions Act 1987* and by any local agreements applicable under their contracts of employment. Note that essential particulars of a teacher's terms and conditions of employment must be presented to a teacher by an employer as a written contract of employment within 13 weeks of the start of the teacher's employment. In county, voluntary-controlled and special agreement schools operating under the LMS arrangements, the contract of employment will continue to be drawn up by the Local Education Authority. In the case of voluntary-aided and independent schools, the contract of employment is normally made with the governing body, although in some independent schools, the employer will be the proprietor.

**Injuries to teachers**

If a teacher is injured in the course of his/her employment, compensation or damages will be payable only if

(i) *it can be established that the injury was the result of negligence on the part of the employer arising,* for example, from inadequate maintenance of equipment, facilities or premises, *or*

(ii) *an appropriate policy of insurance is in force.* For example, employers are commonly party to schemes that provide compensation to employees in the event of death, incapacity, loss of sight or limb, or other major injury. Note, however, that less serious injuries are generally excluded from such schemes. Teachers who wish to insure themselves against injury and perhaps a consequent loss of income therefore should consider taking out personal accident insurance at their own expense.

**Accidents involving pupils**

A teacher is not legally liable for the results of an accident to a pupil unless it is established that the teacher has breached in some way the duty of care that he or she owes to that pupil, i.e. the teacher has been negligent. In considering whether or not negligence is established, it is necessary to consider the duty owed by the teacher to the pupil(s) in his/her charge and then to ask whether or not that duty has been fulfilled. Failure to fulfil that duty might arise from acts either of commission or of omission. Once negligence is established, it becomes important to determine the extent to which the negligence contributed directly to any accident or injury and to decide whether or not the injured pupil contributed in any way to the negligence. Note that SI 650 (1987), *The Education (School Teachers' Pay and Conditions of Employment) Order 1987* requires teachers to maintain 'good order and discipline' among pupils and to safeguard 'their health and safety'. Note also (i) that an employer is responsible for the actions of an employee acting in the course of his/her duty and that employers are required to maintain public liability insurance to meet any claims for damages arising from negligence for which they are directly or vicariously liable, and (ii) that, in delegating a duty to others (e.g. a teaching colleague), a teacher can delegate only the task itself and not the responsibility for it. Particular care is needed, therefore, in delegating tasks to probationary or inexperienced teachers and on no account should non-science teachers be asked to supervise laboratory work.

In considering whether or not an accident involving pupils involves negligence on the part of a teacher, that teacher is

Law Report

**Leaving acid in hand drier was an offence**

regarded as acting *in loco parentis* and as having the duty of care of a 'reasonably careful parent'. In general, the test of reasonableness is to be applied in the context of the school rather than of a pupil's home environment. While schools cannot be expected to provide constant supervision of pupils throughout the school day, it is expected that teachers will act in the light of the 'known propensities' of pupils, e.g. for horseplay and practical jokes.

As far as science teaching is concerned, work in laboratories and workshops presents hazards that are not encountered in conventional classrooms. The duty of a science teacher towards pupils in his or her charge, therefore, might be regarded as that of a reasonably careful parent, acting in the school environment and with the science teacher's expert knowledge.

Compliance with the COSHH *Regulations* is of particular importance in discharging this duty of care in respect of substances hazardous to health. More generally, a science teacher's task is to design the teaching–learning situation in such a way as to remove, or at least minimize, all foreseeable hazards. Pupils should be asked to undertake only those experiments that are commensurate with their age, ability and experience. They must have, and understand, copies of the laboratory rules. They must also be given *explicit* warning of any hazard associated with a particular experiment, technique or material.

In all circumstances, science teachers have a duty to maintain 'good order and discipline'. It follows that pupils should not be left unsupervised in a laboratory, workshop or preparation room. In the event of an accident to a pupil, it is important to seek professional medical opinion unless there is *no doubt* that this is unnecessary. Failure to summon medical attention in such a situation could constitute negligence. If an injury requires the attention of a nurse or doctor, first aid should be given while medical attention is being summoned.

In the case of all but the most obvious minor injuries, a pupil's parents or guardian should be informed as soon as practicable. If teachers decide that a pupil injured at school requires hospital treatment, sending that pupil to the hospital should not be delayed until contact has been established with the pupil's parents or guardian. Teachers confronted with a medical emergency involving a pupil are expected to act as would a reasonably careful parent. This involves acknowledging the seriousness of the situation and acting promptly, appropriately and in good faith by summoning medical attention and administering any necessary first aid (see Chapter 5).

When a pupil is injured at school, a science teacher *may offer or be asked to* take the injured pupil home or to hospital. If the teacher's motor vehicle insurance is restricted in its coverage to social, domestic or pleasure purposes, it could constitute an offence to transport a pupil in this way. However, most Local Authorities have effected suitable Motor Contingent Liability Policies which indemnify teachers in respect of their legal liability for accidents to third parties arising from the use of a car in direct connection with out-of-school activities and insofar as their own insurance arrangements are inadequate for the purpose. It is also a relatively inexpensive undertaking to modify an individual motor insurance policy to provide the necessary cover. Science teachers, like their colleagues, should therefore establish the legal position so far as such insurance is concerned, *before* an emergency or other situation arises.

It is important to make a *factual* report on an accident as soon as it is reasonable to do so and most schools have a standard procedure to be followed in such cases. Since an accident is an uncontrolled situation in which the teacher is emotionally, if not physically, involved, some time for reflection and the consultation of any witnesses, e.g. a laboratory technician, is desirable before a formal account of an accident is submitted. Such an account should be brief and devoid of speculation about or comment upon the causes of the accident. (Even if the cause seems obvious to the teacher, he or she may be mistaken.) It is also sensible to take legal advice from a professional association or other source before providing any fuller written report on an accident that might be requested by an employer.

Note that if an individual is interviewed by a Health and Safety Inspector following an accident, he or she may be 'cautioned' and any statement obtained used as evidence in any subsequent litigation. However, unless the so-called 'judges rules' are followed in obtaining such a statement, it will not be admissible as evidence in a court of law and the interviewee has no entitlement to a copy of the statement prepared by the Inspector. In these latter circumstances, it is sensible for the interviewee to make his or her own notes as the interview proceeds.

Attention is also drawn to the *Reporting of Injuries, Diseases and Dangerous Occurrences Regulations 1985* (SI 2023, 1985), the essential provisions of which are summarized on page 91.

Finally, it should be noted that if any action is brought for negligence, e.g. by a parent, that action may be brought against the employer, the headteacher, the teacher or others allegedly involved in the negligence or jointly against any combination. Any subsequent damages may then be apportioned between those determined as responsible for the negligent act(s). Appropriate insurance cover, therefore, is imperative and this is commonly obtained by membership of one of the teachers' professional associations.

## Legal liabilities of student teachers

The position of a student teacher undertaking teaching practice in a local authority school differs from that of other teachers in the school in that the student teacher is not an employee of that local authority. An LEA provides indemnity for its employees by means of a public liability insurance policy which normally relates to matters arising from the law of negligence, e.g. injury to a pupil or conduct causing injury to a third party. Despite the fact that student teachers have no written contract of service with an employing authority, it is likely that no distinctions will be made between an employee and a student as far as the protection offered by public liability insurance is concerned. Similarly, if a student teacher suffered injury from a pupil or third party while acting as a teacher, he or she would normally receive the same degree of insurance protection as an employee in the same situation.

The legal position of student teachers undertaking teaching practice in independent schools may differ somewhat from that outlined above. However, it is probable that the governors of independent schools, proprietary and voluntary-aided schools will have taken out insurance policies designed to offer cover similar to that provided by LEA public liability insurance.

Science teachers in training by whatever route (articled teachers, licensed teachers, teachers following PGCE or BEd courses) are likely to have relatively little experience of class control and management. This relative lack of experience must be taken into account in determining the tasks that may be appropriately delegated to them. Similar considerations apply, *mutatis mutandis*, to probationary teachers.

Note that the relevant Administrative Memoranda (page 24) include a number of provisions for student teachers using ionizing radiations on teaching practice. For a summary of these provisions, see page 20.

## Out-of-school activities

Science teaching often involves working with pupils away from school premises, e.g. on field trips, industrial visits and school journeys. Any such work must be recognized as an official school function and approved in accordance with any procedures or regulations laid down by a local authority or governing body. Since out-of-school activities are an integral part (or an extension) of an in-school curriculum, the teacher's duty of care remains that of the 'reasonably careful parent'. When pupils are away from home on a residential school visit, the supervising teachers are deemed to be responsible for those in their charge for 24 hours each day. Note, however, that under the *Education (School Teachers' Pay and Conditions of Employment) Order 1987* (SI 650,1987) teachers cannot normally be required by contract to undertake residential visits. Participation by a teacher on a voluntary basis in no way diminishes that teacher's duty of care. For charges that may be made in maintained schools for out of school activities, see DES Circular 2/89. For comment on the organization of field work and educational visits, including insurance matters, see page 63 and *Safety in Outdoor Education* (HMSO, 1989).

It is reasonable to obtain parents' consent to any appropriate medical treatment a child may need on an out-of-school visit or journey, particularly one of several days duration. However, parents cannot be asked to agree to renounce their legal right to seek compensation for any injury to their child arising from negligence by a teacher acting in *loco parentis*. Any attempt to restrict liability for death or personal injury arising from negligence would be in contravention of the *Unfair Contract Terms Act 1977*.

## Experimental work controlled by law

There are a number of Acts of Parliament and Orders in Council which govern the work of any teacher in a school and some of these have particular relevance to the science teacher. In addition, there may be local authority regulations. The following should be noted.

1. Industrial methylated spirit (95% ethanol–water and 5% naphtha) and duty-free spirit (ethanol–water) cannot be obtained without a requisition order from the local office of the Customs and Excise department. It is necessary to give an undertaking that the spirit will be securely stored, used exclusively for science teaching and be accounted for in a return made of the amount used for teaching purposes. If it is required to purify industrial methylated or duty-free spirit, special permission must be obtained. Note that mineralized methylated spirit may be easily purchased although it is, of course, of very limited use in schools.
2. The making of explosive mixtures is governed by the *Explosives Act 1875* which provides that it is unlawful to make explosives without permission under licence from the Home Secretary. Pupils should not be shown how to make fireworks or rocket fuels. Certain procedures, e.g. the mixing of phosphorus or sulphur with potassium chlorate(V) are forbidden by law.

The COSHH *Regulations* (page 11) require: (i) an assessment of the risk associated with the use in schools of any substance hazardous to health and (ii) that steps be taken to prevent, or, where this is not reasonably practicable, adequately to control exposure to these substances. In advising employers how to comply with these *Regulations*, the relevant *Guidance for Schools* (HMSO, 1989) notes that 'a number of general assessments have already been developed for most of the substances and experiments found in school science'. These general assessments are to be found in, for example, *Topics in Safety* (ASE), the *Hazcards* produced by the Consortium of Local Education Authorities for the Provision of Science Services (CLEAPSS) and the Scottish Schools Equipment Research Centre (SSERC). A summary is also provided in Appendix A (page 127). The Guidance note points out that for science subjects, employers have the choice of:

(a) adopting and if necessary adapting to particular circumstances such well researched and established general assessments for school science work;
(b) approaching CLEAPSS or SSERC about the services they intend to offer; and
(c) making their own assessments.

Particular care is needed in undertaking assessments of new substances or materials that may be being used for the first time in a school, e.g. as part of project work.

3. The use of any hazardous material in a school is subject to the COSHH *Regulations* and adequate precautions to secure and monitor the stock are essential. The storage and handling of potentially dangerous substances, e.g. compressed or liquefied gases, flammable liquids, are governed by several Acts of Parliament which were not drawn up with schools particularly in mind. Other *Regulations* on storage, etc. may be laid down by an employer and such *Regulations* are likely to be based on the relevant legislation and the associated Orders. The *Regulations* relating to the storage and use of radioactive materials (DES Administrative Memorandum and SED Circular 1166) and of highly flammable liquids are of particular importance (pages 20 and 86).

Note also that there are stringent regulations governing the disposal of waste materials (page 17) and the transport of radioactive, toxic, flammable or otherwise hazardous materials. A teacher's domestic motor insurance policy could be rendered inoperative if that teacher's car is used to transport apparatus and/or chemicals from one site to another.

4. Work with radioactive materials and ionizing radiations is rigidly controlled in schools. For details see the relevant Administrative Memorandum and SED Circular 1166.

5. The work that can be done with plants and animals in schools is governed by several Acts of Parliament and the legal position has been well summarized in DES Administrative Memorandum 1/89 *Animals and Plants in Schools: Legal Aspects*. The following should be noted.

(i) Animals covered by the *Dangerous Wild Animals Act 1976* must not be brought into schools, i.e. all canines (except domestic dogs and the common red fox), all cats (except domestic animals), almost all monkeys and apes, as well as all crocodiles, alligators and poisonous snakes.

(ii) A school should not sell animals since this may bring the school within the scope of the *Pet Animals Act 1951* under which the school might be categorized as a pet shop. Such a shop requires a licence and is not allowed to sell animals to children below the age of 12.

(iii) Under the *Badgers Act 1973*, no school may receive any badger whether alive or dead or any portion of a badger.

(iv) Where farm or other animals are kept in rural science units, they are likely to be covered by legislation intended to prevent the spread of serious diseases. The health of animals in such units, therefore, should be monitored regularly and, if necessary, veterinary advice obtained.

(v) The *Animals (Scientific Procedures) Act 1986* applies to animals in the wild as well as those in captivity and regulates procedures applied to a vertebrate that 'may have the effect of causing . . . pain, suffering, distress or lasting harm'. The injection of *Xenopus* toads for spawning purposes, anaesthetizing a vertebrate (including a tadpole capable of independent feeding), the examination of live chick embryos after the midway point of incubation, and the pithing of frogs are all forbidden under the Act.

(vi) Under the *Wildlife and Countryside Act 1981*, all wild birds, together with eggs and nests, are protected, except for 13 pest species which may be dealt with only under licence. This protection, which extends to a number of other animals, refers to collecting, buying, selling, killing or injuring an animal and to damaging its habitat. The degree of protection depends upon the species. For example, the crested newt and the Natterjack toad are fully protected by the legislation. Frogspawn, however, may be brought into the classroom to observe the life history of the frog, although surviving frogs should be returned to the area from which the spawn was obtained. For details see

*Protecting Britain's Wildlife: A Brief Guide* (Department of the Environment, 1988) and Administrative Memorandum 1/89, *Animals and Plants in Schools: Legal Aspects* (HMSO, 1989).

(vii) It is an offence to uproot any wild plant without the permission of the land owner. A number of plant species are under additional legislative protection and must not be collected in any circumstances. For details see the sources listed in (vi) above.

(viii) In certain teaching situations, e.g. rural science, where pupils may be working on a farm, other activities will be controlled by specialist regulations. For example, the *Farm Safety Regulations* do not allow children under 13 to ride on a tractor, on farm implements or on trailers (except on the floor of the trailer).

6. The use of micro-organisms in school science teaching is governed by the COSHH *Regulations*. For details of levels of risk, etc. see Chapter 3 and *Microbiology: An HMI Guide for schools and non-advanced further education* (1985).

## The Health and Safety at Work Act

*The Health and Safety at Work etc. Act 1974* applies to all persons at work, except domestic workers in private households. It came into operation on 1 April 1975 and had the effect of making schools and other educational establishments subject to safety legislation comparable with that governing other areas of employment within the UK. Contravention of the Act, e.g. by a teacher failing to observe proper safety precautions, can lead to criminal prosecution. The following general points are of particular importance to school science teachers.

(i) The Act requires all employers to prepare and, where necessary, to revise written statements setting out their *policy* for the health and safety of employees and the procedures for effecting that policy.

(ii) The Act requires that all reasonable practical steps be taken to train employees in health and safety issues. This provision emphasizes the need to ensure that technicians, as well as teachers, are properly trained in safety matters.

(iii) Designers, manufacturers, importers (suppliers of articles or substances) for use in schools and colleges must ensure that, so far as is reasonably practicable, they are safe when properly used. This means that an article must be tested for safety in use and that details must be given of any conditions of use regarding its safety.

(iv) Teachers have a duty under the Act to take reasonable care to avoid injury to themselves or to others by their teaching activities, and to cooperate with employers and others in meeting statutory requirements. The Act also requires employees not to interfere with or misuse anything provided to protect their health, safety or welfare in compliance with the Act. This provision emphasizes the importance of adequate supervision of laboratories at all times and of conducting a systematic check on laboratory safety on a daily, weekly, termly and annual basis.

(v) Section 37 of the Act makes it clear that if an offence against the Act is committed by a corporate body, not only the corporation but also the individual(s) who have been responsible by consent, neglect, connivance etc. may be subject to legal action.

(vi) An employer is required

to give to persons (not being his employees) who may be affected by the way in which he conducts his undertaking, the prescribed information about such aspects of the way he conducts his undertaking as might affect their health or safety.

This sub-section of the Act could be considered as covering risks to pupils in schools and students in colleges and appropriate safety training should be provided.

(vii) The Act provides for recognized Trade Unions to appoint safety representatives from among the employees and requires an employer, if requested by the safety representatives, to appoint a safety committee. These statutory Trades Union representatives must not be confused with safety officers (often a headteacher or senior member of a school staff) appointed by an employer to facilitate communication and disseminate information about safety matters.

Compliance with the provisions of the Act is monitored by Inspectors of the Health and Safety Executive who have the necessary powers of entry to a school as a matter of routine, in response to an invitation or in response to a reported accident. As a result of the visit, the Inspector may raise for discussion a number of matters relating to safety (*not* the curriculum) in the school or any part of it. Where particular matters, such as a failure to provide adequate eye protection for pupils or staff are identified, an Inspector can issue an *improvement notice* requiring that the defect be remedied within a specified period. The more serious *prohibition notice* requires that the activity or activities to which the notice applies must cease until the grounds for its issue no longer apply.

Almost all the safety issues that arise in the course of science teaching and that might be of concern to the HSE can be resolved by discussion, to the mutual benefit of all the parties concerned. In the absence of any national code of practice drawn up by the Health and Safety Executive in respect of safety in schools, the advice and regulations of the government departments with statutory responsibility for education (DES and its counterparts in Scotland, Northern Ireland and Wales) are of particular importance. The relevant publications of the Education Services Advisory Committee of the Health and Safety Commission, the Association for Science Education, and organizations such as CLEAPSS and SSERC are also important. Attention is drawn to the following: Health and Safety Commission Education Service Advisory Committee, *Health and Safety in Education, A Source Book of Reference Material*, Health and Safety Executive, 1987; Health and Safety Executive, Library and Information Services, *Education, A List of HSC/E Publications Relevant to Educational Establishments*, 1987.

A listing of all HSC/E publications is updated twice a year and is available, free of charge. In addition, the HSE Library and Information Services operates three public enquiry points (London, Sheffield and Bootle) and an information service via Prestel. A computer database of published documents on health and safety at work is available on computer disc and a twice weekly update on health and safety publications and legislation from the Health and Safety Executive and Commission is available via an electronic noticeboard.

# THE MANAGE- MENT OF SAFETY

The safe management of school science teaching is an integral part of the wider management of health and safety matters within a school. It involves (i) a clear statement of policy, (ii) a set of objectives derived from that policy, (iii) managerial and administrative arrangements designed to realize those objectives, and (iv) a sensitive and effective means of monitoring and reviewing both the policy and all aspects of its implementation.

The *Health and Safety at Work Act 1974* requires all employers to have a written policy statement in respect of the health and safety of employees and of procedures for effecting that policy. For schools operating under 'local financial management', the employer is the Local Education Authority, although the governors are responsible for staff appointments and for the disbursement of most of the available funds. In the case of independent schools and schools that have 'opted out' of the maintained system, the employers are the governors. In addition to an appropriate policy statement or statements, the *Health and Safety at Work Act* requires an employer to make arrangements for (i) the safety of all plants and systems, (ii) the safe handling (including transport) and storage of materials, (iii) such information, instruction, training and supervision as are necessary to ensure the health and safety of the employees and (iv) the provision of a working environment that is 'safe and healthy' and includes appropriate amenities, e.g. for hygiene, washing, first aid.

The Act also places obligations upon employees, e.g. science teachers, technical and other supporting staff. Employees are required to co-operate with their employers in meeting the requirements of the legislation and not to interfere with or misuse anything provided to protect their health, safety and welfare under the Act. In addition, employees are required to take 'reasonable care' to avoid injury to themselves or others. Note that although pupils are not employees, the Act requires an employer

to give to persons (not being his employees) who may be affected by the way in which he conducts his undertaking, the prescribed information about such aspects of the way he conducts his undertaking as might affect their health and safety.

This sub-section of the Act could be considered as covering

risks not only to pupils but, where appropriate, visitors to a school. Note also that the *Education (School Teachers' Pay and Conditions of Employment) Order 1987* (SI 650, 1987) places a statutory responsibility upon a teacher to safeguard the 'health and safety of pupils'. An employer's statement of policy on health and safety is likely to be drawn directly from the Health and Safety at Work legislation and to specify such matters as those referred to above. This statement provides the framework within which a school will develop its own policy documents and practices relating to health and safety at school, departmental and individual levels.

## The Head of Department's responsibilities

The head of a science department is responsible for ensuring, as far as is reasonably practicable, that the work of the department is carried out (i) in accordance with the policy statements on health and safety prepared by the employer and the school and (ii) in such a way as to safeguard the health, safety and welfare of all those such as technicians, teachers, pupils and visitors who might be affected by the activities undertaken by the department. When the organization of a school provides for heads of subject departments, such as physics, chemistry, biology or technology, each of whom is responsible to a head of science or faculty, then overall responsibility for health and safety matters remains with the head of science, even though many of the relevant tasks will, on a day-to-day basis, be delegated.

The discharge of the responsibilities of a head of a science department requires the development, in conjunction with colleagues, of procedures relating to health, safety and welfare matters arising from the work of that department. These procedures are likely to relate to matters such as the following.

## Information and communication systems

- What mechanisms exist for receiving information about health and safety matters from, for example, the LEA Advisory staff, the Health and Safety Executive, the DES, SED or other Government department?
- Are these mechanisms adequate?
- Is information received on a systematic basis and is a record kept of its receipt?
- Once received in a school or department, how effective are the internal methods of disseminating information and for discussing and taking any necessary action?
- Do the systems of communication encourage teachers to share with colleagues their own knowledge of relevant health and safety issues?
- Do mechanisms exist for informing pupils or others, as appropriate, of relevant new information?

- Are the lines of responsibility and communication clearly understood by all involved? What, for example, is the relationship between the head of the science department, the head of the chemistry department, the school safety officer and a union-appointed school safety representative?

***Monitoring safety equipment and procedures***

The questions that might be asked here are as follows.

- What facilities are available for eye protection?
- Are they in accordance with the relevant regulations?
- Is the stock of, for example, goggles or spectacles in good condition? If appropriate, has it been sterilized?
- What procedures exist for monitoring and maintaining the school's supply of goggles, spectacles or shields?

- Are all the fire extinguishers, fire blankets, first aid boxes, etc. clearly marked and in good working order? Are the sand buckets free from rubbish?
- What are the procedures for maintaining health and safety equipment in good working order and how effective are they?
- Are the fire exits clearly marked and free from obstruction?
- Are the fire alarms working properly?

- Are the locations of mains gas, water and electrical supplies clearly marked, accessible and known to all those who might have proper cause to disconnect one or more of these supplies?
- Has the mains electrical supply been checked by a suitably qualified person? Is there an inventory of electrical apparatus? See *Guidance Note GS23, Electrical Safety in Schools (Electricity at Work Regulations 1989).*

- When pupils and staff are engaged in out-of-school activities, have all the necessary safety procedures been observed?
- What has been learnt from previous activities of this kind and has it been acted upon?

- How often is a safety check carried out in the science department?
- What action was taken as a result of the last check and what record is there of the check and of the action taken?
- Does the check include a discussion among teaching staff, and others, as appropriate, about the hazards of any procedures undertaken in the course of their teaching?
- How adequate are the arrangements for the storage of equipment and materials?
- Do they comply with the relevant regulations?
- How might the storage arrangements be improved?

- What procedures exist for stock control and for discarding chemicals that have a limited shelf life?

**Identifying, labelling and assessing hazards**

- Are all bottles of chemicals properly labelled and are these labels understood by all who might have cause to handle the bottles?
- Where apparatus is running continuously or overnight, does it have a fail-safe mechanism and does it carry a suitable notice?
- Have risk assessments been made of any substance hazardous to health used in the science department, in accordance with the COSHH *Regulations*?
- Is a record kept showing the date of the assessment and the outcome? The advice of the Education Service Advisory Committee of the Health and Safety Commission is that

Whether to record an assessment depends partly on the nature and extent of use of the substance, including the danger it presents. An important test is whether assessments can be repeated easily or followed clearly from the label on the container.

Note that in making their assessments, employers may make their own, seek the advice of organizations such as CLEAPSS or SSERC, or adopt and if necessary adapt to their particular circumstances the well researched and established general assessments that already exist for much of school science teaching. For publications that might be referred to in making a risk assessment, see the Bibliography.

- Is the use of any radioactive materials or ionizing radiation in the science department strictly in accordance with the relevant Administrative Memorandum or Circular issued by the appropriate government department such as the DES or SED? Corresponding questions can be asked about other materials (e.g. asbestos, carcinogenic substances) or items of equipment (e.g. lasers) governed by regulations of this kind.

**Arrangements for new and inexperienced staff**

In addition to experienced staff, the membership of a school science department often includes younger, less-experienced or unqualified staff, e.g. probationary teachers, supply teachers, newly-qualified teachers, support teachers whose qualifications are not in science, articled teachers, licensed teachers and untrained technical staff, as well as students on teaching practice. Arrangements need to be made, therefore, to ensure (i) that such staff are set only those tasks commensurate with their qualifications and experience, and (ii) that their expertise is developed by a suitable programme of staff development and in-service education. This latter consideration may well apply to qualified science teachers who are asked to work outside their own subject disciplines. While some matters can only be learnt by experience and the experienced staff within a science department constitute an important source of advice and support, health and safety issues are an important aspect of staff development and should be seen as such.

Note, however, that inexperienced, new and younger members of a science department can often bring a new perspective to bear upon existing departmental practices. They may be able, therefore, to suggest changes and improvements in the area of health and safety and their suggestions should be encouraged and welcomed.

**The supervision and control of pupils**

Pupils should be allowed in a science laboratory only when they are being supervised by a qualified science teacher. The use of laboratories as 'form rooms' should be discouraged. In addition, *senior* pupils should be allowed to work in laboratories only when their science teacher is satisfied that the pupils are aware of the hazards associated with the task they have been set, are competent to undertake that task and can be relied upon to work competently without immediate supervision. Note that there may be a school, not simply a departmental, policy on leaving pupils to work unsupervised.

Pupils should not have access to storage or preparation rooms or to unattended laboratories. Note, however, that no door must be locked if doing so would prevent evacuation of a room in the event of an emergency.

Discipline and class control are obviously of fundamental importance in ensuring that work with pupils in laboratories is conducted safely. Schools will generally have a clear policy for dealing with breaches of discipline and this policy will obviously apply to work done in the science department. However, it is often helpful to also have a departmental policy dealing with serious or persistent breaches of safety rules. This policy, arrived at by discussion within the science department, can only be effective if it is followed by all members of the department.

When pupils come to laboratory-based lessons, it is the responsibility of the teacher to ensure that bags and coats do not clutter working surfaces and to conduct the lesson in a way that sets an example to pupils of how practical work can be conducted safely. Safety aspects of procedures, together with the reasons for them, should be made explicit. If, in the judgement of the head of department, a laboratory is too small for the numbers of pupils required to undertake practical work safely within it, this should be made known in writing to the headteacher. In the interim, consideration should be given to

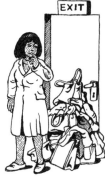

splitting the class for practical lessons, to altering or abandoning the intended practical activity or to carrying out a teacher demonstration, rather than a pupil-based practical laboratory lesson. Attention is drawn to the importance of providing an efficient fume cupboard where noxious fumes are likely to be produced. More generally, Guidance Note EH22, *Ventilation of Buildings: Fresh Air Requirements*, issued by the Health and Safety Executive, offers advice about the ventilation of buildings.

## Curriculum initiatives

The development and introduction of innovatory courses and schemes of work often entails experimental work with which teachers may be unfamiliar. The hazards associated with such work need to be identified and an assessment made of the associated degree of risk. A similar procedure should be followed whenever any material or experimental procedure is introduced into school science teaching, e.g. when senior pupils are undertaking project work. Note, however, that many procedures and items of equipment are unique to school science teaching and that the hazards associated with a material or procedure may become known only after considerable experience has been gained of working with that material or of following an initially unfamiliar procedure.

Health and safety issues should be an explicit and integral part of lesson planning, of the organization of pupils' learning, and more generally, of the conduct of the work of the science department. Many routine and familiar laboratory operations present opportunities not merely to highlight safety matters but also to explain the scientific ideas upon which such matters depend.

## Work with living organisms

If the school maintains a stock of live animals, particular attention must be given to the arrangements for their containment and nutrition and for monitoring their well-being. The relevant questions thus include:

- Are the animal cages, aquaria or other containers cleaned on a regular basis?
- Is any cage, aquarium or other container in need of repair or replacement?
- Are the arrangements for feeding the livestock adequate, particularly during school holidays?
- By what means, and how frequently, is the condition of the animals monitored?
- When micro-organisms are used in school science teaching, are they used in accordance with the advice given in *Microbiology: An HMI Guide for schools and non-advanced further education* (HMSO, 1985)?

- Are all those working with micro-organisms familiar with the relevant regulations and advice?
- When staff and pupils are on field trips or similar activities, are they aware of the relevant statutory provisions (e.g. about uprooting wild plants) and of the hazards posed by the field environment?

**Chemical storage** The *Health and Safety at Work Act* imposes a general duty of care in respect of the storage of hazardous materials. The storage of some categories of materials (e.g. highly flammable liquids, petroleum) is also subject to statutory regulation. In addition, a local authority or other employer may have a code of practice designed to ensure compliance with the law in matters of storage and to promote the health and safety of employees and others who might be affected by the legislation.

In addition to the legislative framework and any code of practice laid down by an employer, the following are important when considering the storage of chemicals and other hazardous materials.

1. The storage system must be as straightforward as possible and allow materials to be located easily. Commonly, this involves storing materials in alphabetical order by name or grouping by class of material, e.g. flammable substances, toxic substances, corrosive substances, general chemicals of low toxicity, chemicals that are particularly hazardous (e.g. white phosphorus). All materials should be date stamped upon receipt and such receipt recorded.

   All containers of chemicals must be clearly labelled to show the name of the substance contained and the hazard(s) associated with it. It is also good practice to include on the label the action to be taken in the event of accidental spillage.
2. The amount of each substance to be stored should be considered carefully in the light of (i) its stability (e.g. hydrogen peroxide), (ii) the degree of hazard associated with it (e.g. concentrated sulphuric acid, '0.880' aqueous ammonia), (iii) the amount and cycle of use, and (iv) the available storage space.
3. Stock records may be kept in a stock book or in a computerized form. The records must show the quantity of each substance received, the date of receipt, the associated hazard(s) and, if necessary, where the substance is stored. Computerized stock control facilitates the monitoring and re-ordering of stock, including those materials of a limited 'shelf life'.
4. The storage facilities must be secure and include a fire-

resistant store or cupboard. Access to stored substances should be limited to members of the teaching and technical staff. A laboratory or a fume cupboard is not a suitable place for the long-term storage of chemicals. Adequate ventilation of a storage facility is essential, although a fire-resistant cupboard should not have an air vent.

5. Substances within a storage facility should not be stored above head height and stock bottles of different reagents should not be stored immediately behind each other.

6. For the storage of gas cylinders, see page 33. For radioactive materials, see page 20.

The facilities available for the storage of hazardous materials differ greatly from one school to another. Where an outside chemical store is available, this must be secure, properly-vented and sited to minimize exposure to direct sunlight, and heated only to the level necessary to prevent condensation. Internally, it must incorporate a facility for containing any spillage. Shelving should be of plastic-covered wood and the security of the shelving and its supports should form part of a regular safety check. For a suggested internal layout of a chemical store, see *Topics in Safety* (Association for Science Education, 1988).

### Laboratory maintenance

The wear and tear on a school science laboratory is substantial and attention should be given on a regular basis to the condition of the sinks, floors, ventilation systems (including fume cupboards), and mains services. Some laboratories have an inherently safer design than others (although not necessarily for all activities) and any shortcomings in the design cannot always be remedied immediately. In such circumstances, minimizing the level of risk is the first priority. The inadequacies should be noted and made known, in writing, to the employer through the appropriate channel. For a guide to laboratory design, see C. Elliott, *Building for Science: A Laboratory Design Guide*, Association for Science Education, 1989.

### Action in an emergency

Relevant questions here include the following:

- Do all staff and pupils know the procedures to be followed in the event of an emergency, e.g. a fire, a bomb threat, the escape of a significant quantity of toxic fumes, the sudden collapse of a teacher through illness?
- How often is there a fire drill and what has been learnt from previous exercises of this type?
- Do staff and pupils know which fire extinguisher should, or should not, be used to deal with a particular type of fire?

- Are staff and pupils competent at basic first aid procedures, including artificial ventilation?
- Are the criteria and procedures for summoning professional medical help clearly understood and have the arrangements worked satisfactorily?

**Conducting a safety check**

This can be done most conveniently by means of a suitable checklist, drawn up to reflect the issues referred to in the paragraphs above. For an example of a checklist, see *Topics in Safety*, Association for Science Education, and *Education in Science*, November 1986.

In constructing such a checklist, it is helpful to distinguish items on the basis of the frequency with which they need to be checked, e.g. daily, weekly, monthly, termly or annually. It is also helpful to maintain a separate record of the safety checks undertaken in each of the laboratories, preparation rooms, dark rooms and other ancillary rooms, and offices within the science department. Any safety check is, of course, of little value unless the matters that require attention are subsequently addressed in an appropriate manner.

# SELECT BIBLIOGRAPHY

**1. General**

Assistant Masters and Mistresses Association, *Out of School*, 1987, AMMA, London.

Association for Science Education, *Be Safe—Some Aspects of Safety in Science and Technology for Primary Schools*, 1988, ASE, Hatfield.

Association for Science Education, *Topics in Safety*, 1988, ASE, Hatfield.

Bretherick, L., *Handbook of Reactive Chemical Hazards*, 1990, Butterworths, London.

Bretherick, L., *Hazards in the Chemical Laboratory*, 1986, The Royal Society of Chemistry, London.

British Standard 4163, *Recommendations for Safety in Workshops of Schools and Colleges of Education*, 1984.

British Standard 4803, part 2, *Radiation Safety of Laser Products and Systems: Specification for Manufacturing Requirements for Laser Products*, 1983.

British Standard 2092, *Eye-protectors for Industrial and Non-industrial Uses*, 1987.

Consortium of Local Education Authorities for the Provision of Science Services (CLEAPSS), *Storage and Handling of Chemicals*, 1988, Brunel University.

*ibid.*, School Science Service, *HAZCARDS*, 1989, CLEAPSS, Brunel University.

*Dangerous Chemicals: An Emergency First Aid Guide*, Croner Publications.

*Dangerous Chemicals: An Emergency Spillage Guide*, Croner Publications.

Department of Education and Science (DES):

Administrative Memoranda

3/70 *Avoidance of Carcinogenic Aromatic Amines in Schools and Other Educational Establishments.*

7/70 *The Use of Lasers in Schools and Other Educational Establishments.*

6/76 *The Laboratory Use of Dangerous Pathogens.*

2/86 *Children at School and Problems Related to AIDS.*

3/86 *The Use of Asbestos in Educational Establishments.*

1/89 *Animals and Plants in Schools: Legal Aspects.*

*ibid.*, Building Bulletins

No. 7 *Fire and the Design of Educational Buildings*, sixth edition, 1988, HMSO, London.

No. 50 *Furniture and Equipment, Working Heights and Zones for Practical Activities*, 1973, HMSO.

No. 62 *Body Dimensions of the School Population*, 1985, HMSO.

No. 63 *Craft, Design and Technology: Accommodation in Secondary Schools*, 1986, HMSO.

No. 64 *Adaptable Facilities in Further Education for Business and Office Studies*, 1986, HMSO.

*Safety in Education*, Bulletin issued occasionally and supplements the advice given by HMI in the DES *Safety Series* and other publications.

*Safety in Further Education*, 1976, HMSO.

*Safety in Outdoor Education*, 1989, HMSO.

*Safety in Practical Studies*, 1985, HMSO.

*Safety in Science Laboratories*, 3rd edn., 1987, HMSO.

Laboratories Investigations Unit, *Designing for Science*, 1987, HMSO.

Department of Education for Northern Ireland, *The Use of Ionising Radiations in Educational Establishments*, 1986.

DENI Safety Series. 1. *Safety in Science Laboratories*, 1984.

Health and Safety Commission:

*Genetic Manipulation Regulations 1989: Guidance on Regulations*, 1989.

*Approved Code of Practice and Guidance Notes: Preventing Accidents to Children in Agriculture*, 1988.

*Control of Substances Hazardous to Health and Control of Carcinogenic Substances, Approved Code of Practice*, 1989.

*The Noise at Work Regulations: Guidance on the Regulations*, 1989.

Health and Safety Commission, Education Service Advisory Committee:

*Educational Establishments—Unattended Operation of Experimental Apparatus Outside Normal Working Hours*, 1986.

*Health and Safety in Education: A Source Book of Reference Material*, 1987.

*COSHH: Guidance for Schools*, 1989.

*What you should know about allergy to laboratory animals*, 1990.

Health and Safety Executive, *Occupational Exposure Limits*, Guidance Note EH40, issued annually.

*ibid.*, Guidance Note EH22, *Ventilation of Buildings: Fresh Air Requirements*, 1979.

*ibid.*, *First Aid at Work, Health and Safety (First-Aid) Regulations 1981 and Guidance*, 1990.

*ibid.*, Guidance Note GS23, *Electrical Safety in Schools, (Electricity at Work Regulations 1989)*, 1990.

*ibid.*, Memorandum of guidance on the *Electricity at Work Regulations 1989*, 1989.

*ibid.*, *A Guide to the Reporting of Injuries, Diseases and Dangerous Occurrences Regulations 1985*, HS(R)23, 1986.

*ibid.*, *A Guide to the Pressure Systems and Transportable Gas Containers Regulations 1989*, 1990.

*ibid.*, *Storage and Use of Highly Flammable Liquids in Educational Establishments* 2/86, 1986.

*ibid.*, *Prevention of Accidents*, AS12, 1986.

*ibid.*, *Working with VDUs*, 1986.

*ibid.*, *COSHH Assessments, A Step-by-Step Guide to Assessment and the Skills Needed for It*, 1988.

*ibid.*, *Pesticides*, AS27, 1988.

*ibid.*, *Toxicity Review*, No. 1, *Styrene*; No. 2, *Formaldehyde*; No. 3, *Carbon Disulphide*; No. 4, *Benzene*; No. 6, *Trichloroethylene*; No. 9, *1,1,1,Trichloroethane*; No. 12, *Dichloromethane*; No. 18, *n-Hexane*; No. 19, *Nickel and its Inorganic Compounds*; No. 20, *Toluene*; No. 21, *Chromium and its Inorganic Compounds*.

Health and Safety Executive, Library and Information Services, *Education, A List of HSC/E Publications Relevant to Educational Establishments*. 1987, HSE, Sheffield.

Pitt, M. J., Pitt, E., *Handbook of Laboratory Waste Disposal*, 1985, Ellis Horwood/Wiley, Chichester.

Royal Society of Chemistry, *COSHH in Laboratories*, 1989, RSC, London.

Royal Society of Chemistry, *Safe Practices in Chemical Laboratories*, 1989, RSC, London.

Royal Society of Chemistry, *Solvents in Common Use, Health Risks to Workers*, 1988, RSC, London.

St. John's Ambulance, *Emergency Aid in Schools*, 1986, The Order of St. John, London.

Scottish Education Department (SED):

*Procedures for the Use of Ionising Radiations in Educational Establishments.* Circular 1166, 1987.

*Use of Carcinogenic Substances in Educational Establishments*, Circular 825, 1972.

*Use of Asbestos in Educational Establishments*, Circular 1113, 1984.

*Inhalation of Asbestos Dust. Preventive Measures*, Memorandum 6/68, 1968.

*Laboratory Use of Dangerous Pathogens*, Memorandum 15/76, 1976.

*Lead in the Environment*, SDD11/83.

*Computer Rooms: Making Room for Information Technology*, 1984.

Statutory Instruments:

*The Protection of Eyes Regulations 1974*, No. 1681, 1974.

*The Health and Safety (Agriculture) (Poisonous Substances) Regulations 1975*, No. 282, 1975.

*Safety Signs Regulations* No. 1471, 1980.

*The Health and Safety (First Aid) Regulations 1981, Approved Code of Practice*, No. 917, 1981.

*Ionising Radiations Regulations 1985* No. 1333, 1985.

*The Reporting of Injuries, Diseases and Dangerous Occurrences Regulations 1985*, No. 2023, 1985.

*Classification, Packaging and Labelling of Dangerous Substances Regulations 1986*, No. 1922; 1988, No. 766.

*Education (School Teachers' Pay and Conditions of Employment) Order 1987*, No. 650, 1987.

*Control of Substances Hazardous to Health Regulations 1988* No. 1657, 1988.

Warren, P. J. (ed.) *Dangerous Chemicals: Emergency Spillage Guide*, 1985, Wolters Samson.

## 2. Biological hazards

Altmann, H., *Poisonous Plants and Animals*, 1980, Chatto and Windus, London.

Association for Science Education, *Issues Surrounding the Use of Animals in Science Lessons: A Resource Pack*, 1988, ASE, Hatfield.

Association for Science Education, Safety in School Biotechnology, *Education in Science*, 1988, 126.

Barrass, R., *The Locust: A Laboratory Guide*, 1980, Heinemann, London.

British Agrochemicals Association, *Directory of Garden Chemicals*, BAA.

Bunyan, P., Safety and the school pond, *School Science Review* 1987, **69**(247), 286.

Collins, C. H., *Safety in Biological Laboratories*, 1985, Institute of Biology, London.

Consortium of Local Education Authorities for the Provision of Science Services (CLEAPSS) School Science Service, *Aquaria–Electrical Safety*, Guide No. L124.

Department of Education and Science (DES), *AIDS: Some Questions and Answers—Facts for Teachers, Lecturers and Youth Workers*, 1987, HMSO.

*ibid.*, *Keeping Animals in Schools: A Handbook for Teachers*, 1971.

*ibid.*, *Microbiology: An HMI Guide for schools and non-advanced further education*, 1985, HMSO.

Department of the Environment, *Protecting Britain's Wildlife: A Brief Guide*, 1988, HMSO, London.

Dixon, A., *Issues Surrounding the Use of Animals in Science Lessons: A Resource Pack*, A.S.E., Hatfield, 1988.

Forsyth, A. A., *British Poisonous Plants*, Ministry of Agriculture, Fisheries and Food, 1980, HMSO, London.

Gadd, L., *Deadly Beautiful: The World's Most Poisonous Animals and Plants*, 1980, London, Macmillan.

Haskell, P. T., *Pesticide Application*, 1985, OUP, London.

Kelly, P. J., Wray, J. D. (eds), *Educational Use of Living Organisms—A Source Book*, 1975, EUP, London.

Nature Conservancy Council, *Wildlife, the Law and You*, NCC.

Nichols, D., *Safety in Biological Fieldwork: Guidance Notes for Codes of Practice*, 1983, Institute of Biology, London.

Nonis, V., *Mushrooms and Toadstools*, 1982, David and Charles, London.

O'Donoghue, P. N., The law and animals in schools, *Journal of Biological Education.*, 1988, **22**(1).

Pinching, A. J., Aids and the AIDS virus (HIV): Facts and Implications, *School Science Review*, 1987, **69**(247), 205.

Robinson, D. F., Zoonoses—are they a school problem? *School Science Review*, 1983, **64**(228), 453.

Royal Society for the Prevention of Cruelty to Animals, *Alternatives to Dissection*, 1984, RSPCA, Horsham.

*ibid.*, *Small Mammals in Schools*, 1986, RSPCA, Horsham.

*ibid.*, *Animals in Schools—General Guidelines*, 1984, RSPCA, Horsham.

*ibid.*, *Visiting Animals Schemes*, RSPCA, Horsham.

Schools Council, *Animal Accommodation in Schools*, 1974, Hodder and Stoughton, Sevenoaks.

Tomlins, B., 'Sense and safety in school biology', *Education in Science*, 1988, **128**, 25.

Universities Federation for Animal Welfare, *Humane Killing*, 1978, UFAW, Potters Bar.

*ibid.*, *Handbook on the Care and Management of Laboratory Animals*, 1987, Churchill Livingstone, Edinburgh.

Woodward, L., *Poisonous Plants, A Colour Field Guide*, 1985, David and Charles, London.

## 3. Laboratory design, management and organization

Archenhold, W. F., Jenkins, E. W., Wood-Robinson, C. *School Science Laboratories, A Handbook of Design, Management and Organisation*, 1979, John Murray, London.

Cipfa *et al.*, *Local Management in Schools, A Practical Guide*, 1988, Local Management in Schools Initiative, London.

Crellin, J. R., School fume cupboards, *Education in Chemistry*, 1984, **21**, 185.

DES, *Design Note 29: Fume Cupboards in Schools*, 1982, HMSO.

Kibblewhite, J., *Microcomputer Applications in Safety Management*, 1989, H. and H. Scientific Consultants Ltd, Leeds.

*Manual for Heads of Science*, Croner Publications.

Nellist, J., Nicholl, B., *ASE Science Teachers' Handbook*, 1986, Hutchinson, London.

## 4. Education and the law

Assistant Masters and Mistresses Association, *The School Minibus and the Law*, 1986, AMMA, London.

Barrell, G. R., Partington, J. A., *Teachers and the Law*, 1985, sixth edition, Methuen, London.

*Croner's the Head's Legal Guide*, Croner Publications.

*Education and the Law*, 3 issues p.a., Longmans, London.

Leonard, M., *The Education Act 1988—A Practical Guide for Schools*, 1988, Blackwell, Oxford.

Lowe, C., *The School Governor's Legal Guide*, 1989, Croner, London.

Nice, D. (ed.), *Education and the Law*, 1986, Councils and Education Press, London.

Partington, J., *Law and the New Teacher*, 1984, Holt, Rinehart and Winston, Eastbourne, Sussex.

Secondary Heads Association, *Education Reform Act 1988*: *Implications for School Management*, 1988, SHA, London.

# APPENDIX A
# Hazard information and advice

The COSHH *Regulations* require that an assessment is made of the use at work of substances that are hazardous to health, and that steps be taken to prevent, or where this is not reasonably practicable, adequately to control exposure to those substances.

The *Regulations* categorize the following substances as hazardous to health.

---

(a) substances defined as very toxic / toxic / harmful / corrosive / irritant — as dangerous for supply in part 1A of the Approved List under the *CPL Regulations*[1]

(b) substances which have an MEL (Maximum Exposure Limit) or an OES (Occupational Exposure Standard) — as listed in HSE Guidance Note EH40/89 *Occupational Exposure Limits*

(c) micro-organisims which create a hazard to the health of any person, where the hazard arises out of or in connection with work which is under the control of the employer. For example, contracting a disease from a laboratory animal is included, but catching a cold from a co-worker is not;

(d) dust of any kind when present at a substantial concentration in air (where there is no indication of the need for a lower value); substantial concentrations are: $-10$ mg/m$^3$ total inhalable dust $-5$ mg/m$^3$ respirable dust

(e) any other substance which creates a comparable risk to health to any of the above.

However, the *Regulations* do not apply to activities where the *Control of Asbestos at Work Regulations* or the *Control of Lead at Work Regulations* apply, or where the risk is solely from radiation, noise, pressure, flammability, heat or cold.

---

1. *The Classification, Packaging and Labelling of Dangerous Substances Regulations 1984*

Note that hazardous substances found in schools are not confined to science laboratories and preparation rooms. Such substances may also be found in other locations such as rural science buildings, cleaners' stores, and workshops.

In ensuring that work in school science complies with the COSHH *Regulations*, the Education Service Advisory Committee of the Health and Safety Commission advises that employers have the choice of

1. adopting and if necessary adapting to particular circumstances well researched and established general assessments for school science work (such as the assessments in the ASE's *Topics in Safety* and the *Hazcards* produced jointly by CLEAPSS and SSERC).

2. approaching CLEAPSS or SSERC about the services they intend to offer.

3. making their own assessments.

For fuller details on compliance with the COSHH *Regulations*, see COSHH, *Guidance for Schools*, HMSO, 1989.

The entry for each of the substances listed in this Appendix is intended to facilitate compliance with the COSHH *Regulations*. Each entry provides (1) information about known or suspected hazards, (2) advice on storage, where relevant, and (3) comments upon the appropriateness for use of the substance by teachers and by pupils at particular stages of education (years 1 to 13), together with comments upon related experimental procedures.

Note (i) that the Appendix does not include data about micro-organisms (see Chapter 3) and (ii) that the absence of information about a particular substance should not be taken to imply anything about the hazard(s) associated with that substance or its use or storage in schools or elsewhere, and (iii) that technical staff are not identified as a separate category in the risk assessments. Clearly, the qualifications and experience of technical staff are of particular importance in determining the tasks they can properly be asked to undertake.

For further advice on COSHH, see: The Royal Society of Chemistry, *COSHH in Laboratories*, RSC, 1989; Health and Safety Executive, *COSHH Assessments, A Step-by-Step Guide to Assessment and the Skills Needed for It*, HMSO, 1989; Health and Safety Commission, Education Service Advisory Committee, *COSHH: Guidance for Schools*, HMSO, 1989.

**Aerosol sprays**

1. Contain material under pressure; some propellant gases cause damage to the ozone layer.

2. Store away from sunlight and heat and in accordance with the manufacturer's instructions; do not puncture or burn even when used.

3. Consider 'dipping' as an alternative to spraying; always use an aerosol in a fume cupboard; confine use to teachers and senior pupils unless close supervision of younger pupils (years 9,10 and 11) is possible.

**Aluminium**

1. Reacts with acids and alkalis to form flammable hydrogen; reactions with halogens vigorous, even violent; as a powder, aluminium can react explosively with oxidizing agents, sulphur, alcohols and some chlorinated hydrocarbons; burning metal difficult to extinguish (use dry sand or soda ash).

2. Treat the powder as a flammable solid for storage purposes;

keep all forms of aluminium away from oxidizing agents and from mercury.

3. Restrict use to teachers and to pupils in year 9 and above, unless close supervision of younger secondary pupils is possible; fume cupboard required for all reactions with halogens; wear gloves and use a fume cupboard when 'cleaning' aluminium foil with aqueous mercury(II) chloride.

**Aluminium carbide**
1. Reacts with water to form flammable gases.
2. Store in small quantities in dry conditions.
3. Restrict use to teacher.

**Aluminium chloride (anhydrous)**
1. Reacts vigorously with water, generating hydrochloric acid and much heat; corrosive, dangerous to eyes and skin.
2. Dry storage essential; pressure can build up in a container due to entry of atmospheric moisture.
3. Restrict use to teachers and to pupils in years 12 and 13; wear eye protection and gloves when handling; work in a fume cupboard when preparing from the constituent elements or when using the substance in a Friedel Crafts reaction. Note that ALUMINIUM BROMIDE presents comparable hazards.

**4-Aminobiphenyl**  Prohibited from use.

**Ammonia**
1. Gas is strongly irritating and toxic by inhalation; can form explosive products with halogens; product of reaction with aqueous silver nitrate may be explosive; 38% w/w or '0.880' aqueous solution is very corrosive.
2. Store aqueous ammonia in a cool place, away from sunlight or heat.
3. In many cases, '0.880' aqueous ammonia can be replaced by a less concentrated and, therefore, less hazardous solution; '0.880' solution should be used only by teachers or senior pupils; dilute solutions in the range 2–5 M can be used by pupils in year 9 and above or by pupils in years 7 and 8 with close supervision; fume cupboard required for the preparation of ammonia gas; safety screen advisable when conducting the 'fountain experiment'; do not store 'ammoniacal silver nitrate' (Tollen's reagent) but dilute with an excess of water and discard as soon as the reagent is no longer required; catalytic oxidation of ammonia using oxygen and a '0.880' solution must be done in a fume cupboard in an 'open' apparatus (air and 10 M aqueous ammonia is a less hazardous alternative).

**Ammonium dichromate(VI)**
1. Decomposes thermally at 190°C, with the emission of a large volume of green powdered $Cr_2O_3$. Insoluble compounds

of chromium(VI) are covered by the *Control of Carcinogenic Substances, Approved Code of Practice*, 1988 and the associated *Regulations* but a proposed amendment, if accepted, would restrict control to the manufacture of dichromate(VI) from chromite ore.

2. Store as an oxidizing agent and away from flammable materials.

3. Must not be heated with powdered metals; exposure to the solid product of the thermal decomposition should be prevented; teacher use only.

**Ammonium nitrate**

1. May cause fire in contact with combustible materials; forms explosive mixtures with a number of reagents, e.g. aluminium, phosphorus, potassium manganate(VII), ethanoic acid; may explode on heating, particularly larger crystals.

2. Store as a powerful oxidizing agent and away from flammable materials.

3. Do not grind; wherever possible, replace by a mixture of ammonium chloride and sodium nitrate; do not recrystallize from aqueous solution; suitable for use by teachers and senior pupils only.

**Ammonium sulphide (aqueous)**

1. Corrosive and releases highly toxic hydrogen sulphide with acids.

2. Small quantities only to be stored securely as a highly toxic chemical.

3. Suitable for use by teachers, senior pupils and, if necessary, by pupils in year 9 and above under close supervision.

**Antimony**

1. All soluble antimony compounds are toxic and some cause skin irritation and dermatitis; the chlorides are readily hydrolyzed.

2. Secure storage of small quantities may be appropriate.

3. In general, work with antimony or its compounds should be confined to teacher demonstration or exhibition purposes and then only after an appropriate COSHH assessment.

**Arsenic**

Arsenic or arsenic compounds should not be stored or used in schools.

**Asbestos**

Asbestos and asbestos products (e.g. tape, mats, gloves) must not be stored or used in schools. A variety of replacements is available (e.g. leather gloves, ceramic wool).

**Azo dyes**

1. Some azo dyes are carcinogenic and others may contain small quantities of carcinogenic impurities.

2. Store only small quantities of those permitted under the regulations (see page 19).

3. Wherever possible, prepare water-soluble azo dyes; ensure that diazotization is complete before proceeding to the next stage of a preparation; do not prepare azo dyes that involve the use of 1- or 2-naphthol or other carcinogenic materials or the formation of any of these compounds as intermediates.

**Barium compounds**

1. All soluble barium compounds are toxic; aqueous barium hydroxide is corrosive; barium nitrate is a strong oxidizing agent; barium chromate precipitated from aqueous solution should not be isolated; solid barium chromate should not be kept or used; for barium peroxide, see peroxides below.

2. Store securely as toxic chemicals.

3. Pipette filler essential for pipetting barium solutions; 0.2 M solution adequate for most purposes (e.g. flame test, precipitation of sulphate); solid barium compounds should be used only by senior pupils or teachers; solutions can be used by younger pupils under close supervision.

**Benzene**

1. Highly toxic, flammable and should be treated as a carcinogen; LEA or other employer may have banned altogether the use of benzene in schools.

2. Store securely and as a flammable liquid.

3. Do not use as a solvent; wherever possible, replace by less toxic alternatives such as methylbenzene (as solvent or in Friedel–Crafts syntheses), cyclohexane (in measuring lowering of a freezing point) as appropriate; any use to be confined to teachers and senior pupils; fume cupboard required.

**Benzenecarbonyl chloride**

1. Fumes in moist air, producing hydrochloric acid; corrosive; fumes irritate skin and eyes, the liquid itself causing serious damage.

2. Store small quantities in a cool, dry place, away from light.

3. Use only in a fume cupboard, wear gloves when handling and confine use to teachers and senior pupils.

**Benzenediamines**

1. Both the 1,3- and the 1,4-isomers are very toxic and may also cause skin irritation and dermatitis.

2. Store securely as toxic chemicals.

3. Gloves and eye protection needed when working with these materials; use restricted to teachers and senior pupils.

**Benzene diols**

1. Harmful and irritant substances that burn the skin; react vigorously with concentrated nitric acid; test solutions of benzene-1,3-diol in ethanol and propanone are highly

flammable; test solution of benzene-1,3-diol in ethanoic acid is corrosive.

2. Store as corrosive solids.

3. Handle with care and use eye protection; restrict use to teachers, senior pupils and to pupils in year 9 and above under close supervision.

**Benzenesulphonic acid**

1. Causes burns and irritation of the eyes and skin.

2. Store as a corrosive substance.

3. Restrict use to teachers and senior pupils; wear eye protection and gloves.

**Benzene-1,2,3-triol**

1. Harmful and irritant substance that burns the skin; reacts vigorously with concentrated nitric acid.

2. Store as a corrosive solid.

3. Its saturated solution ('saturated pyrogallol') is sometimes used to absorb oxygen (and carbon dioxide). This solution is hazardous to make and use (eye protection and gloves required) and, in most cases, a saturated solution of benzene-1,2,3-triol in sodium hydrogencarbonate constitutes a safer, alternative method of oxygen absorption (such a solution does not absorb carbon dioxide). Restrict use to teachers and senior pupils.

**Benzene-1,3,5-triol**

1. and 2., as for benzene-1,2,3-triol.

3. Solution in ethanol and concentrated hydrochloric acid is flammable (eye protection and fume cupboard required in its preparation); restrict use to teachers and senior pupils.

**Benzonitrile**

1. Harmful and irritant liquid that should be assumed to be toxic; vapour irritating to eyes and respiratory system.

2. Store securely as a toxic chemical.

3. Use only in a fume cupboard, avoid contact with skin or eyes and restrict use to teachers and senior pupils.

**Beryllium**

Beryllium and its compounds must not be kept or used in schools.

**Biphenyl-4,4-diamine**

Not to be kept or used in schools.

**Bismuth**

1. Bismuth and its compounds should be regarded as toxic.

2. Small quantities only are likely to be needed in schools and these should be stored securely.

3. Work with bismuth and its compounds should be restricted to teachers and senior pupils.

**Bleaching powder**   1. Corrosive, strong oxidizing agent; liberates chlorine with acids; vigorous reactions with alcohols and a range of other organic compounds; decomposes on standing.
2. Store in a cool, dry place as a corrosive solid with a limited shelf life. Old (18 months and older) stock should be discarded.
3. Requires eye protection and gloves when handled; restrict use to teachers and pupils at year 9 or above.

**Boric acid**   1. Mildly toxic if ingested.
2. No special storage requirements.
3. Eye protection and gloves needed when fused with other oxides to make glasses; acceptable level of risk for pupils from year 7 and upwards.

**Boron trihalides**   React vigorously or violently with water; toxic or very toxic; $BBr_3$ boils at 90°C, $BCl_3$ at 12.5°C and $BF_3$ (b.p. $-100$°C) is a gas under normal conditions; any work must be done in a fume cupboard but each of the trihalides probably presents an unacceptable degree of risk to allow its use in schools under the conditions commonly prevailing.

**Bromine**   1. Powerful oxidizing agent; violent or explosive reactions with alkali metals, aluminium, magnesium, concentrated aqueous ammonia and a range of organic compounds; liquid causes severe burns to the skin; the vapour attacks the eyes, nose, throat and lungs.
2. Small quantities only (100 $cm^3$ or less) to be kept in a cool secure store; ampoules should be kept in their protective packaging.
3. Open ampoules or bottles of bromine only in a fume cupboard; use gloves and eye protection when working with bromine; work confined to teachers and senior pupils under close supervision; dissolve in cyclohexane, *not* tetrachloromethane, to show effect of solvent on colour; avoid reactions leading to, or involving the formation of, carcinogenic 1,2-dibromoethane. BROMINE WATER is best prepared in fume cupboard using an ampoule of bromine broken under the water with the aid of a pliers (eye protection, gloves needed). It is much less of a hazard than bromine itself and, when dilute, is suitable for work with pupils from year 9 onwards.

**Bromobenzene**   1. Flammable, irritating to the skin.
2. Store as a flammable liquid.
3. Although little is known of its toxicity, work should be restricted to teachers and senior pupils and carried out in a fume cupboard.

**Bromobutanes**
1. Harmful materials; 1-bromobutane has a flash point of 24°C.
2. Store in small quantities as flammable liquids.
3. Restrict use to teachers and senior pupils and work in a fume cupboard unless very small quantities (ca. 5 cm$^3$) are involved.

**Bromoethane**
1. Harmful by inhalation; vapour has toxic and narcotic effects; liquid is also toxic, causing kidney damage.
2. Store in small quantities as a flammable liquid (b.p. 38°C).
3. Restrict use to teachers and senior pupils and work in a fume cupboard unless very small quantities (ca. 5 cm$^3$) are involved.

**Bromomethane**
1. Very toxic by inhalation (b.p. 4°C); vapour and liquid cause severe eye damage; liquid burns the skin; substance penetrates rubber.
2. Usually supplied as ampoule or cylinder.
3. Work involving bromomethane is not suitable for pupils at school.

**Bromopropanes**
1. Harmful materials.
2. Store in small quantities in a cool place.
3. Restrict use to teachers and senior pupils and work in a fume cupboard unless small quantities (ca. 5 cm$^3$) are involved.

**3-bromoprop-1-ene**
1. Highly flammable; very toxic by inhalation; irritating to skin, eyes and respiratory system.
2. Store in small quantities as a flammable liquid.
3. Restrict use to teachers and senior pupils and work always in a fume cupboard.

**Butanal**
1. Highly flammable (flash point −6.7°C); irritant.
2. Store as highly flammable liquid.
3. Restrict use to teachers and to pupils above year 9, and work always in a fume cupboard unless small quantities (ca. 5cm$^3$) are involved.

**Butanoic acid**
1. Oily liquid which causes burns.
2. Store as corrosive material.
3. Restrict use to teachers and senior pupils.

**Butanols**
1. Flammable; harmful by inhalation; vapour may irritate eyes and respiratory system.
2. Store as flammable liquids.

3. Risk appropriate for work with teachers and with pupils at year 9 and beyond; use fume cupboard unless quantities are small (ca. 5 cm$^3$).

**Butanone**
1. Highly flammable (flash point $-7°C$); inhalation of vapour may cause drowsiness, headache, nausea; liquid irritates the eyes and may cause severe damage.
2. Store as a highly flammable liquid.
3. Risk appropriate for work with teachers and with pupils at year 9 and beyond; use a fume cupboard unless quantities are small (ca. 5 cm$^3$).

**Cadmium**
There is little cause to use cadmium or its compounds in school laboratory work. Lead(II) bromide is to be preferred to cadmium iodide in electrolysis experiments. Cadmium chloride is carcinogenic.

**Calcium**
1. Metal reacts steadily with moisture, more rapidly with acids to form hydrogen; reaction with heated sulphur is explosive.
2. Store away from water and oxidizing agents.
3. When reacting with water, use an excess of water to minimize the risk of the heat of the reaction igniting the hydrogen; burning calcium is difficult to extinguish (use dry sand or soda ash); reaction with dry chlorine requires a fume cupboard.

**Calcium dicarbide**
1. Contact with water liberates highly flammable gases.
2. Store in a dry place as a flammable material.
3. Restrict use to teachers or to senior pupils under close supervision.

**Calcium hydride**
1. Contact with water liberates highly flammable gas.
2. Store in a dry place as a flammable material.
3. Restrict use to teachers or senior pupils under close supervision.

**Calcium oxide**
1. Irritant; reacts violently with water, releasing much heat.
2. Store in small quantities in dry conditions and away from acids.
3. Wear eye protection when adding to water; acceptable level of risk for teachers and for pupils in year 9 and above; younger secondary school pupils require close supervision.

**Calcium phosphide**
Not recommended for school use.

**Calcium sulphide**

1. Contact with acid liberates toxic gas.
2. Store in small quantities in dry conditions.
3. Use only in fume cupboard; restrict work to teachers and senior pupils.

**Camphor**

1. Harmful substance.
2. Store away from heat.
3. Appropriate for work undertaken by teachers and pupils from year 9 onwards.

**Carbon dioxide**

1. In solid form, causes skin 'burns'; large volumes of gas can asphyxiate.
2. Store cylinders securely away from sources of heat (see page 33); quantities of 'dry ice' can be kept for a few days in an insulated container but this must not be sealed.
3. Wear gloves when handling solid carbon dioxide; keep a cylinder firmly clamped when in use; although the gas presents an acceptable level of risk for the usual work with pupils of secondary school age, only teachers and senior pupils should be allowed to operate cylinders or 'handle' solid carbon dioxide.

**Carbon monoxide**

1. Highly flammable; forms explosive mixtures with air; very toxic by inhalation.
2. There seems little case for storing cylinders of carbon monoxide in schools.
3. Any preparation of the gas (teachers and senior pupils only) must be in a fume cupboard and on a small scale (as a liquid–liquid mixture the reaction between concentrated sulphuric acid and methanoic acid is easier to control than that between concentrated sulphuric acid and sodium methanoate); wherever possible, use an alternative to carbon monoxide as a gaseous reductant; any reduction with carbon monoxide requires a safety screen and should only be carried out by a teacher; ensure that all air has been expelled from an apparatus before lighting an emergent jet of carbon monoxide.

**Carbon disulphide**

1. Highly volatile; very low flashpoint ($-30°C$); very toxic.
2. Store in small quantities as a highly flammable liquid but consider carefully whether the substance should be used at all in school science teaching; some employers have banned carbon disulphide from schools and the ASE recommends that it is not 'normally held or stored'.
3. Dimethylbenzene can be used instead of carbon disulphide as a solvent for sulphur, although it is less efficient; 3-phenyl propenoate (ethyl cinnamate) can be used to replace carbon

disulphide in the hollow prism experiment but the prism must be washed out with propanone immediately afterwards.

**Carbonyl chloride**   Not recommended for preparation or use in schools.

**Chlorates(I)**
1. Release toxic chlorine with acids; solutions irritating to eyes and skin.
2. Store small quantities only, away from sunlight and heat.
3. Dilute solutions (<1% 'available chlorine') are appropriate for use by pupils from year 7 onwards; the use of more concentrated chlorate(I) solutions should be restricted to teachers and older pupils (e.g. year 9 onwards with supervision as appropriate).

**Chlorates(V)**
1. Strong oxidizing agents; react violently with a range of easily oxidized materials, e.g. sulphur, powdered metals, organic materials.
2. Store in a cool place away from combustible materials.
3. Restrict use to teachers and senior pupils.

**Chlorates(VII)**
1. Extremely powerful oxidizing agents; mixtures of chlorates(VII) and combustible materials are readily ignited and some react explosively.
2. Do not store in a school.
3. The hazards presented by chlorates(VII) are such that the use of these compounds in schools is not normally justified.

**Chlorine**
1. Very toxic; causes lung damage but effects of exposure can be delayed.
2. Chlorine cylinders should not be stored in schools; some employers forbid such storage.
3. Use fume cupboard and wear eye protection for all experiments involving the gas; do not mix gaseous chlorine and hydrogen and then ignite the mixture but lower a jet of safely burning hydrogen into a gas jar of chlorine; when preparing the gas from potassium manganate(VII) and concentrated hydrochloric acid, it is *essential* to check that the correct acid is being used (alternatively, use 5M hydrochloric acid and moistened bleaching powder); do not mix with ammonia; do not attempt to prepare oxides of chlorine; do not mix volumes of gaseous chlorine and ethyne (ASE advises that the simultaneous generation of these gases by adding dilute hydrochloric acid to a mixture of bleaching powder and calcium dicarbide (fume cupboard, safety screen) is acceptable as a teacher demonstration); small scale (test tube) reactions should be the norm for pupils' work with chlorine and much of

this should be confined to pupils beyond year 9; pupils below years 12 and 13 should not prepare chlorine.

**Chlorobenzenes**

1. Chlorobenzene is highly flammable, harmful by inhalation and may cause drowsiness; treat 1,4-dichlorobenzene as a suspected carcinogen.
2. Store chlorobenzene as a flammable liquid.
3. Wear eye protection and gloves when using any of the dichlorobenzenes; when 1,4-dichlorobenzene is used as a substitute for colchicine, rinse the treated biological material thoroughly before handling; keep chlorobenzene away from sources of ignition; any work with these substances is appropriate only for teachers and senior pupils.

**Chlorobutanes**

1. Flammable; flash points of 1- and 2- chlorobutane are $-9°C$ and $-10°C$ respectively.
2. Store as flammable liquids.
3. Work requires a fume cupboard and should be restricted to teachers and senior pupils.

**Chloroethane**

1. Extremely flammable liquid/gas (b.p. 12.4°C); flash point $-50°C$; mild irritant; used as a local anaesthetic.
2. Cylinders should not be kept in a school.
3. Work requires a fume cupboard and should be restricted to teachers and senior pupils.

**Chloroethene**

The monomer is not to be kept or used in schools.

**Chloroethanoic acids**

1. All three acids cause severe burns; monochloroethanoic acid perhaps the most toxic.
2. Store as corrosive materials.
3. Work should be restricted to teachers and senior pupils.

**(Chloromethyl)-benzene**

1. Irritates eyes, skin and respiratory system.
2. Store as a general organic chemical.
3. Work requires a fume cupboard and should be restricted to teachers and senior pupils.

**Chlorosulphonic acid**

1. Reaction with water is violent, even explosive; fumes cause severe irritation of skin, eyes and respiratory system; causes severe burns; powerful oxidizing agent.
2. Store small quantities in dry conditions, away from sources of heat.
3. Work requires a fume cupboard and is appropriate only for teachers and senior pupils.

**Chromates(VI) and dichromates(VI)**

1. Irritate the eyes, skin and respiratory system; many are toxic; calcium chromate(VI), strontium chromate(VI) and zinc chromates(VI), including zinc potassium chromate(VI) are carcinogenic (see also page 130).

2. Carcinogenic chromates(VI) should not be stored, kept, used or prepared in schools.

3. Non-carcinogenic insoluble chromates(VI) should not be isolated if precipitated from aqueous solution; do not use 'chromic acid' to clean laboratory glassware; restrict work with water soluble chromates(VI) and dichromates(VI) to teachers and to pupils beyond year 9.

**Colchicine**

Do not store or use in a school; 1,4-dichlorobenzene (see above) and 1-bromonaphthalene have been suggested as alternatives.

**Copper compounds**

1. The copper compounds commonly used in school science teaching are harmful only if taken internally or if ground to a fine dust.

2. Store as general inorganic chemicals but note that copper(II) nitrate is a powerful oxidizing agent.

3. Generally suitable for work throughout the secondary school with close supervision of pupils below year 9.

**Crude oil**

1. Flammable; harmful; 'crude oil' supplied for school use is a reconstituted mixture of petroleum fractions and is unlikely to contain the small quantities of carcinogenic hydrocarbons that may be present in real crude oil.

2. Store as a flammable liquid.

3. Distillation in a fume cupboard may be thought appropriate; do not attempt to clean the tubes used in small-scale distillations; suitable for pupils from year 7 onwards when appropriately supervised.

**Cyanides**

1. Extremely poisonous and contact with acids liberates highly toxic hydrogen cyanide.

2. Cyanides should not normally be kept or stored in a school and may be the subject of a ban by an employer.

**Cyanogen**

This highly flammable and toxic gas (b.p. $-21°C$) should not normally be prepared, used or stored (cylinder) in schools.

**Cyclohexane**

1. Highly flammable; irritates the eyes, skin and respiratory system.

2. Store as a highly flammable liquid.

3. Use a fume cupboard for all but small-scale work;

appropriate for use by teachers and by pupils from year 9 onwards.

**Cyclohexanol**

1. Harmful and may irritate the eyes, skin and respiratory system.
2. Store as a general organic chemical.
3. Appropriate for work by teachers and senior pupils; consider use of fume cupboard for some experiments.

**Cyclohexanone**

1. Flammable; harmful by inhalation.
2. Store as a general organic chemical.
3. Appropriate for work by teachers and senior pupils; consider use of fume cupboard for some experiments.

**Cyclohexene**

1. Highly flammable; irritating to the respiratory system; forms unstable peroxides over a long period.
2. Store as a highly flammable liquid with a limited shelf life.
3. Appropriate for use by pupils from year 9 onwards; consider use of fume cupboard for some experiments.

**DDT**

This substance (1,1-*bis*(4-chlorophenyl)-2,2,2-trichloroethane) should not be kept, stored, prepared or used in a school.

**Decanedioyl dichloride**

1. Toxic and corrosive; reacts vigorously with water to form hydrochloric acid.
2. Available in 25cm$^3$ packs and as 5% w/w solution in tetrachloromethane (see below) but cyclohexane (see above) is to be preferred as a solvent for the 'nylon rope' experiment; store away from moisture.
3. Appropriate for use by teachers, senior pupils and, with close supervision, by pupils at year 9 or above.

**1,6-Diaminohexane**

1. Irritates the eyes.
2. Store as a corrosive solid.
3. For use in the 'nylon rope' experiment, dissolve in cyclohexane and wear eye protection; appropriate for use by teachers, senior pupils and, with close supervision, pupils at year 9 or above.

**Di(benzenecarbonyl) peroxide**

1. An extremely hazardous substance, liable to explode when subjected to shock, friction or heat; normally supplied moistened with about 30% water.
2. Because of the hazards associated with this substance and the fact that less hazardous substitutes are usually available, it should not be kept, stored, used or made in a school.

| | |
|---|---|
| **1,2-Dibromoethane** | 1. Toxic; narcotic; suspected carcinogen.<br>2. Do not store, keep, use or prepare in a school.<br>3. Use with dilute aqueous bromine to test for C=C permissible. |
| **Dichlorobiphenyl-4,4'-Diamines** | Not to be kept, stored, used or prepared in schools; reactions in which they may be formed as intermediates must not be undertaken. |
| **1,2-Dichloroethane** | 1. Highly flammable (flash point 13°C); toxic by inhalation; irritates eyes and respiratory system.<br>2. Store as flammable liquid.<br>3. Use only in a fume cupboard and restrict use to teachers. |
| **Dichloromethane** | 1. Harmful by inhalation (b.p. 40°C); irritates eyes and respiratory system.<br>2. Store in a cool place.<br>3. Use in a fume cupboard; appropriate for work by teachers and senior pupils. |
| **2,4-Dichlorophenol** | 1. Harmful in contact with the skin and eyes, causing irritation or burns.<br>2. Store as a general organic chemical.<br>3. Work with eye protection; fume cupboard sometimes appropriate; appropriate for work by teachers and senior pupils. |
| **Di(dodecanoyl) peroxide** | 1. Highly flammable; very dangerous to the eyes; very powerful oxidizing agent.<br>2. Store only in small quantities (not more than 100 g) and store away from flammable liquids and easily oxidized substances; normally supplied moist.<br>3. Eye protection essential; use instead of di(benzenecarbonyl) peroxide (see above); appropriate for use by teachers, senior pupils and, with close supervision, pupils at year 9 and above. |
| **Diethylamine** | 1. Highly flammable (flash point −26°C); irritates the eyes and respiratory system.<br>2. Store as highly flammable liquid.<br>3. Fume cupboard required unless used in dilute aqueous solution; the latter is suitable for work by teachers and by pupils at year 9 and above, otherwise restrict work to teachers and senior pupils. |
| **Diethyl sulphate** | Do not store, keep or use in schools. |

| | |
|---|---|
| ***Diiodine hexa-chloride*** | Harmful solid and vapour that cause severe burns; gloves, eye protection, and fume cupboard essential; any work to be restricted to the teacher or to senior pupils under close supervision. |
| ***3,3'-Dimethoxy-biphenyl-4,4'-diamines*** | Not to be kept, stored, used or prepared in schools; reactions in which they may be formed as intermediates must not be undertaken. |
| ***Dimethylamine*** | 1. Highly flammable gas at ordinary temperatures (b.p. 7°C, flash point −50°C); irritates the eyes and respiratory system. <br> 2. Work in a fume cupboard unless used in dilute aqueous solution; the latter is suitable for work by teachers and by pupils at year 9 and above, otherwise restrict work to teachers and senior pupils. |
| ***Dimethylforma-mide*** | 1. Harmful in contact with the skin; vapour from heated liquid irritates the eyes and respiratory system. <br> 2. Store as a general organic chemical. <br> 3. Use only in a fume cupboard and restrict work to teachers and senior pupils. |
| ***Dimethyl sulphate*** | Do not store, keep or use in schools. |
| ***Dimethylsul-phoxide*** | 1. Harmful; irritates the eyes and skin. <br> 2. Store as a general organic chemical. <br> 3. Use (gloves, eye protection) only in a fume cupboard and restrict use to teachers. |
| ***Dinitrobenzenes*** | 1. Toxic or very toxic. <br> 2. Store securely as toxic materials. <br> 3. Restrict use to teachers and to senior pupils under close supervision. |
| ***4,4-Dinitrobiphenyl*** | Not to be kept, stored, used or prepared in schools; reactions in which it may be formed as an intermediate must not be undertaken. |
| ***2,4-Dinitro-bromobenzene*** | Toxic; a powerful skin sensitizer; should not be stored, kept or used in schools. |
| ***2,4-Dinitro-chlorobenzene*** | Toxic; a powerful skin sensitizer; should not be stored, kept or used in schools. |

**2,4-Dinitro-fluorobenzene**
See preceding entry; should not be stored, kept or used in schools.

**Dinitrogen oxide**
1. Anaesthetic properties.
2. Cylinders of the gas should not be stored or used in schools.
3. Laboratory preparation appropriate for teachers and senior pupils.

**Dinitrophenols**
1. Toxic; skin contact may cause dermatitis.
2. Store as general organic chemicals.
3. Restrict use to teachers and senior pupils under close supervision.

**2,4-Dinitro-phenylhydrazine**
1. Toxic; skin contact may cause dermatitis; reacts vigorously with oxidizing agents; when dry, sensitive to shock, heat or friction.
2. Normally supplied moist and must be kept so; store securely as a toxic chemical.
3. Wear eye protection when preparing a solution for use as a reagent to detect carbonyl compounds; appropriate for use by teachers and senior pupils.

**Dioxan**
1. Highly flammable; may form explosive peroxides on exposure to air.
2. Store as a highly flammable liquid with a limited shelf life.
3. Restrict use to teachers or, with close supervision, to senior pupils.

**Diphenylamine**
1. Toxic; may cause dermatitis; pure grade minimizes risk of carcinogenic impurities; commonly used dissolved in concentrated sulphuric acid (corrosive).
2. Store securely as a toxic substance.
3. Dilution of the solution in concentrated sulphuric acid requires eye protection and gloves; pupils should not have access to solid diphenylamine; restrict use of the solution to teachers and senior pupils under close supervision.

**Disulphur dichloride**
1. Reacts violently with water producing toxic and irritating fumes; liquid causes burns.
2. Store as a corrosive liquid.
3. Use a fume cupboard; restrict work to teachers and senior pupils under close supervision.

**Enzymes**
1. Some may be irritant or allergenic.
2. Store as general organic chemicals.
3. Avoid skin contact and inhalation; use gloves and eye protection when preparing solutions, especially of lipolytic

and proteolytic enzymes; solutions suitable for work by teachers and by pupils from year 7 onwards with appropriate supervision; restrict work with solid enzymes to teachers.

**Ethanal**

1. Highly flammable (flash point $-38°C$); irritates the eyes and respiratory system; readily forms peroxides; very reactive with a range of organic compounds.
2. Store in a cool place as a highly flammable and volatile liquid (b.p. $21°C$).
3. Use a fume cupboard; restrict work with this substance and its trimer to teachers and senior pupils; work with the tetramer 'metaldehyde' may be appropriate for pupils in year 9.

**Ethane**

1. Highly flammable; can act as an asphyxiant.
2. Ethane cylinders should not be stored in schools.
3. Work with small volumes of the gas (test-tube scale) appropriate for teachers and senior pupils.

**Ethane-1,2-diamine**

1. Flammable; liquid and vapour irritate the eyes and skin.
2. Store as a corrosive material; the hydrate has a higher flash point ($57°C$) than the diamine itself ($34°C$).
3. Use a fume cupboard; restrict work to teachers and senior pupils.

**Ethanedioic acid**

1. Toxic and irritant; reacts vigorously with oxidizing agents.
2. Store securely as a toxic chemical.
3. Restrict use of the aqueous acid and its salts to teachers, senior pupils and, with close supervision, to pupils in year 9 or above; use of pipette filler essential in volumetric analysis; work with solid acid or ethandioates should be restricted to teachers and senior pupils.

**Ethanoic acid**

1. Glacial acid is corrosive; vapour irritates the eyes and respiratory system.
2. Store as a corrosive liquid.
3. Wear gloves and eye protection when diluting the concentrated acid; work with the concentrated acid (fume cupboard, eye protection) should be restricted to teachers, senior pupils and, with close supervision, to pupils in year 9 or above; dilute solutions (not more than 5 M) may be appropriate for closely supervised pupils in year 7 or above.

**Ethanoic anhydride**

1. Corrosive; vapour irritates the eyes, skin and respiratory system; reacts vigorously with a range of oxidizing agents.
2. Store as a corrosive chemical.
3. Restrict work (fume cupboard) to teachers and senior pupils.

**Ethanol**

1. Flammable; narcotic; reacts vigorously or violently with oxidizing agents.
2. Store as a flammable liquid.
3. Do not use near a source of ignition; do not react with potassium; do not mix with nitric acid, bromine or comparable oxidizing agents; explosive compounds can be formed with silver nitrate or mercury(II) nitrate; appropriate for use by teachers, senior pupils and, with close supervision, by pupils in year 7 or above.

**Ethanoyl chloride**

1. Highly flammable (flash point 4°C); corrosive; reacts with water to produce toxic and corrosive fumes that irritate the eyes, skin and respiratory system; reacts vigorously with a range of organic compounds.
2. Store as a corrosive, flammable liquid.
3. Restrict work (fume cupboard, eye protection) to teachers and senior pupils.

**Ethene**

1. Highly flammable; asphyxiant.
2. Cylinders of ethene should not be stored in schools.
3. Do not explode ethene with oxygen; ignition of ethene–air mixtures on a test-tube scale appropriate for pupils from year 9 onwards.

**Ethenyl ethanoate**

1. Highly flammable (flash point −8°C); vapour may be narcotic.
2. Store as a highly flammable liquid.
3. Use in fume cupboard and restrict use to teachers and to senior pupils under close supervision.

**Ethoxyethane**

1. Highly flammable; volatile to produce a dense intoxicating vapour that can cause a 'flash back' from a source of ignition.
2. Store in a cool, dark place as a flammable liquid; test for peroxide formation (potassium iodide in concentrated ethanoic acid) on a termly basis; if peroxides are found to be present, shake the ethoxyethane with about half of its volume of M iron(II) sulphate, separate and repeat until the peroxide test is negative; do not store ethoxyethane from which peroxides have been removed.
3. Before use, extinguish all sources of ignition; use in a fume cupboard; do not place in a refrigerator unless this has been spark-proofed; consider less flammable solvents; appropriate for work by teachers, senior pupils and, with close supervision, pupils in year 9 or above.

**Ethoxyethanol**

1. Flammable; harmful, irritant vapour.
2. Store as a flammable liquid.

3. Use a fume cupboard; appropriate for work by teachers, senior pupils and, with close supervision, pupils in year 9 or above.

*Ethylamine*

1. Flammable; highly volatile (b.p. 17°C); irritates the eyes and the respiratory system. 70% w/w aqueous solution is adequate for most school purposes.
2. Store as a flammable liquid.
3. Use a fume cupboard for work with ethylamine; work appropriate for teachers, senior pupils and, with close supervision, pupils in year 9 or above.

*Ethylbenzene*

1. Highly flammable (flash point 15°C); irritates the eyes, skin and respiratory system.
2. Store as a flammable liquid.
3. Appropriate for use by teachers, senior pupils and, with close supervision, pupils in year 9 or above; fume cupboard appropriate for some work.

*Ethyl ethanoate*

1. Highly flammable; vapour may irritate the eyes and respiratory system.
2. Store as a highly flammable liquid.
3. Appropriate for work by teachers and pupils in year 9 or above; a fume cupboard may be appropriate for some work.

*Ethyne*

1. Highly flammable; asphyxiant; forms explosive compounds with some metals and explosive mixtures with air.
2. Cylinders of ethyne should not be stored or used in school science teaching.
3. Do not explode with oxygen; explosion with air must be on a small scale (test tube) and be done by the teacher; see also CHLORINE above.

*Fehling's solution*

1. Fehling's solution No. 2 contains caustic sodium hydroxide and is mixed with solution No. 1 (aqueous copper(II) sulphate) immediately before use.
2. Store the alkaline solution as a corrosive substance.
3. Wear eye protection when testing with Fehling's solution and heat gently (consider a water bath); consider Benedict's solution or Barfoed's solution as an alternative; appropriate for use by teachers, senior pupils and, with close supervision, by pupils in year 9 or above.

*Fluorine*

No attempt should be made to prepare, or undertake work with, fluorine in a school. Note that many FLUORIDES are toxic and can irritate the eyes, skin and respiratory tract. Work with solid fluorides should be restricted to teachers. Work with fluorides in aqueous solution is normally appropriate for teachers, senior pupils and, with close supervision, pupils in year 9 or above.

**Heptane**

1. Highly flammable; narcotic.
2. Store as a highly flammable liquid.
3. Appropriate for work by teachers and pupils in year 9 or above; fume cupboard appropriate for some work.

**Hexacyano-ferrates(II) and Hexacyano-ferrates(III)**

1. Contact with mineral acids releases toxic hydrogen cyanide.
2. Store as general inorganic chemicals.
3. Restrict use of solids to work by teachers and senior pupils; solutions, which must not be heated or treated with mineral acid, are appropriate for work by teachers, senior pupils and, with close supervision, by pupils in year 9 or above.

**Hexane**

1. Highly flammable; narcotic vapour.
2. Store as a flammable liquid.
3. Appropriate for work by teachers and pupils in year 9 or above; fume cupboard appropriate for some work.

**Hexanedioyl chloride**

1. Corrosive; volatile; also supplied as a 5% w/w solution in tetrachloromethane (see below).
2. Store as a corrosive liquid in a cool, dry place; stores less well than decanedioyl dichloride (see above).
3. Use in a fume cupboard; appropriate for work by teachers, senior pupils and, with close supervision, pupils in year 9 or above.

**Hydrazine**

1. Anhydrous hydrazine should not be kept, stored or used in schools; the hydrazine salts are corrosive and cause severe irritation to the eyes and skin; hydrazine hydrate may be carcinogenic.
2. If it is necessary to store hydrazine chloride, hydrate or sulphate in a school, the quantities should be small and the stock regarded as toxic and corrosive.
3. Work should normally be restricted to teachers.

**Hydrochloric acid**

1. Corrosive; vapour severely irritates the eyes, skin and respiratory system; reacts vigorously with many metals.
2. Store as a corrosive liquid.
3. Work with concentrated hydrochloric acid should normally be confined to teachers and senior pupils; work with dilute acid (5 M or less) is appropriate for teachers and pupils in year 9 and beyond and, with close supervision, for pupils in years 7 and 8; use a fume cupboard when hydrogen chloride

would otherwise be released into the atmosphere; use eye protection and gloves when working with the concentrated acid; when added to nitric acid to produce aqua regia, do not store the mixture; do not allow to come into contact with methanal.

**Hydrofluoric acid**  The hazards associated with this material are such that it should not be kept, stored, prepared or used in a school.

**Hydrogen**  1. Highly flammable; explosion limits in air of 4–75%; common cause of accidents in schools.
2. Hydrogen cylinders should be securely stored, away from sources of heat.
3. Use of a hydrogen cylinder should be confined to the teacher; do not use powdered metals in the laboratory preparation of hydrogen; if the gas is to be dried, use silica gel not concentrated sulphuric acid; test tube scale preparation, collection and testing appropriate for teachers and for pupils from year 9 onwards with close supervision; large-scale preparation to be undertaken only by the teacher; burning of hydrogen in air or in chlorine suitable for the teacher only; explosion in air or oxygen suitable for the teacher only; reduction of metal oxides normally suitable for the teacher only; igniting hydrogen in the presence of air or oxygen presents major hazards so great care is needed in lighting a jet of hydrogen to be used to reduce a heated metal oxide: no attempt should be made to light such a jet until all the air has been purged from the apparatus and this has been confirmed by collecting and testing a sample of the escaping gas; a safety screen and eye protection will be necessary precautions for most school experiments involving gaseous hydrogen.

**Hydrogen cyanide**  The hazards associated with this material are such that it should not be kept, stored, prepared or used in a school.

**Hydrogen peroxide**  1. '100 volume' hydrogen peroxide is corrosive and causes severe irritation of the eyes, skin and respiratory system; powerful oxidizing agent; hazardous reactions with a range of easily oxidized materials, including many common organic compounds.
2. Has a limited shelf life; store '100 volume' in a dark, cool place as a corrosive chemical away from easily oxidized materials; open with care and dilute only immediately before use; '20 volume' hydrogen peroxide, purchased as such, may be stored as a general inorganic chemical but should also be kept away from light and heat.
3. '100 volume' solution should be used only by the teacher;

'20 volume' or less concentrated solutions are appropriate for use by teachers, by pupils in or beyond year 9 and, with close supervision, by pupils in years 7 and 8.

**Hydrogen sulphide**

1. Flammable; toxic; forms explosive mixtures with air; anaesthetizes the sense of smell.
2. Cylinders of hydrogen sulphide should not be kept in a school; the gas should be prepared, on a small scale in a fume cupboard, as required.
3. Work with hydrogen sulphide should be restricted to teachers and senior pupils; all work with the gas requires a fume cupboard; work with aqueous hydrogen sulphide in a well-ventilated laboratory may be acceptable.

**2-Hydroxybenzoic acid**

1. Harmful, causing nausea.
2. Store as a general organic chemical.
3. Appropriate for use by teachers and pupils in or beyond year 9.

**Indicators**

1. In powder form, some indicators are irritant and some may be, or may contain, small quantities of one or more suspected carcinogens; solutions of indicators in, for example, ethanol are flammable.
2. Store powdered indicators as general inorganic chemicals.
3. Wear disposable gloves when working with a powder and restrict use to teachers; wear eye protection when preparing solutions in flammable solvents; solutions of indicators normally appropriate for use by teachers, by pupils in year 9 or above, and, with close supervision, by pupils from year 7 onwards.

**Iodic(V) acid**

1. Strong oxidizing agent; may ignite on contact with combustible material; dust and solution irritate the eyes, skin and respiratory system.
2. Store away from combustible material.
3. Restrict use of acid and of IODATES(V) to work by the teacher and senior pupils.

**Iodine**

1. Vapour and solid irritate the eyes; vapour irritates the respiratory system; reacts vigorously with powdered metals; forms explosive addition compounds with ammonia.
2. Store as a corrosive solid.
3. Fume cupboard essential whenever the vapour would otherwise be released into the atmosphere, e.g. reaction with metals, demonstration of sublimation; in a well-ventilated laboratory, heating a small quantity (not more than 0.1 g) in a

test tube, plugged with cotton wool, may present an acceptable degree of risk; do not dissolve in tetrachloromethane (use cyclohexane instead to demonstrate the effect of solvent on colour); appropriate for work by teachers, senior pupils and, with close supervision, pupils in year 7 or above.

**Iodobutane**

1. Harmful; flash point 36°C.
2. Store as a general organic chemical.
3. Use a fume cupboard and restrict work to teachers and senior pupils.

**Iodoethane**

1. Harmful; vapour narcotic.
2. Has a limited shelf life since it is affected by light and air; store in a cool, dark place.
3. Use a fume cupboard and restrict work to teachers and senior pupils.

**Iodopropane**

1. Harmful.
2. Store as a general organic chemical.
3. Use a fume cupboard and restrict work to teachers and senior pupils.

**Iron(III) chloride**

1. Reaction with water produces corrosive hydrochloric acid.
2. Store a general inorganic chemical.
3. Anhydrous solid and solution appropriate for use by teachers and pupils in year 9 or beyond; pupils in years 7 and 8 should not work with anhydrous iron(III) chloride and should be closely supervised when using the solution.

**Iron(II) sulphide**

1. Produces very toxic hydrogen sulphide in contact with acid.
2. Store as a general inorganic chemical.
3. Restrict use to teachers and to pupils in year 9 or above.

**Lead and its compounds**

1. Lead is a cumulative poison and it and all its compounds should be regarded as harmful or toxic; lead(II) nitrate is a strong oxidizing agent.
2. Store lead as a general inorganic chemical and its compounds as toxic materials; do not store lead chromate (VI).
3. Wash hands after handling metallic lead; avoid release of vapour or dust of lead or lead compounds into the atmosphere; do not work with lead alkyls; electrolysis of molten lead(II) bromide requires a fume cupboard (or an effective localized method of extracting fumes) and should be restricted to teachers, senior pupils or, with close supervision, pupils in year 9 or above; decomposition of lead(II) nitrate requires a fume cupboard and, on a test tube scale, is appropriate for

teachers and pupils in year 9 or above; work with lead oxides is normally appropriate for teachers, pupils in or above year 9, and, with close supervision, for pupils in years 7 and 8; reduction of small quantities of ores as a class experiment requires a well ventilated laboratory and, with close supervision, may be appropriate for pupils in year 7 or above.

**Lithium and its compounds**

1. The metal produces flammable hydrogen on contact with water; lithium hydroxide is caustic and corrosive; lithium nitrate is an oxidizing agent; lithium tetrahydridoaluminate(III) produces flammable hydrogen with water; lithium hydride ignites in moist air.
2. Store the metal away from moisture and oxidizing agents.
3. Heating lithium in air requires eye protection and a safety screen and should be done only by the teacher; work with lithium hydride and the tetrahydridoaluminate(III) requires a fume cupboard and should be restricted to the teacher; addition of small pieces of lithium to water (eye protection) is not appropriate for pupils below year 9; restrict work with lithium hydroxide to teachers and senior pupils.

**Magnesium**

1. Burning metal difficult to extinguish; reactions of the powdered metal can be violent or explosive, e.g. with sulphur, halogens and metal oxides; reaction of metal with acids produces flammable hydrogen.
2. Store as a flammable solid, away from oxidizing agents.
3. Work with magnesium ribbon or turnings is generally appropriate for teachers, for pupils in year 9 or above, and, with close supervision, for pupils in years 7 or 8; work with the powdered metal should be restricted to teachers, senior pupils and, with close supervision, to pupils in year 9 or above; avoid looking directly at the light emitted by burning magnesium; note that burning magnesium in glass apparatus can produce magnesium silicide; do not use a mixture of magnesium and potassium carbonate as a substitute for sodium in sodium fusion tests.

**Magnesium chorate(VII)**

1. A powerful oxidizing agent that forms explosive or unstable mixtures with a variety of organic compounds and other readily oxidized materials; toxic and irritates the skin, eyes and respiratory tract.
2. The hazards of this material are such that it should not be kept, stored, used or made in schools; as a desiccant, it can be replaced by silica gel or anhydrous calcium sulphate.

**Manganese(IV) oxide**

1. An oxidizing agent that can react vigorously with combustible materials.

2. Store as an oxidizing agent.

3. Prepare oxygen from aqueous hydrogen peroxide rather than by heating the so-called oxygen mixture of manganese(IV) oxide and potassium chlorate(V); when fusing with alkali to make manganate(VII) (teachers or senior pupils only), wear eye protection and gloves and use a safety screen; oxidation of hydrochloric acid by manganese(IV) oxide unnecessary as a method of preparing chlorine (see above).

**Mercury and its compounds**

1. Mercury vapour is toxic and the compounds of the metal are also highly poisonous; mercury(II) nitrate is an oxidizing agent; mercury reacts vigorously or violently with powdered aluminium, alkali metals and halogens.

2. Store securely as toxic materials.

3. If possible, avoid all exposure of metal to the atmosphere (minimize exposure in simple barometric work and incorporate arrangements for spillage); fume cupboard essential for amalgamation experiments and for work that involves heating the metal or its compounds (e.g. the oxide or nitrate) and for reaction with iodine; avoid using Millon's reagent (Cole's modification is a suggested alternative); use a syringe or pooter to collect small drops of spilled mercury (e.g. from a broken thermometer); if the drops are inaccessible (e.g. in small cracks in the floor) treat with a 1:1 mixture of calcium hydroxide and powdered sulphur.

**Methanal**

1. Toxic; methanal vapour irritates the eyes, skin and respiratory system; the 37–41% aqueous solution is corrosive, has a flash point of 50°C and is usually supplied containing 11–14% methanol.

2. Store as a flammable liquid.

3. Wear eye protection when using methanal solution; work in a fume cupboard unless the solution is very dilute; do not allow to come into contact with hydrochloric acid or hydrogen chloride; consider using 70% ethanol as an alternative preservative for biological material; when 'formalin' is used as preservative, soak the preserved specimen(s) in water or 30% ethanol for a minimum of one hour, then rinse thoroughly before examination; aqueous solution appropriate for work by teachers, senior pupils and, with close supervision, by pupils in years 9–11.

**Methanoic acid**

1. Corrosive; vapour causes severe irritation of the eyes, skin and respiratory system.

2. Store as a corrosive liquid.

3. Wear eye protection and gloves when using the concentrated acid; appropriate for use by teachers, senior pupils and,

with close supervision, by pupils in year 9 or above; a fume cupboard will be required for some experiments.

**Methanol**
1. Highly flammable; toxic.
2. Store as a flammable liquid.
3. Appropriate for work by teachers, senior pupils and, with close supervision, pupils in years, 9,10 and 11.

**Methoxyphenyl-amines**
1. 2-Methoxyphenylamine (liquid, b.p. 224°C), the 4-isomer (solid, m.p. 59°C) and their vapours are both very toxic.
2. Store as toxic substances.
3. Use in a fume cupboard and restrict use to teachers and senior pupils.

**Methylamine**
1. Gas (b.p. $-6.3$°C) is very flammable and irritates the eyes, skin and respiratory system; solution (commonly 25–30% in water or ethanol) also flammable and irritating.
2. Store solution as a flammable liquid.
3. Wear eye protection, consider the use of a fume cupboard and restrict use to teachers and senior pupils.

**Methylbenzene**
1. Highly flammable; inhalation of vapour causes nausea, dizziness and headache; absorption via the skin or by ingestion causes poisoning.
2. Store as a flammable liquid.
3. Restrict use to teachers, senior pupils and, with close supervision, to pupils in year 9 or above; consider use of a fume cupboard; note that although the dimethylbenzenes are less volatile than methylbenzene and thus present a reduced fire risk, they may be more toxic.

**Methyl ethanoate**
1. Highly flammable; vapour irritates the eyes, skin and respiratory system.
2. Store as a flammable liquid.
3. Restrict use to teachers and pupils in year 9 or above; consider the use of a fume cupboard.

**Methyl ethyl ketone peroxide**
1. Oxidizing agent.
2. Store as an oxidizing agent away from combustible materials.
3. Restrict use to teachers and to pupils in year 9 or above.

**Methyl methanoate**
1. Flammable and irritant.
2. Store as a flammable liquid.
3. Restrict use to teachers and to pupils in year 9 or above; consider the use of a fume cupboard.

**Methyl 2-methylpropanoate**
1. Highly flammable and causes irritation of the eyes, skin and lungs.
2. Store as a flammable liquid.
3. Use in a fume cupboard and restrict use to teachers and senior pupils.

**Millon's reagent**
See under MERCURY AND ITS COMPOUNDS above. Cole's modification is appropriate for use by teachers, senior pupils and, with close supervision, by pupils in year 9 or above.

**Naphthalen-1-amine and naphthalen-2-amine**
These compounds must not be kept, stored, used or prepared in schools; avoid reactions in which either of these compounds is likely to be formed as an intermediate. Note, however, that *pure* naphthalen-1-amine is not carcinogenic.

**Naphthalene**
1. Combustible; harmful.
2. Store as a flammable solid and away from oxidizing agents.
3. Do not use naphthalene in an open laboratory; use alternatives to naphthalene where possible (e.g. hexadecan-1-ol, octadecan-1-ol, hexadecanoic acid or octadecanoic acid, for cooling curve experiments); do not nitrate; appropriate for use by teachers and by pupils in year 9 or above.

**Nessler's reagent**
1. Very toxic (see MERCURY AND ITS COMPOUNDS above); corrosive.
2. Store securely as a poison.
3. Consider whether the use of the reagent can be avoided and, if not, restrict use to teachers and senior pupils.

**Nickel and its compounds**
1. The metallic dust and many nickel compounds commonly found in schools irritate the skin, eyes and lungs; many of these compounds are also harmful.
2. Store as general inorganic chemicals.
3. Restrict work with powdered nickel or solid nickel salts to teachers and senior pupils; work with aqueous solutions of nickel salts appropriate for teachers and for pupils in year 9 or above.

**Ninhydrin**
1. Solution in butan-1-ol flammable.
2. Store solid in refrigerator; store aerosol away from heat and in accordance with the manufacturer's instructions.
3. Do not allow pupils to work with solid ninhydrin; undertake all work with a ninhydrin aerosol or solution in a fume cupboard and restrict such work to teachers, senior pupils and, with close supervision, pupils in year 9 or above.

**Nitric acid**
1. Corrosive; vapour injures the eyes, skin and respiratory system; powerful oxidizing agent which reacts vigorously or violently with combustible materials.
2. Store as a corrosive liquid, away from flammable materials; caution needed (eye protection, gloves, fume cupboard) in opening a bottle of fuming (98%) nitric acid.
3. Restrict work (fume cupboard, etc.) with fuming acid to teachers and, with close supervision, to senior pupils; work with dilute acid (less than 5 M) is appropriate for teachers, pupils in year 9 or above and, with close supervision, pupils in years 7 and 8; work with concentrated acid (70%) should be restricted to teachers, senior pupils and, with close supervision, pupils in years 9–11; do not mix nitric acid with alcohol; restrict laboratory preparation on anything other than a test-tube scale to teachers; do not nitrate naphthalene; any organic nitrations (fume cupboard normally required) should be restricted to teachers and senior pupils; reactions that produce nitrogen dioxide require a fume cupboard; for aqua regia, see HYDROCHLORIC ACID.

**Nitrites**
1. Toxic; oxidizing agents.
2. Store away from combustible materials and acids.
3. Nitrites in solution are appropriate for use by teachers and by pupils in year 9 or above; the use of solid nitrites should be restricted to teachers and senior pupils; see also AZO DYES.

**Nitrobenzene**
1. Very toxic; vapour can cause severe breathing problems.
2. Store as a toxic liquid.
3. Use in a fume cupboard and restrict use to teachers and senior pupils.

**4-Nitrobiphenyl**
This substance must not be kept, stored, used or prepared in schools.

**Nitrogen dioxide**
1. Very toxic; effects of inhalation (headache, nausea, cyanosis etc.) sometimes evident only after a long delay.
2. Do not store cylinders of nitrogen dioxide in schools.
3. Preparation requires a fume cupboard; restrict preparation to teachers and senior pupils.

**Nitrogen monoxide**
1. Very toxic; rapidly oxidized in air to nitrogen dioxide.
2. Do not store cylinders of nitrogen monoxide in school.
3. Preparation requires a fume cupboard; restrict preparation to teachers and senior pupils; reaction with CARBON DISULPHIDE (see above) not recommended. For DINITROGEN OXIDE, see above.

**Nitromethyl-benzenes**

These substances should not be kept, stored, used or prepared in schools.

**Nitronaphthalenes**

These substances must not be kept, stored, used or prepared in schools.

**Nitrophenols**

1. Harmful; 2-nitrophenol is more volatile than its isomers.
2. Store as general organic compounds.
3. Restrict work to teachers and to senior pupils under close supervision.

**4[(4-Nitro-phenyl)azo]benzene-1-3-diol (magneson I) and 4[(4-nitro-phenyl)azo]naphthalen-1-ol (magneson II)**

1. Solid reagents are harmful and their solutions in sodium hydroxide are corrosive.
2. Store as general organic chemicals.
3. Use of the solutions appropriate for teachers and pupils in year 9 or above; restrict use of solids to teachers.

**Nitrosamines**

These substances must not be kept, stored, used or prepared in schools. Avoid reactions in which they might be formed as intermediates.

**Nitrosophenols**

Do not keep, store, use or prepare 2- or 3-nitrosophenols in schools. If work with 4-nitrosophenol (toxic, irritant) cannot be avoided, restrict such work to teachers and senior pupils under close supervision.

**Octane**

1. Flammable (flash point 13°C).
2. Store as a flammable liquid.
3. Appropriate for use by teachers and pupils in year 9 or above; consider the use of a fume cupboard.

**Oleum**

This substance should not normally be kept, stored, used or prepared in schools.

**Osmic acid**

This substance should not normally be kept, stored, used or prepared in schools. Alternative stains for microscopy are available (e.g. the Sudan dyes).

**Oxygen**

1. Enhances combustion.
2. Store cylinders securely and away from sources of heat.
3. Restrict use of cylinders to teachers and senior pupils; reaction with AMMONIA is hazardous (see above); do not prepare using 'oxygen mixture' (see MANGANESE(IV) OXIDE above).

**Pentane**
1. Highly flammable (flash point −48°C); very volatile (b.p. 30°C); vapour is narcotic.
2. Store as a flammable liquid.
3. Appropriate for use by teachers and by pupils in year 9 or above; consider the use of a fume cupboard.

**Pentanols**
1. Flammable; vapour irritates the eyes and the respiratory system.
2. Store as flammable liquids.
3. Appropriate for use by teachers and by pupils in year 9 or above; consider the use of a fume cupboard.

**Pentan-2-one and pentan-3-one**
1. Highly flammable; vapour irritates the eyes and the respiratory system.
2. Store as flammable liquids.
3. Appropriate for use by teachers and by pupils in year 9 or above; consider the use of a fume cupboard.

**Pentyl ethanoate**
1. Flammable; vapour can cause headache.
2. Store as a flammable liquid.
3. Appropriate for use by teachers and by pupils in year 9 or above; consider the use of a fume cupboard.

**Potassium peroxodisulphate(VI)**
1. Strong oxidizing agent; toxic.
2. Store away from organic solvents and other combustible materials.
3. Restrict use to teachers and senior pupils.

**Petroleum spirit (b.p. <80°C)**
1. Highly flammable; volatile, producing a flammable, narcotic vapour that can flash back from a source of ignition.
2. Store as flammable liquids.
3. Do not use in the same room as a source of ignition; restrict use to teachers and senior pupils; work in a fume cupboard; PETROLEUM SPIRIT with a higher boiling point, i.e. >80°C also presents a considerable fire hazard but may be appropriate for use by pupils in years 9–11 under close supervision.

**Phenol**
1. Corrosive; toxic.
2. Store securely as a toxic chemical.
3. Prevent eye and skin contact; use dilute nitric acid (ca. 4M) to nitrate phenol; in reactions involving diazotization, ensure that diazotization is complete before proceeding to the next stage; in preparing phenol-methanal resins, do not use hydrochloric acid as a catalyst; restrict use of solid to teachers and senior pupils under close supervision; work with dilute aqueous phenol appropriate for teachers and for pupils in year 9 or above.

| | |
|---|---|
| ***Phenylamine*** | 1. Toxic; vapour can cause headache, drowsiness, cyanosis, etc. |
| | 2. Store as a toxic chemical. |
| | 3. Use phenylammonium chloride instead of phenylamine in diazotization reactions; in such reactions, ensure that diazotization is complete before proceeding to the next stage (see also AZO DYES above); work with phenylamine (fume cupboard) and its salts is appropriate for teachers and senior pupils. |
| ***Phenylethanone*** | 1. Irritant. |
| | 2. Store as a general organic chemical. |
| | 3. Appropriate for work by teachers, by pupils in year 9 or above and with close supervision, by pupils in years 7 and 8. |
| ***Phenylethene*** | 1. Flammable, irritates the eyes and respiratory system; readily polymerizes with evolution of heat. |
| | 2. Store away from light in small quantities as a flammable liquid. |
| | 3. Use a fume cupboard and restrict work to teachers and senior pupils. |
| ***Phenylhydrazine*** | 1. Toxic vapour; dust or vapour irritating to the eyes and skin and can be allergenic. |
| | 2. Store as a general organic chemical. |
| | 3. Restrict work with phenylhydrazine or its salts to teachers and senior pupils. |
| ***Phenylthiourea*** | 1. Usually sold as strips of impregnated paper and, in this form, presents an acceptable level of risk. |
| | 2. Store paper strips in accordance with manufacturer's instructions. |
| | 3. Restrict work with the strips to teachers, senior pupils and, with close supervision, pupils in years 9–11. |
| ***Phosphoric(V) acid*** | 1. Corrosive; exothermic reaction with water. |
| | 2. Store as a corrosive liquid. |
| | 3. When used to prepare hydrogen halides, a fume cupboard is essential; work with the concentrated acid should be restricted to teachers and senior pupils; work with dilute solutions ($<5M$) is appropriate for teachers and for pupils in year 9 or above. |
| ***Phosphorus*** | 1. Red phosphorus is highly flammable and explodes on mixing with a range of oxidizing substances; white phosphorus also ignites spontaneously in air and is highly toxic. |
| | 2. Store red and white forms of phosphorus away from oxidiz- |

ing agents; store white phosphorus securely under water and replace the water regularly; work with white phosphorus requires a fume cupboard and should be confined to teachers; cut white phosphorus under water with a sharp knife; work with red phosphorus is appropriate for teachers, senior pupils, and, with close supervision, pupils in years 9–11.

**Phosphorus chlorides**

1. Corrosive; vapour attacks eyes, skin and respiratory system; react violently with water, producing corrosive fumes.
2. Store in small quantities as corrosive chemicals and keep away from moisture.
3. Work in a fume cupboard, use eye protection and restrict work to teachers and senior pupils under close supervision.

Similar hazards are presented by PHOSPHORUS(III) BROMIDE and by PHOSPHORUS TRICHLORIDE OXIDE and similar precautions are required.

**Phosphorus(V) oxide**

1. Corrosive; irritates the eyes, skin and respiratory system; reacts violently with water producing corrosive liquid and fumes; produces carbon monoxide with methanoic acid.
2. Store in small quantities as a corrosive chemical and keep away from moisture.
3. Consider alternatives (e.g. silica gel, anhydrous calcium sulphate) as a desiccant; use a fume cupboard whenever hydrogen chloride is likely to be produced, e.g. preparation of acid anhydrides; restrict work to teachers and senior pupils.

**Potassium**

1. Reacts violently with water, producing hydrogen (which usually ignites) and corrosive aqueous potassium hydroxide; metal burns vigorously.
2. Store a small quantity as a flammable substance and keep away from moisture; note that old stock may contain peroxides, leading to explosion when an attempt is made to cut the metal; destroy old stock, which sometimes has a yellowish appearance, by dissolving small amounts in 2-methylpropan-2-ol.
3. Work with potassium (eye protection, safety screen) should be restricted to the teacher; do not burn potassium in chlorine; do not add the metal to chlorinated hydrocarbons.

**Potassium amide**

Reacts violently with water; this substance should not normally be kept, stored, used or prepared in schools.

**Potassium chlorate(V)**

1. Strong oxidizing agent; irritates the skin; reacts vigorously with combustible materials; forms explosive chlorine oxides with concentrated sulphuric acid.

2. Store as an oxidizing agent away from organic solvents and other combustible materials.

3. Do not use in the preparation of oxygen (aqueous hydrogen peroxide and manganese(IV) oxide preferred); consider the use of anhydrous sodium tetraborate as an alternative in solubility experiments; when fused with potassium hydroxide to prepare potassium manganate(VII), wear eye protection and use a safety screen.

*Potassium chromate(VI)*

1. Oxidizing agent; irritates the eyes, skin and respiratory system.

2. Store as a toxic chemical and away from flammable materials.

3. Aqueous solutions appropriate for work by teachers and pupils beyond year 9; see CHROMATES(VI) and DICHROMATES(VI) above.

*Potassium cyanide*

See CYANIDES above.

*Potassium hexa-cyanoferrate(II) and potassium hexacyano-ferrate(III)*

See HEXACYANOFERRATES(II) and HEXACYANOFERRATES(III) above.

*Potassium hydroxide*

1. Corrosive; dissolution in water highly exothermic.

2. Store as a corrosive solid.

3. Restrict use of solid to teachers and senior pupils; dilute solutions (2 M or less) appropriate for use by teachers, pupils in year 9 or above and, with close supervision, by pupils in years 7 and 8; eye protection essential in all cases.

*Potassium iodate(V)*

1. Oxidizing agent; reacts vigorously or violently with a number of common chemicals, e.g. carbon, sulphur, magnesium.

2. Store as an oxidizing agent and away from combustible materials.

3. See IODIC(V) acid above.

*Potassium manganate(VII)*

1. Strong oxidizing agent.

2. Store as a strong oxidizing agent and away from combustible materials.

3. Eye protection essential when decomposing the manganate(VII) by heating; do not mix with phosphoric acid or with concentrated sulphuric acid, see CHLORINE above; appropriate for use by teachers, by pupils in year 9 and above, and, with close supervision, by pupils in year 7 and 8.

**Potassium nitrate**    1. Oxidizing agent; reacts vigorously or violently with easily oxidized substances.
2. Store as an oxidizing agent and away from combustible materials.
3. Appropriate for work by teachers, pupils in year 9 or above, and, with close supervision, by pupils in years 7 and 8.

**Potassium nitrite**    See NITRITES above.

**Propanal**    1. Highly flammable and volatile liquid (flash point $-38°C$, b.p. $21°C$); irritates eyes, skin and respiratory system.
2. Prepare as required or store in a cool place as a flammable, volatile liquid.
3. Use in a fume cupboard and restrict use to teachers and to pupils in year 9 or above.

**Propanoic acid**    1. Corrosive; irritates eyes, skin and respiratory system.
2. Store as a corrosive material.
3. Use in a fume cupboard and restrict use to teachers and to pupils in year 9 or above.

**Propanols**    1. Highly flammable; react vigorously with oxidizing agents; vapours irritate the eyes and respiratory system.
2. Store as flammable liquids; risk of peroxide formation when propan-2-ol is exposed to sunlight for prolonged periods; store propan-2-ol in a dark place and for not longer than two years.
3. Appropriate for use by teachers and by pupils in year 9 or above.

**Propanone**    1. Highly flammable (flash point $-18°C$); vapour irritates the eyes and respiratory system; reacts vigorously with oxidizing agents.
2. Store as a flammable liquid.
3. Do not mix with trichloromethane; do not mix with nitric acid; use fume cupboard for all but small-scale reactions; appropriate for use by teachers, by pupils in year 9 or above and, with close supervision, by pupils in years 7 and 8.

**Propylamines**    1. Flammable (flash point of each isomer $-37°C$); volatile and vapour irritates the eyes, skin and respiratory system.
2. Store as flammable liquids.
3. Restrict use (fume cupboard) of amines to teachers and senior pupils; work with aqueous solutions may also be appropriate for pupils in year 9 or above.

**Propyl ethanoate**
1. Highly flammable.
2. Store as a flammable liquid.
3. Restrict use to teachers and to pupils in year 9 or above; consider the use of a fume cupboard.

**Pyridine**
1. Highly flammable (flash point 20°C); vapour irritates the respiratory system and may cause nausea and vomiting.
2. Store as flammable liquid.
3. Use a fume cupboard and restrict use to teachers and senior pupils.

**Silicon tetra-chloride**
1. Corrosive; reacts vigorously with water; vapour irritates the eyes, skin and respiratory system.
2. Store small quantities in dry conditions, e.g. in a desiccator; do not keep stock for more than two years; open container (gloves, eye protection) in a fume cupboard.
3. Use a fume cupboard and restrict work to teachers and senior pupils.

**Silver nitrate**
1. Corrosive; toxic.
2. Store securely (dark bottle) as a toxic chemical.
3. Aqueous solution appropriate for use by teachers, senior pupils and, with close supervision, pupils in years 9–11; restrict use of solid to teachers and senior pupils; see also AMMONIA above.

**Sodium**
1. Reacts vigorously with water producing flammable hydrogen; reacts violently with many oxidizing agents e.g. chlorine, bromine; forms explosive mixtures with chlorinated hydrocarbons, e.g. tetrachloromethane.
2. Store securely in small quantities as a flammable metal and ensure that the metal is always covered by liquid paraffin.
3. Appropriate for work by teachers and, with close supervision, senior pupils; eye protection essential when working with the metal; use Middleton's test in preference to the sodium fusion test.

**Sodium amide**
Reacts violently with water; this substance should not normally be kept, stored, prepared or used in schools.

**Sodium chlorate(I)**
See CHLORATES(I) above.

**Sodium chlorate(V)**
See CHLORATES(V) above.

**Sodium hydroxide**
1. Corrosive; dissolves very exothermically in water.

2. Store as a corrosive solid.

3. Restrict work with the solid to teachers and, with close supervision, senior pupils; work with dilute aqueous sodium hydroxide (2 M or less) appropriate for teachers, pupils in year 9 and above, and, with close supervision, for pupils in years 7 and 8; eye protection essential when working with solid, melt or aqueous solutions.

**Sodium nitrate**

1. Oxidizing agent.

2. Store as an oxidizing agent and away from combustible materials.

3. Appropriate for work by teachers and, with appropriate supervision, by pupils from year 7 onwards.

**Sodium nitrite**

See NITRITES above.

**Sodium penta-cyanonitrosyl-ferrate(II)**

1. Toxic.

2. Store securely as a toxic solid.

3. Restrict use to teachers and senior pupils.

**Sodium peroxide**

1. Corrosive; strong oxidizing agent; reacts vigorously with water to form a corrosive solution; violent or explosive reaction with many organic compounds.

2. Store in dry conditions as a corrosive solid and away from combustible materials.

3. Eye protection essential when working with this substance; not recommended as a means of preparing oxygen; restrict work to teachers and, with close supervision, senior pupils.

**Sulphur**

1. Forms corrosive sulphur dioxide on combustion; forms very reactive mixtures with some powdered metals, e.g. aluminium, magnesium; forms explosive mixtures with chlorates(V) and with silver nitrate.

2. Store as a flammable solid.

3. Appropriate for work by teachers and by pupils in year 7 or above; fume cupboard required whenever sulphur dioxide would otherwise be released into the laboratory; safety screen and eye protection needed when heating with iron filings or powdered copper; do not heat sulphur with magnesium; do not use CARBON DISULPHIDE (see above) as a solvent for sulphur.

**Sulphur dichloride dioxide**

1. Reacts violently with water forming corrosive sulphuric and hydrochloric acids; corrosive; vapour irritates the eyes, skin and respiratory system.

2. Store away from moisture as a corrosive liquid.

3. Use in a fume cupboard and restrict use to teachers and, with close supervision, senior pupils.

**Sulphur dichloride oxide**

1. Reacts violently with water forming corrosive hydrochloric acid and sulphur dioxide; corrosive; vapour irritates the eyes, skin and respiratory system.
2. Store away from moisture as a corrosive liquid.
3. Use in a fume cupboard and restrict use to teachers and, with close supervision, senior pupils.

**Sulphur dioxide**

1. Toxic; irritates the eyes, skin and respiratory system.
2. Store as a canister in a cool, corrosion-free atmosphere.
3. Work with the gas requires a fume cupboard; preparation from sodium sulphite and dilute sulphuric acid is safer than heating copper with concentrated sulphuric acid; use of a canister should be restricted to teachers and, with close supervision, senior pupils; when using a canister, do not overtighten the valve; preparation on a test tube scale from dilute acid and sulphite appropriate for teachers, senior pupils and, with close supervision, pupils in years 9–11.

**Sulphuric acid**

1. Very corrosive; highly exothermic reaction with water.
2. Store as a corrosive liquid.
3. Eye protection and gloves essential when handling the concentrated acid; do not mix with chlorates, manganates(VII), white phosphorus; when diluting the concentrated acid, add slowly, with stirring, to a large excess of water; avoid use of the concentrated acid as a desiccant; restrict work with the concentrated acid to teachers, senior pupils and, with close supervision, pupils in years 9–11; work with dilute sulphuric acid (5 M or less) appropriate for teachers, pupils in year 9 or above and, with close supervision, by pupils in years 7 and 8.

**Tetrachloro-methane**

1. Toxic; vapour irritates the eyes; reacts explosively with alkali metals.
2. Store securely as a toxic chemical.
3. Wherever possible, avoid the use of tetrachloromethane; alternative and less toxic solvents are usually available; any work with tetrachloromethane requires a fume cupboard and should be restricted to teachers and, with close supervision, senior pupils.

**Thallium and its compounds**

These substances should not be kept, stored, used or prepared in schools.

**Thiocyanates**

1. Harmful.
2. Store as general inorganic chemicals.

3. Do not heat or react with acid; restrict use of solids to teachers and senior pupils; work with solutions appropriate for teachers and pupils in year 9 or above.

**Thorium compounds**

Radioactive and perhaps toxic; any storage or use must be in strict accordance with the relevant regulations from the DES or DENI as appropriate (see page 20); note that SED Circular 1166, 1987 forbids the use of thorium compounds in Scottish schools.

**Tin chlorides**

1. Tin(IV) chloride is corrosive and the vapour irritates the eyes; it reacts vigorously with water forming corrosive hydrogen chloride; tin(II) chloride reacts vigorously with oxidizing agents.
2. Store tin(IV) chloride as a corrosive substance and in dry conditions (e.g. in a desiccator); store tin(II) chloride as a general inorganic chemical.
3. Work with tin(IV) chloride (eye protection, fume cupboard) should be restricted to teachers and senior pupils; tin(II) chloride is appropriate for work by teachers and by pupils in year 9 or above.

**Titanium(IV) chloride**

1. Corrosive; reacts violently with water forming corrosive hydrogen chloride; vapour irritates the eyes, skin and respiratory system.
2. Store in small quantities in dry conditions.
3. Use a fume cupboard and restrict work to teachers.

**1,1,1-Trichloroethane**

1. Harmful vapour; reacts violently or explosively with alkali metals.
2. Store as a general organic chemical.
3. Appropriate for use by teachers, senior pupils and, with close supervision by pupils in years 9–11; consider use of a fume cupboard.

**2,2,2-Trichloro-ethanediol**

1. Toxic; irritates the eyes and skin.
2. Store securely as a toxic chemical.
3. Use a fume cupboard and restrict work to teachers and senior pupils.

**Trichloroethanoic acid**

See CHLOROETHANOIC ACIDS above.

**Trichloroethene**

1. Harmful vapour; reacts violently or explosively with alkali metals.
2. Store as a general organic chemical.

3. Use a fume cupboard and restrict work to teachers and, with close supervision, senior pupils.

**Trichloromethane** 1. Toxic; vapour irritates eyes; anaesthetic; reacts violently with alkali metals; can form an explosive mixture with propanone.
2. Store securely as a toxic chemical.
3. Consider carefully whether the use of this substance is necessary; other, less toxic solvents are usually available; work with trichloromethane requires a fume cupboard and should be confined to teachers and, with close supervision, senior pupils.

**2,4,6-Trinitrophenol** 1. Toxic; risk of explosion by shock, friction or heat.
2. Solid must be kept damp; store in a bottle sealed with a waxed cork not a screw top; keep away from sources of heat.
3. Restrict work with the solid to teachers; work with the solution appropriate for teachers and senior pupils.

**Triiodomethane** 1. Irritant.
2. Store as a general organic chemical.
3. Use a fume cupboard and restrict work to teachers and senior pupils.

**Uranium compounds** Toxic and radioactive. Any storage or use must be in strict accordance with the relevant regulations (see page 20) from the DES, SED or DENI as appropriate.

**Vanadium(V) oxide** 1. Harmful by inhalation.
2. Store as a general inorganic compound.
3. Restrict use to teachers and senior pupils. The use of solid VANADATES(V) should be similarly restricted; work with aqueous vanadates(V) is appropriate for teachers, senior pupils and, with close supervision, pupils in years 9–11.

**Zinc and its compounds** 1. Zinc dust is flammable; reacts vigorously with acids and alkalis to form flammable hydrogen; reacts violently on heating with sulphur; vigorous reaction with iodine; zinc chloride and zinc bromide are corrosive.
2. Store zinc and its compounds as general inorganic chemicals but do not store zinc chromate(VI) which is a suspected carcinogen.
3. Zinc powder appropriate for work by teachers and, with close supervision, pupils in year 9 or above; do not allow zinc dust to enter the atmosphere; fume cupboard and eye protection essential for the reaction of zinc with iodine; do not use zinc dust when heating (small-scale only) the metal with

sulphur; restrict work with zinc chloride or bromide to teachers and senior pupils; do not use zinc chromate(VI); other common zinc compounds normally appropriate for work by teachers, by pupils in year 9 or above and, with close supervision, by pupils in years 7 and 8.

# APPENDIX B
# Hazards reported

This Appendix lists the major hazards which have been reported in *The School Science Review* from its first publication in 1919 to 1990 and in *Education in Science* since its first publication as the *Bulletin* of the Association for Science Education. Hazards reported in *Education in Science* are cited in italics.

It is envisaged that it will provide a handy source of reference for teachers and students, both for identifying those hazards which have been reported and as a record of various improved experimental procedures useful in school science teaching.

Although most of the principal hazards have been reported from time to time, the sources quoted in the Bibliography will be found helpful in any more exhaustive search.

The hazards reported in this Appendix are classified using the nomenclature adopted in the original source. In cases where doubt or confusion may arise, systematic names are also given and appropriate cross-references provided.

| Compound, Substance, Subject | Details, Reaction etc. | Author | Reference |
|---|---|---|---|
| Accidents | Advice on insurance position | — | *1967, 23, 30* |
| Accidents | Some legal advice | E. A. Philpots | 1933, 56, **14**, 488 |
| Accidents | Safeguards: comprehensive article | C. W. W. Read | 1940, 83, **21**, 964 |
| Accidents and incidents | Article—General survey of accidents | — | 1928, 38, **10**, 97 |
| Acetal (1,1-diethoxyethane) | Explosive under distillation | A. J. Mee | 1940, 85, **22**, 95 |
| Acetates (ethanoates) | Cacodyl experiment | C. W. W. Read | 1940, 83, **21**, 969 |
| Acetic acid (ethanoic acid) | Preparation by oxidation of ethyl alcohol: explosion on distilling product | E. N. Annable | 1951, 117, **32**, 249 |
| Acetic acid, glacial | Phosphorus trichloride. Preparation of acetyl chloride. Report of explosion | T. A. H. Peacocke | 1962, 152, **44**, 217 |
| Acetic anhydride (ethanoic anhydride) | Preparation | C. W. W. Read | 1940, 83, **21**, 976 |
| Acetone | *See* Propanone | | |
| Acetyl chloride (ethanoyl chloride) | Preparation | C. W. W. Read | 1940, 83, **21**, 976 |
| Acetyl peroxide | Explosive when crystallizing small quantity | A. J. Mee | 1940, 85, **22**, 95 |
| Acetylene (ethyne) | Respect under pressure, storage | F. Johnstone | 1941, 88, **22**, 448 |
| Acetylene (ethyne) | Chlorine: 'a safe way of performing' | F. Johnstone | 1931, 47, **12**, 296 |
| Acetylene (ethyne) | Chlorine | C. W. W. Read | 1940, 83, **21**, 977 |
| Acetylene (ethyne) | Copper. Explosive compounds. Copper must not be used in oxyacetylene blowlamp | R. H. Smith | 1936, 70, **18**, 281 |

| Compound, Substance, Subject | Details, Reaction etc. | Author | Reference |
|---|---|---|---|
| Acetylene (ethyne) | Oxygen. Explosion | G. Fowles | 1940, 85, **22**, 6 |
| Acetylene (ethyne) | Oxygen. Explosion: extreme danger | C. Holt | 1962, 152, **44**, 161 |
| Acetylene (ethyne) | Oxygen. Violent explosion on ignition | P. D. Arculus | 1963, 154, **44**, 706 |
| Acetylene (ethyne) | Oxygen. Explosion: precautions | T. A. H. Peacocke | 1964, 156, **45**, 459 |
| Acids | Mineral. Toxic | C. G. Vernon | 1927, 34, **9**, 97 |
| Acids | Reports of accidents | — | 1928, 38, **10**, 98, 102 |
| Acids | Effect on skin | A. St. G. Huggett | 1929, 41, **11**, 19 |
| Acrolein (propenal) | Lachrymator | P. A. Ongley | 1963, 154, **44**, 249 |
| Acrylic esters (propenoates) | Some toxic | A. J. Mee | 1940, 85, **42**, 95 |
| Air pistol | Advice on use | — | *1985, 112, 18* |
| Alcohol (ethanol) | Flammable | C. W. W. Read | 1940, 83, **21**, 973 |
| Alcohol (ethanol) | Air oxidation to formaldehyde. Danger of ignition. Safer equipment | C. Holt | 1955, 131, **37**, 135 |
| Alcohol (ethanol) | Iodine, phosphorus, ethyl iodide preparation dangerous | C. W. W. Read | 1940, 83, **21**, 967 |
| Alcohol (ethanol) | Fires | — | *1986, 116, 15* |
| Alkalis | Strong. Toxic | C. G. Vernon | 1927, 34, **9**, 97 |
| Alkalis | Pipetting | C. W. W. Read | 1940, 83, **21**, 977 |
| Alkaloids | Poisons | C. W. W. Read | 1940, 83, **21**, 971 |
| Alkyl fluorides | High toxicity | J. Ormston | 1945, 99, **26**, 148 |
| Allergy | Locusts, advice and warning | P. H. F. White | *1968, 28, 22* |
| Allyl alcohol (prop-2-en-1-ol) | Lachrymator | P. A. Ongley | 1963, 154, **44**, 749 |
| Aluminium | Ammonium nitrate. Mixture explosive | D. J. Lyness, K. Hutton | 1953, 125, **35**, 139 |
| Aluminium | Caustic alkali. Beware of hydrogen formed | D. R. Browning | 1968, 168, **49**, 606 |
| Aluminium | Sulphur | C. W. W. Read | 1940, 83, **21**, 977 |
| Aluminium | Iodine. Slight moisture results in ignition. | S. Asmathullah *et al.* | 1956, 134, **38**, 107 |
| Aluminium | Use of milk bottle tops | — | *1980, 88, 19* |
| Aluminium chloride | Preparation | C. W. W. Read | 1940, 83, **21**, 969 |
| Aluminium chloride | Dust corrosive, burns caused | D. R. Browning | 1967, 166, **48**, 718 |
| Aluminium chloride | Explosion danger in sealed tubes | A. F. Kitching | 1930, 45, **12**, 79 |
| Aluminium formate (methanoate) | Explosive | A. J. Mee | 1940, 85, **22**, 95 |
| Amido derivatives of benzene | Toxic. Some are absorbed by skin | C. G. Vernon | 1927, 34, **9**, 97 |
| Amines, aromatic | Many suspected to be carcinogenic | D. R. Browning | 1967, 167, **49**, 278 |
| Amino alcohols | Poisons | C. W. W. Read | 1940, 83, **21**, 971 |
| Aminosulphonic acid | *See* Sulphamic acid | | |
| Ammonia | Poison | C. W. W. Read | 1940, 83, **21**, 972 |
| Ammonia | Dangerous in case of leakage when used as refrigerant | V. A. Carpenter | 1952, 120, **33**, 173 |
| Ammonia | Beware of pressure build-up in bottles | V. A. Carpenter | 1963, 154, **44**, 739 |
| Ammonia | Preparation | C. W. W. Read | 1940, 83, **21**, 976 |
| Ammonia | Chlorine passed into. Nitrogen trichloride formed | C. W. W. Read | 1940, 83, **21**, 969 |
| Ammonia | Chlorine | C. W. W. Read | 1940, 83, **21**, 976 |
| Ammonia | Oxygen. Oxidation reaction: pass $NH_3$ over platinized asbestos. Beware vigorous reaction | D. Nealy | 1935, 63, **16**, 410 |

| Compound, Substance, Subject | Details, Reaction etc. | Author | Reference |
|---|---|---|---|
| Ammonia | Oxygen. Oxygen bubbled through NH₃ | E. J. Williams | 1935, 63, **16**, 410 |
| Ammonia | Oxygen. Platinum spiral catalyst. Safe but violent | L. T. Taylor | 1935, 63, **16**, 410 |
| Ammonia | Burns in oxygen | C. W. W. Read | 1940, 83, **21**, 976 |
| Ammonia | Burns in oxygen. Details of experiment | H. D. Marshall | 1968, 168, **49**, 504 |
| Ammonia | Silver oxide ppt. When hot, explosion. Fulminate possibly formed. *See* Ammonium, Silver | J. R. Morse | 1955, 131, **37**, 147 |
| Ammonia | Catalytic oxidation. Hazardous advice in textbook | — | *1979, 84, 34* |
| Ammonia | Explosion when preparing and reducing copper oxide | M. A. McElroy | *1971, 71, 21* |
| Ammonium compounds | Sodium hydroxide boiling with | C. W. W. Read | 1940, 83, **21**, 969 |
| Ammonium dichromate(VI) | Explosive when mixed with Mg. | — | *1972, 47, 24* and *1974, 56, 39* |
| Ammonium dichromate(VI) | Decomposition hazardous | — | *1979, 83, 20* |
| Ammonium ions | Silver. Heated with NaOH to expel ammonia; Devarda's alloy added: violent explosion | J. Baldwin | 1967, 165, **48**, 586 |
| Ammonium nitrate | Heat. Explosive above 240°C | — | 1927, 34, **9**, 127 |
| Ammonium nitrate | Extensive details of reaction | E. Coddington | 1928, 35, **9**, 209 |
| Ammonium nitrate | Explosion possible | E. A. Philpots | 1933, 56, **14**, 489 |
| Ammonium nitrate | Unpredictable explosive behaviour | S. I. Levy | 1936, 68, **17**, 496 |
| Ammonium nitrate | Heat | C. W. W. Read | 1940, 83, **21**, 968 |
| Ammonium nitrate | Heat | C. W. W. Read | 1940, 83, **21**, 976 |
| Ammonium nitrate | Aluminium. Mixture explosive | D. J. Lyness, K. Hutton | 1953, 125, **35**, 139 |
| Ammonium nitrate | Thermal decomposition. Report of details including explosion | J. H. Lee | 1965, 160, **46**, 697 |
| Amyl nitrate (pentyl nitrate) | Toxic; blood rush to head when inhaled | C. G. Vernon | 1927, 34, **9**, 97 |
| Aniline (phenylamine) | Toxic, absorbed by skin | C. G. Vernon E. Hough | 1927, 34, **9**, 97 1968, 168, **49**, 607 |
| Aniline (phenylamine) | Inhalation of vapour and absorption through skin—consequences | D. R. Browning | 1967, 166, **48**, 718 |
| Antimonial compounds | Poisons | C. W. W. Read | 1940, 83, **21**, 971 |
| Arsenic compounds | Toxic | C. G. Vernon | 1927, 34, **9**, 97 |
| Arsenic compounds | Poison | E. A. Philpots | 1933, 56, **14**, 489 |
| Arsenic compounds | Biological methylation of | F. Challenger | 1936, 68, **17**, 575 *et seq.* |
| Arsenic compounds | Poisons | C. W. W. Read | 1940, 83, **21**, 971 |
| Arsine, chlor-diphenylamino-diphenyl chlor-diphenyl cyano- | Nose irritants | F. F. Crossley | 1940, 84, **21**, 1049 |
| Asbestos | Suspected carcinogenic | D. R. Browning | 1967, 167, **49**, 278 |
| Asbestos | Calcium, molten, dropped on asbestos square caused explosion | P. J. Scott | 1967, 167, **49**, 251 |
| Asbestos | Explosion when heating solder on asbestos mat | R. D. Harris | 1967, 166, **48**, 853 |
| Asbestos | McKechnie fibre substitute | A. Cochrane | *1979, 81, 26* |
| Asbestos | Types and hazards | — | *1975, 64, 16* |
| Asbestos paper | Combustion spoon substitute | — | *1977, 75, 26* |

| Compound, Substance, Subject | Details, Reaction etc. | Author | Reference |
|---|---|---|---|
| Asbestos substitute | *See* Rocksill | | |
| Asbestos wool | Hazards of | — | *1968, 26, 28* |
| Azides | Explosive | W. E. Garner | *1933, 55, **14**, 247* |
| Bacteriological cultures | Advice on spp. | K. M. Jack *et al.* | *1969, 31, 29–30* |
| Barium azide | Explosive | W. E. Garner | *1933, 55, **14**, 250* |
| Barium salts | Except sulphate, poisonous | C. W. W. Read | *1940, 83, **21**, 971* |
| Barium salts | Poisonous | A. Adair | *1964, 156, **45**, 460* |
| Battery | Explosion on recharging an expendable battery | J. Lewis | *1976, 69, 21* |
| Bell jars | Implosion on evacuation | — | *1983, 103, 21* |
| Benzene | Inflammable | C. W. W. Read | *1940, 83, **21**, 973* |
| Benzene | Fire risk when distilling | A. W. Wellings | *1941, 88, **42**, 430* |
| Benzene | May lead to leukaemia | D. R. Browning | *1967, 166, **48**, 918* |
| Benzene | Suspected carcinogenic | D. R. Browning | *1967, 167, **49**, 278* |
| Benzene | Blood disease caused | D. R. Browning | *1967, 166, **48**, 718* |
| Benzene | Toxic, absorbed by skin | A. W. Bamford | *1970, 177, **51**, 957* |
| Benzene | Nitric acid, fuming; Nitrobenzene prepn. | — | *1928, 38, **10**, 98* |
| Benzene | Phosgene; benzophenone preparation relatively safe on small scale | J. T. Stock, M. A. Fill | *1961, 149, **43**, 130* |
| Benzene | DES advice | — | *1974, 58, 22* |
| Benzene-1,3-diol | *See* Resorcinol | | |
| Benzene-1,2-dicarboxylic anhydride | *See* Phthalic anhydride | | |
| Benzene and some homologues | Toxic | C. G. Vernon | *1927, 34, **9**, 97* |
| Benzidine (biphenyl-4,4′-diamine) | Suspected carcinogenic | D. R. Browning | *1967, 167, **49**, 278* |
| Benzoyl peroxide | Advice | — | *1967, 25, 26* |
| Benzyl chloride | *See* (chloromethyl)benzene | | |
| Benzyl chloride (chloromethyl)benzene | Preparation to be avoided? | C. W. W. Read | *1940, 83, **21**, 969* |
| Beryllium | Highly poisonous, acute lung disease | P. A. Philbrick | *1950, 114, **31**, 263* |
| Beryllium | Poisoning details | H. F. Boulind | *1950, 115, **31**, 415* |
| Beryllium | Poisoning. Precautions similar to those for radioactive material reqd. | N. F. Hall | *1964, 158, **46**, 32* |
| Beryllium and compounds | Health hazard described. Dust or vapour often proves fatal | H. L. Walker | *1954, 127, **35**, 351* |
| Beryllium fluoride | Magnesium. Violently exothermic | H. L. Walker | *1954, 127, **35**, 348* |
| Bleaching powder | Liable to explode if stored in warm | G. Fowles | *1937, 73, **19**, 23* |
| Blood sampling | Recommended procedures | — | *1979, 82, 27–28* |
| Bracken | Poisonous | H. G. Andrew | *1976, 201, 57, 783* |
| Brick solvent store | Danger from excessive heat or cold | R. J. Mitchell | *1979, 82, 29* |
| Bromide, ethyl (bromoethane) | Preparation of, using phosphorus | C. W. W. Read | *1940, 83, **21**, 976* |
| Bromine | A suggested first-aid treatment | — | *1929, 41, **11**, 20* |
| Bromine | Poison | E. A. Philpots | *1933, 56, **14**, 489* |
| Bromine | Absorption by respirator | C. L. Bryant | *1940, 83, **21**, 913* |
| Bromine | Corrosive | C. W. W. Read | *1940, 83, **21**, 973* |
| Bromine | Sixth formers and teachers only to use it | C. W. W. Read | *1940, 83, **21**, 976* |
| Bromine | Persistent and non-persistent gas | E. A. Wilson | *1943, 94, **24**, 335* |
| Bromine | Liquid causes severe and slow-healing burns | G. W. Young | *1952, 120, **33**, 244* |
| Bromine | Corrosive | P. A. Ongley | *1963, 154, **44**, 747* |

| Compound, Substance, Subject | Details, Reaction etc. | Author | Reference |
|---|---|---|---|
| Bromine | Keep clear of skin | T. C. Swinfen | 1965, 160, **46**, 669 |
| Bromine | Disposal of in fume cupboard | W. S. Motz | 1966, 164, **48**, 179 |
| Bromine | Preparation of | C. W. W. Read | 1940, 83, **21**, 976 |
| Bromine | Molten lead bromide electrolysis, bromine liberated. Hazardous; precautions described | C. A. Pryke | 1967, 166, **48**, 862 |
| Bromine | Ethyl bromide preparation dangerous | C. W. W. Read | 1940, 83, **21**, 967 |
| Bromine | Gallium: violent combination at room temperature | H. L. Walker | 1956, 132, **37**, 196 |
| Bromine | Organic preparations. Possible danger in handling. Small-scale experiment described | J. H. Wilkinson, N. Ferry | 1953, 125, **35**, 122 |
| Bromine | Phosphorus, water. Explosion danger | A. J. Mee | 1940, 85, **22**, 95 |
| Bromine trifluoride | Well ventilated fume cupboard needed to handle | J. M. Fletcher | 1952, 120, **33**, 158 |
| Bromoacetates (bromoethanoates) | Lachrymators | P. A. Ongley | 1963, 154, **44**, 747 |
| Bromobenzene | Preparation to be avoided? | C. W. W. Read | 1940, 83, **21**, 969 |
| Bromoethane | *See* Ethyl bromide | | |
| Burning gases at jets | More appropriate for teachers to perform than pupils | C. W. W. Read | 1940, 83, **21**, 977 |
| Butane | Gas cartridge. Beware of high temperature near cartridge | J. I. Fell | 1963, 154, **44**, 728 |
| Calcium | Asbestos. Molten calcium dropped on asbestos square caused explosion | P. J. Scott | 1967, 167, **49**, 251 |
| Calcium | Burning in oxygen hazard | — | *1981, 93, 21* |
| Calcium hypochlorite | Can cause burns | D. R. Browning | 1968, 168, **49**, 606 |
| Calcium phosphide | Explosion of bottle | — | *1970, 36, 41–42* |
| Capacitors | Explosion due to excess current | — | *1988, 129, 12* |
| Carbon dioxide | Poisonous in large doses | W. L. Clark | 1945, 99, **26**, 219 |
| Carbon disulphide | Burning. Precautions | J. A. Cochrane | 1928, 35, **9** 234 |
| Carbon disulphide | Explosion possible | E. A. Philpots | 1933, 56, **14**, 489 |
| Carbon disulphide | Inflammable | C. W. W. Read | 1940, 83, **21**, 973 |
| Carbon disulphide | Poisonous, explosive | A. J. Mee | 1940, 85, **22**, 95 |
| Carbon disulphide | Danger of explosive mixture of vapour with air | A. Towers | 1948, 109, **29**, 307 |
| Carbon disulphide | Highly explosive | G. A. Dickens | 1950, 114, **31**, 264 |
| Carbon disulphide | Further details, concerning ignition temperature | A. Webster | 1950, 115, **31**, 415 |
| Carbon disulphide | Inflammable, narcotic | D. R. Browning | 1967, 166, **48**, 718 |
| Carbon disulphide | Burn nitric oxide with | C. W. W. Read | 1940, 83, **21**, 977 |
| Carbon disulphide | Nitric oxide, burns with blue flash | F. A. Halton | 1963, 154, **44**, 701 |
| Carbon disulphide | Survey of hazards | D. M. Wharry | 1973, 191, **55**, 417 |
| Carbon monosulphide | Readily polymerizes with explosive violence | T. G. Pearson | 1938, 78, **20**, 189 |
| Carbon monoxide | Toxic | C. G. Vernon | 1927, 34, **9**, 97 |
| Carbon monoxide | Poison | E. A. Philpots | 1933, 56, **14**, 489 |
| Carbon monoxide | Poison | F. Briers | 1935, 65, **17**, 36 |
| Carbon monoxide | Prepare in small quantities only | C. W. W. Read | 1940, 83, **21**, 969 |
| Carbon monoxide | Poison | C. W. W. Read | 1940, 83, **21**, 973 |
| Carbon monoxide | Preparation | C. W. W. Read | 1940, 83, **21**, 976 |

| Compound, Substance, Subject | Details, Reaction etc. | Author | Reference |
|---|---|---|---|
| Carbon monoxide | Volume composition of | C. W. W. Read | 1940, 83, **21**, 976 |
| Carbon monoxide | Explosion when made from $C + O_2$ | W. E. Jones | *1967, 23, 42–43* and *1967, 21, 47–48* |
| Carbon monoxide | Explosion when made from HCOOH | — | *1972, 46, 22* |
| Carbon suboxide | Preparation. Gas poisonous | D. B. Briggs | 1931, 48, **12**, 380 |
| Carbon tetrachloride (tetrachloromethane) | Extinguishers. Oxidation to phosgene in confined spaces | R. W. Thomas | 1965, 160, **46**, 775 |
| Carbon tetrachloride | Damage may prove fatal. Details | D. R. Browning | 1967, 166, **48**, 718 |
| Carbon tetrachloride | Fumes | D. R. Browning | 1967, 166, **48**, 918 |
| Carbon tetrachloride | Alternative in preparing $SnI_4$ | M. A. Coles *et al.* | *1977, 206, 59, 158* and *1978, 208, 59, 561* |
| Carbonyl chloride | *See* Phosgene | | |
| Carbonyl compounds | Advice on oxidation | — | *1981, 93, 21* |
| Carbylamine test | Teachers' opinions on its use | C. W. W. Read | 1940, 83, **21**, 969, 976 |
| Carcinogenesis | Substances causing | D. R. Browning | 1968, 168, **49**, 607 |
| Carcinogens | Survey of hazards | — | *1979, 84, 17–21* |
| Carius expts. | Should not be conducted in schools | C. W. W. Read | 1940, 83, **21**, 977 |
| Centrifuges | BS standard and advice on use | — | *1983, 103, 21* and *1984, 106, 14* |
| Charcoal | Sulphur, potassium nitrate. Grind: explosive | — | 1923, 18, 5 112 |
| Charcoal blocks | Fire risk | C. W. W. Read | 1940, 83, **21**, 969 |
| Chlorate mixture | Discussion on use of a fuse in Thermit process | Editors of *Science Master's Book*, IV, 2 | 1966, 162, **47**, 560 |
| Chlorate mixtures | Dangerously sensitive | H. K. Black | 1963, 153, **44**, 462 |
| Chlorates | Explosion possible. *See also* Potassium chlorate | E. A. Philpots | 1933, 56, **14**, 489 |
| Chlorhydrin | Potentially toxic | A. J. Mee | 1940, 85, **22**, 96 |
| Chloric(VII) acid | *See* Perchloric acid | | |
| Chlorides, anhydrous | Preparation | C. W. W. Read | 1940, 83, **21**, 976 |
| Chlorine | Toxic | C. G. Vernon | 1927, 34, **9**, 97 |
| Chlorine | Advice on drying | — | *1980, 88, 19* |
| Chlorine | Poison | — | 1929, 41, **11**, 22 |
| Chlorine | Poison | E. A. Philpots | 1933, 56, **14**, 489 |
| Chlorine | Poison | C. W. W. Read | 1940, 83, **21**, 973 |
| Chlorine | Lung irritant | F. F. Crossley | 1940, 84, **21**, 1049 |
| Chlorine | Gassing danger | C. W. W. Read | 1941, 87, **22**, 340 |
| Chlorine | Preparation | C. W. W. Read | 1940, 83, **21**, 976 |
| Chlorine | Preparation by dropping conc. hydrochloric acid on $KMnO_4$: explosion reported | J. C. Curry | 1965, 160, **46**, 770 |
| Chlorine | Preparation and preservation of liquid chlorine at room temperature | J. G. Silcock | 1968, 168, **49**, 496 |
| Chlorine | Acetylene. 'A safe way of performing?' | — | 1931, 47, **12**, 296 |
| Chlorine | Acetylene | C. W. W. Read | 1940, 83, **21**, 977 |
| Chlorine | Ammonia. Passed into $NH_3$ soln. Nitrogen trichloride formed | C. W. W. Read | 1940, 83, **21**, 969 |
| Chlorine | Ammonia | C. W. W. Read | 1940, 83, **21**, 976 |
| Chlorine | Hydrogen, explosion with | C. W. W. Read | 1940, 83, **21**, 969, 976 |

| Compound, Substance, Subject | Details, Reaction etc. | Author | Reference |
|---|---|---|---|
| Chlorine | Hydrogen, explosion with. Precautions needed, e.g. avoid sunlight | J. Lambert | 1948, 109, **29**, 364 |
| Chlorine | Hydrogen. Explosion on thorough mixing on dull day | L. H. Angus | 1950, 115, **31**, 402 |
| Chlorine | Hydrogen, explosion with | C. Holt | 1962, 152, **44**, 161 |
| Chlorine | Hydrogen, explosion with: precautions | T. A. H. Peacocke | 1964, 156, **45**, 459 |
| Chlorine | Hydrogen. Photocatalytic explosion demonstration | A. Adair | 1966, 164, **48**, 159 |
| Chlorine | Methane. Sometimes explosive violence | G. H. James | 1966, 164, **48**, 46 |
| Chlorine | Methyl alcohol. Fire | A. J. Mee | 1940, 85, **42**, 96 |
| Chlorine | Soda, molten. Dangerous | J. Bradley | 1968, 168, **49**, 454 |
| Chlorine trifluoride | Well ventilated fume cupboard needed to handle | J. M. Fletcher | 1952, 120, **33**, 158 |
| Chlorobenzene | Avoid preparation? | C. W. W. Read | 1940, 83, **21**, 969 |
| Chlorodinitrobenzene | Beware. Special note on vapour when in solution | C. G. Vernon | 1927, 34, **9**, 98 |
| 1-chloro-2,4-dinitrobenzene | Potent sensitizer | — | 1977, 204, **58**, 582 |
| Chloroform (trichloromethane) | Poison | C. W. W. Read | 1940, 83, **21**, 972 |
| Chloroform | Photochemical oxidation in air, giving phosgene | P. F. R. Venables | 1942, 92, **24**, 26 |
| Chloroform | Anaesthetic. Causes conjunctivitis, poisonous by mouth | D. R. Browning | 1967, 166, **48**, 718 |
| Chloroform | Sodium, violent reaction with | D. R. Browning | 1967, 166, **48**, 718 |
| Chloroform | Explosion on mixing with propanone | E. H. Coulson | 1974, 192, **55**, 596 |
| Chloroform | Explosion with propanone | — | *1974, 57, 38* |
| (Chloromethyl)benzene | Possible carcinogen | D. Hodgson | *1974, 58, 32* |
| Chloropicrin (trichloronitromethane) | Lung irritant | F. F. Crossley | 1940, 84, **21**, 1049 |
| Chlorosilanes | Hydrolysis strongly exothermic, severe burns caused to skin, very inflammable, plant unit kept under small positive pressure of nitrogen | S. J. Hart | 1959, 141, **40**, 260 |
| Chloro-vinyl-dichlorarsine (Lewisite) | Vesicant | F. F. Crossley | 1940, 84, **21**, 1049 |
| Chromates, dichromates | Absorption: disease, results, details | D. R. Browning | 1967, 166, **48**, 718 |
| Coal dust | Explosion | F. Briers | 1935, 65, **17**, 36 |
| Coal dust | Details for performing experimental 'safe' explosions | W. Railston | 1937, 74, **19**, 173 |
| Coal gas | Toxicity should not be exaggerated | G. Fowles | 1940, 85, **22**, 5 |
| Coal gas | 'Deadly poison' | C. W. W. Read | 1941, 87, **22**, 341 |
| Coal gas | Possible explosion | E. A. Philpots | 1933, 56, **14**, 489 |
| Coal gas | Poison | C. W. W. Read | 1940, 83, **21**, 972 |
| Coal gas | Bernouilli effect; precautions when showing | C. McGarry | 1966, 162, **42**, 504 |
| Coal gas | Reduction of oxides | C. W. W. Read | 1940, 83, **21**, 976 |
| Coal gas, oxygen blow pipe | Warnings about, e.g. explosion, fire, melted metals | G. W. Young | 1948, 109, **29**, 368 |
| Coal tar | Fractional distillation yields poisonous corrosive phenolic products | M. S. Parker | 1965, 159, **46**, 345 |
| Colchicine | Toxic/carcinogenic | — | *1981, 94, 22* |
| Combustion tubes | Hazards of cleaning | — | *1983, 103, 21* |

| Compound, Substance, Subject | Details, Reaction etc. | Author | Reference |
|---|---|---|---|
| Commercial chemicals | How 'safe' are they? | C. W. W. Read | 1940, 83, **21**, 977 |
| Conservation of matter | Enclosed experiments for | C. W. W. Read | 1940, 83, **21**, 977 |
| Copper | Acetylene. Explosive compound, therefore copper must not be used for oxyacetylene blow lamps | R. H. Smith | 1936, 70, **18**, 281 |
| Copper | Hydrochloric acid boiling. Explosion when cooled (corked flask). Possible explanation | — | 1924, 21, **6**, 55 |
| Copper | Sulphuric acid conc. Caution when adding copper to hot sulphuric acid: violent reaction | G. Fowles | 1927, 34, **9**, 90 |
| Copper | Sulphuric acid. Dangerous preparation of $SO_2$ | D. A. Campbell | 1939, 80, **20**, 631 |
| Copper | Sulphuric acid: $SO_2$ preparation | C. W. W. Read | 1940, 83, **21**, 969 |
| Copper oxalate | Explosion possible on heating | W. E. Garner | 1933, 55, **14**, 247 |
| Copper oxide | Anhydrous, with phthalic anhydride: explosive when overheated | A. J. Mee | 1940, 85, **22**, 95 |
| Copper oxide | Reduction by hydrogen. Explosion | C. W. W. Read | 1941, 87, **22**, 340 |
| Copper oxide | In Thermit process: explosion | T. E. W. Browne | 1967, 166, **48**, 921 |
| Copper(II) oxide | Reduction by CO; explosion | — | *1972, 46, 22* |
| Copper(II) oxide | Reduction by $NH_3$ explosion | M. A. McElroy | *1979, 71, 21* |
| Creosote | Poison | C. W. W. Read | 1940, 83, **21**, 972 |
| Critical state expt. | Danger of tube 'blow out': minimization of danger | W. K. Mace | 1957, 136, **38**, 466 |
| Critical state expt. | Precautions for handling tubes at high pressure | I. W. Jones *et al.* | 1962, 152, **44**, 173 |
| Crude oil | *See* petroleum | | |
| Cyanide, hydrogen | Not recommended | A. W. Wellings | 1941, 88, **22**, 429 |
| Cyanide, potassium | Use only by teachers | C. W. W. Read | 1940, 83, **21**, 976 |
| Cyanides | Poison | E. A. Philpots | 1933, 56, **14**, 489 |
| Cyanides | Poison: precautions | — | 1935, 65, **17**, 146 |
| Cyanides | Poison | C. W. W. Read | 1940, 83, **21**, 972 |
| Cyanides | Toxic | P. A. Ongley | 1963, 154, **44**, 747 |
| Cyanides | Danger of using such highly poisonous solution as electrolyte | F. E. L. Parsons | 1935, 66, **17**, 179 |
| Cyanogen | Preparation | C. W. W. Read | 1940, 83, **21**, 977 |
| Cyanogen compounds | Toxic | C. G. Vernon | 1927, 34, **9**, 97 |
| Cyclotron | Neutrons emitted: possible harmful effects | R. Pardoe | 1944, 97, **25**, 286 |
| Cylinders | *See* Gas cylinders | | |
| Detergent | *See* Sodium | | |
| Detonations and solid reactions | Review of a paper | — | 1935, 65, **17**, 150 |
| Devarda's alloy | Silver and ammonium ions. NaOH, heat to expel $NH_3$. Addition of alloy caused violent explosion | J. Baldwin | 1967, 165, **48**, 586 |
| 1,2-Dibromoethane | Carcinogenic | — | *1981, 93, 21* |
| Dichloro-diethyl sulphide (mustard gas) | Vesicant | F. F. Crossley | 1940, 84, **21**, 1049 |
| Dichromates | Absorption-disease, details | D. R. Browning | 1967, 166, **48**, 718 |
| 1,1-Diethoxyethane | *See* Acetal | | |
| Di-isocyanates | Extreme toxicity | E. G. Meek | 1975, 198, **57**, 187 |
| Dimethyl sulphate | Lung and sight injury | D. R. Browning | 1967, 166, **48**, 718 |
| Dinitro compounds | Poison | C. W. W. Read | 1940, 83, **21**, 971 |
| Dinitrobenzene | Beware of on skin | C. G. Vernon | 1927, 34, **9**, 97 |
| 2,4-dinitrobenzene | Powerful sensitizer | — | *1976, 67, 15* |

| Compound, Substance, Subject | Details, Reaction etc. | Author | Reference |
|---|---|---|---|
| 2,4-dinitrofluorobenzene | Powerful sensitizer | — | 1976, 67, 15 |
| Dinitrophenol | Beware of on skin | C. G. Vernon | 1927, 34, **9**, 97 |
| Dioxan (diethyl dioxide) | Particularly explosive | G. N. Copley | 1939, 82, **21**, 871 |
| Dioxan (diethyl dioxide) | Potentially toxic | A. J. Mee | 1940, 85, **22**, 95 |
| Diphenyl chlor-arsine | Nose irritant | F. F. Crossley | 1940, 84, **21**, 1049 |
| Diphenyl cyanoarsine | Nose irritant | F. F. Crossley | 1940, 84, **21**, 1049 |
| Diphenylamine chlor-arsine | Nose irritant | F. F. Crossley | 1940, 84, **21**, 1049 |
| Dissection | Advice for schools | — | 1976, 70, 25 and 1975, 64, 29 |
| Dust explosions | Use of plastic bag | R. G. Bray | 1967, 165, **48**, 510 |
| Eclipses of the sun | Advice on viewing | — | 1982, 98, 22–4 |
| Electrical hazards | Advice and recommendations | — | 1979, 83, 20–21 |
| Electrical sockets | Advice on testing safety of | M. D. Ellse | 1977, 205, 58, 820–22 |
| Electrical plugs | Advantage of sleeved pins | — | 1990, 137, 28 |
| Electrical safety | ASE advice | — | 1983, 101, 15–17 |
| Enclosed expts. for conservation of matter | Should only be done by teachers | C. W. W. Read | 1940, 83, **21**, 977 |
| Epoxyethane | *See* Ethylene oxide | | |
| Ethanedioic acid | *See* Oxalic acid | | |
| Ethanol | *See* Ethyl alcohol | | |
| Ethene | *See* Ethylene | | |
| Ethenone | *See* Ketene | | |
| Ether (ethoxyethane) | Safe for sixth formers to prepare | C. W. W. Read | 1940, 83, **21**, 977 |
| Ether (ethoxyethane) | Care | G. Fowles | 1940, 85, **22**, 6 |
| Ether (ethoxyethane) | Explosion possible | E. A. Philpots | 1933, 56, **14**, 489 |
| Ether (ethoxyethane) | Old stocks may contain much explosive peroxide | — | 1937, 71, **18**, 447 |
| Ether (ethoxyethane) | Dangers of peroxide impurity | B.D.H. | 1937, 74, **19**, 189 |
| Ether (ethoxyethane) | Evaporation by fan: ensure motor of fan does not come into contact with vapour | A. Adair | 1963, 153, **44**, 418 |
| Ether (ethoxyethane) | Recovery: peroxide risk | C. W. W. Read | 1940, 83, **21**, 977 |
| Ether, di-isopropyl | Peroxide formation | G. N. Copley | 1939, 82, **21**, 871 |
| Ether peroxide | Peroxide, acetaldehyde etc. impurities in ether. Nausea caused. Explosion in case of peroxide | P. F. R. Venables | 1942, 92, **24**, 26 |
| Ether, preparation | Lower ethers hazardous because of inflammability and volatility | W. H. Dovell | 1964, 156, **45**, 407 |
| Ethers | Explosive peroxide formation, removal of | G. N. Copley | 1939, 82, **21**, 871 |
| Ethers | Explosions possible | A. J. Mee | 1940, 85, **22**, 95 |
| Ethyl alcohol (ethanol) | Oxidation to acetic acid: explosion on distilling product (*see also* Alcohols) | E. N. Annable | 1951, 117, **32**, 249 |
| Ethyl bromide (bromoethane) | Preparation using phosphorus | C. W. W. Read | 1940, 83, **21**, 976 |
| Ethyl iodide (iodoethane) | Preparation | C. W. W. Read | 1940, 83, **21**, 967 |
| Ethyl iodo-acetate (iodoethanoate) | Lachrymator | F. F. Crossley | 1940, 84, **21**, 1049 |
| Ethylene (ethene) | Oxygen, explosion. Precautions | T. A. H. Peacocke | 1964, 156, **45**, 459 |
| Ethylene derivatives | Volatile derivatives toxic | A. J. Mee | 1940, 85, **22**, 95 |
| Ethylene oxide (epoxyethane) | Toxic, potentially | A. J. Mee | 1940, 85, **22**, 95 |

| Compound, Substance, Subject | Details, Reaction etc. | Author | Reference |
|---|---|---|---|
| Ethyne | *See* Acetylene | | |
| Explosions | Some potentially explosive reactions | E. A. Philpots | 1933, 56, **14**, 489 |
| Explosives | Home Office advice | — | *1965, 12, 33–34* |
| Explosives, nitro | — | S. I. Levy | 1935, 67, **17**, 341 |
| Explosives, nitro | — | S. I. Levy | 1936, 68, **17**, 488 |
| Eye protection | Clarification of DES advice | N. Booth | *1976, 70, 20* |
| Eye protection | ASE advice | — | *1981, 93, 27–30* |
| Faulty apparatus | Responsibility for | — | *1976, 67, 14–15* |
| Ferric oxide (iron(III) oxide) | Reduction by carbon monoxide. Danger of forming explosive iron pentacarbonyl at low temps. (0–150°C) | C. W. Othen | 1964, 156, **45**, 459 |
| Fire | Background to fire control | W. J. Leggett | 1974, 195, **56**, 406 |
| Fire extinguishers | Carbon tetrachloride type dangerous with incendiary bombs etc.: explosion phosgene | A. J. Mee | 1940, 85, **22**, 95 |
| First aid | Common first-aid procedures (some now obsolete) | — | 1929, 41, **11**, 17 |
| Fittig's reaction | Suitable for teachers or sixth formers | C. W. W. Read | 1940, 83, **21**, 977 |
| Flammable liquids | Storage advice | — | *1976, 67, 14* |
| Fluoride, hydrogen | High toxicity | J. Ormston | 1945, 99, **26**, 148 |
| Fluorides, alkyl | High toxicity | J. Ormston | 1945, 99, **26**, 148 |
| Fluorine | Corrosive: precautions in handling | J. M. Fletcher | 1952, 120, **33**, 155 |
| Fluorine | 'The Manufacture and use of Fluorine and its Compounds'. Book review. Gives details of risk involved in school preparation of fluorine | A. J. Rudge | 1962, 152, **44**, 242 |
| Fluorine | Health hazard | H. L. Walker | 1954, 127, **35**, 346 |
| Fluorine | With hydrogen: explosive | J. M. Fletcher | 1952, 120, **33**, 156 |
| Fluorine | Organic molecules, Copper gauze catalyst used to prevent explosions, also fluorine diluted | J. Ormston | 1944, 98, **26**, 30 |
| Fluorine | Organic compounds. Explosive vapours diluted with $N_2$ and reactor filled with silver-plated copper turnings | J. M. Fletcher | 1952, 120, **33**, 157 |
| Fluoroacetates (fluoroethanoates) and derivatives | Toxic, details | B. C. Saunders | 1952, 121, **33**, 325 |
| Fluorophosphine oxides, diamino | Toxic generally | B. C. Saunders | 1952, 121, **33**, 324 |
| Fluorophosphonates | Toxic; details | B. C. Saunders | 1952, 121, **33**, 320 |
| Food calorimeter | Explosion using peanut | I. Nuttall | 1977, 205, **58**, 817 |
| Formaldehyde (methanal) | Poison | C. W. W. Read | 1940, 83, **21**, 972 |
| Formaldehyde | Preparation from air and methyl alcohol using Cu or Pt catalyst. Explosion possible | P. H. Arnold | 1952, 120, **33**, 267 |
| Formaldehyde | Preparation: safe method | G. F. Hood | 1952, 121, **33**, 416 |
| Formaldehyde | Preparation: further details | D. T. Radford | 1953, 124, **34**, 426 |
| Formaldehyde | Resorcinol resin: explosion | — | *1971, 45, 36* |
| Formaldehyde | Toxicity, advice on use | — | *1982, 98, 21–2* |
| Friedel-Crafts reaction | — | C. W. W. Read | 1940, 83, **21**, 977 |
| Gallium | Bromine, violent combination at room temperature | H. L. Walker | 1956, 132, **37**, 196 |

| Compound, Substance, Subject | Details, Reaction etc. | Author | Reference |
|---|---|---|---|
| Gas | Hazard in preparing from oil | — | 1972, 46, 22 |
| Gas cylinders | Storage advice | — | 1970, 36, 47 |
| Gas taps | Design and installation | — | 1985, 114, 14 |
| Gaseous explosions | 'Flame and combustion in Gases'. Ref. book, deals with gaseous explosions | W. A. Bone et al. | 1928, 37, **10**, 80 |
| Gaseous explosions | Use of plastic bag in | R. G. Bray | 1967, 165, **48**, 570 |
| Gaseous mixtures | Explosion of: dangerous | C. W. W. Read | 1940, 83, **21**, 965 |
| Gaseous mixtures | Explosions. Method | P. D. Arculus | 1963, 154, **44**, 706 |
| Gaseous mixtures | Explosion of: use balloon | B. Poole | 1964, 158, **46**, 230 |
| Gaseous mixtures | Explosion of: details and precautions | T. A. H. Peacocke | 1964, 156, **45**, 459 |
| Gases | Explosion and fires in coal mines | F. Briers | 1935, 65, **17**, 36 |
| Gases | Explosive mixtures of | C. W. W. Read | 1941, 87, **22**, 340 |
| Gases | Flame and Combustion in. Ref. book, deals with gaseous explosions | W. A. Bone et al. | 1928, 37, **10**, 80 |
| Gases | Jets, burning at | C. W. W. Read | 1940, 83, **21**, 977 |
| Gases | Poisonous: coal gas, CO, $CO_2$, $Cl_2$, $SO_2$, $H_2$ | — | 1929, 41, **11**, 22 |
| Gases | Poisonous: $SO_2$, $H_2S$, $Cl_2$, $N_2O_4$, NO, $NH_3$, $Br_2$, S | C. W. W. Read | 1940, 83, **21**, 968 |
| Gases | Respirator, absorption by | C. L. Bryant | 1940, 83, **21**, 913 |
| Gases | Techniques for smelling | — | 1988, 127, 32 |
| Gases | Toxic: $H_2S$, $PH_3$, CO, $Cl_2$, oxides of N | C. G. Vernon | 1927, 34, **9**, 97 |
| Gases | Warfare, used in | F. F. Crossley | 1940, 84, **21**, 1049 |
| Gases | Warfare, used in | E. A. Wilson | 1943, 94, **24**, 335 |
| Glass tubing | Dangers of | C. W. W. Read | 1941, 87, **22**, 341 |
| Glycerol (propane-1,2,3-triol) | Nitration of, with conc. sulphuric and nitric acids. Reaction can become uncontrollable | S. I. Levy | 1935, 67, **17**, 344 |
| Goggles | See Eye protection | | |
| Groundsel | Hazards of | H. G. Andrew | 1976, 201, **57**, 783 |
| Groundsel | See Senecio sp. | | |
| Gunpowder | Preparation | C. W. W. Read | 1940, 83, **21**, 977 |
| Hair styles | Hazard | — | 1988, 127, 17 |
| Halogen acids | Can be safely prepared | G. Fowles | 1940, 85, **22**, 6 |
| Halogen acids | Preparation | C. W. W. Read | 1940, 83, **21**, 977 |
| Halogenated D.N.B. | Powerful sensitizers | — | 1976, 67, 15 |
| 'Hazards' | BDH Dealing with spillage of hazardous chemicals. Wall chart on hazards available | B.D.H. | 1965, 159, **46**, 471 |
| Health and Safety legislation | — | — | 1977, 72, 19–20 |
| Health and Safety legislation | ASE statements | — | 1976, 66, 25 and 1975, 64, 13 |
| Hepatitis | Risk of, blood group determination | — | 1976, 67, 16 |
| Heptane | Technique for heating | — | 1984, 106, 14 |
| Hydrazine hydrate | Poisonous | G. Fowles | 1963, 154, **44**, 692 |
| Hydrazine hydrate | Further details. Caustic | A. Adair | 1964, 156, **45**, 460 |
| Hydrocarbons, polycyclic aromatic | Carcinogenic | C. F. Cullis | 1968, 168, **49**, **402** |
| Hydrochloric acid | Poison | C. W. W. Read | 1940, 83, **21**, 972 |
| Hydrochloric acid | Conc. on to potassium permanganate. Explosion took place | J. C. Curry | 1965, 160, **46**, 770 |

| Compound, Substance, Subject | Details, Reaction etc. | Author | Reference |
|---|---|---|---|
| Hydrofluoric acid | Danger to skin | — | 1929, 42, **11**, 152 |
| Hydrogen | Preparation. Sodium on water, collection | C. W. W. Read | 1940, 83, **21**, 976 |
| Hydrogen | Preparation. Acid on metal | C. W. W. Read | 1940, 83, **21**, 977 |
| Hydrogen | Preparation. Safer method using tap funnel for acid | C. Mangham | 1964, 158, **46**, 233 |
| Hydrogen | Preparation. Safe generator, burner | A. V. Pitter | 1964, 157, **45**, 685 |
| Hydrogen | Air. Why quiet burning of inverted jar? | — | 1922, 14, **4**, 97 |
| Hydrogen | Air. Reply to query above | — | 1922, 16, **4**, 215 |
| Hydrogen | Burning of | C. W. W. Read | 1940, 83, **21**, 976 |
| Hydrogen | Chlorine, explosion with | C. W. W. Read | 1940, 83, **21**, 969 |
| Hydrogen | Chlorine, explosion with | C. W. W. Read | 1940, 83, **21**, 976 |
| Hydrogen | Chlorine, explosion with: details of precautions | J. Lambert | 1948, 109, **29**, 364 |
| Hydrogen | Chlorine, explosion with. Explosion on thorough mixing on dull day | L. H. Angus | 1950, 115, **31**, 402 |
| Hydrogen | Chlorine, explosion with | C. Holt | 1962, 152, **44**, 161 |
| Hydrogen | Chlorine: explosion with: precautions | T. A. H. Peacocke | 1964, 156, **45**, 459 |
| Hydrogen | Chlorine: photocatalytic explosion demonstration | A. Adair | 1966, 164, **48**, 159 |
| Hydrogen | Fluorine, explosive | J. M. Fletcher | 1952, 120, **33**, 156 |
| Hydrogen | Jet: beware explosive mixture with air | — | 1928, 38, **10**, 99 |
| Hydrogen | Jets, danger of | E. A. Philpots | 1933, 56, **14**, 489 |
| Hydrogen | Jets. Safe methods of igniting using test tube full of collected gas | K. G. Price | 1964, 158, **46**, 187 |
| Hydrogen | Oxygen. Explanation why no explosion with hot silver wire | C. N. Hinshelwood | 1927, 31, **8**, 171 |
| Hydrogen | Oxygen. Explosion with certain volumes, in eudiometer: dangers | R. D. Reid | 1928, 38, **10**, 149 |
| Hydrogen | Oxygen. Form soap bubbles: harmless explosions | R. R. Finney | 1935, 65, **17**, 137 |
| Hydrogen | Oxygen. Explosions hazardous | C. W. W. Read | 1940, 83, **21**, 976 |
| Hydrogen | Oxygen. Explosion with: extra care required | C. Holt | 1962, 152, **44**, 161 |
| Hydrogen | Oxygen. Explosion with: precautions | T. A. H. Peacocke | 1964, 156, **45**, 459 |
| Hydrogen | Oxygen. Explosion with: demonstration using polythene flask | J. W. Davis | 1964, 157, **45**, 649 |
| Hydrogen | Oxygen. Explosion with: demonstration using polythene bottle | E. V. Ogden | 1964, 157, **45**, 674 |
| Hydrogen | Oxygen. Explosion with: use balloon | B. Poole | 1964, 158, **46**, 230 |
| Hydrogen | Oxygen. Explosion with: 'Safe experiment' described | M. J. Clark | 1965, 161, **47**, 177 |
| Hydrogen | Reduction of copper oxide by | C. W. W. Read | 1941, 87, **22**, 340 |
| Hydrogen | Reduction of metal oxides: dangerous | C. W. W. Read | 1940, 83, **21**, 965 |
| Hydrogen | Reduction of oxides | C. W. W. Read | 1940, 83, **21**, 976 |
| Hydrogen | Reduction of oxides: method of avoiding danger | H. E. Watson | 1943, 93, **24**, 211 |
| Hydrogen | Danger when used as reductant | — | *1970, 40, 32,* |
| Hydrogen | Relative merits of thistle and tap funnel in preparation | — | *1975, 61, 33* |
| Hydrogen chloride | Vapour: industrial absorption | S. I. Levy | 1934, 62, **16**, 154 |
| Hydrogen chloride | Respiratory damage caused | D. R. Browning | 1967, 166, **48**, 718 |

| Compound, Substance, Subject | Details, Reaction etc. | Author | Reference |
|---|---|---|---|
| Hydrogen cyanide | Sex-linked ability to smell | G. J. Cooper | 1967, 24, 33 |
| Hydrogen fluoride | Risk of burns can be reduced, although very dangerous to handle | A. J. Rudge | 1962, 151, 43, 672 |
| Hydrogen fluoride | High toxicity | J. Ormston | 1945, 99, 26, 148 |
| Hydrogen fluoride | Mercuric oxide. Mercuric fluoride produced reacts with organic molecules: highly exothermic reaction | J. Ormston | 1944, 98, 26, 32 |
| Hydrogen sulphide | Toxic | C. G. Vernon | 1927, 34, 9, 97 |
| Hydrogen sulphide | Poison | F. Briers | 1935, 65, 17, 36 |
| Hydrogen sulphide | Poison | C. W. W. Read | 1940, 83, 21, 973 |
| Hydrogen sulphide | Poisonous | A. W. Wellings | 1942, 92, 24, 83 |
| Hydrogen sulphide | Toxic | B. E. Dawson | 1961, 147, 42, 214 |
| Hydrogen sulphide | Toxicity comparable to hydrogen cyanide | D. R. Browning | 1967, 166, 48, 919 |
| Hydrogen sulphide | High concentrations fatal; inflammable | D. R. Browning | 1967, 166, 48, 718 |
| Hydrogen sulphide | Ignited by trace of $Na_2O_2$ or rusty pipes | A. J. Mee | 1940, 85, 22, 95 |
| Hydrogen sulphide | Preparation; synthesis, use of | C. W. W. Read | 1940, 83, 21, 976 |
| Hydrogenation | Catalytic. Hershberg apparatus. Exclusion of air vital, otherwise explosion over catalyst. Safety screen advisable | — | 1966, 163, 47, 808 |
| Ice | Caution needed in dislodging | M. A. McElroy | 1977, 71, 21 |
| Immersion heater | Explosion of | K. A. Hall | 1979, 84, 34 |
| Immersion heater | Risks of old equipment | — | 1983, 103, 21 |
| Incendiary bombs etc. | Carbon tetrachloride extinguisher may cause explosion and large quantities of phosgene | A. J. Mee | 1940, 85, 22, 95 |
| Incubators | Advice on use | — | 1985, 112, 18 |
| Infra red lamps | Water, speck of, causes implosion | A. T. Neuff | 1967, 165, 48, 489 |
| Iodine | Aluminium: slight moisture results in ignition | S. Azmathullah | 1956, 134, 38, 107 |
| Iodine | Phosphorus, alcohol: ethyl iodide preparation dangerous | C. W. W. Read | 1940, 83, 21, 967 |
| Iodoethane | See Ethyl iodide | | |
| Iodomethane | Cancer hazard | D. Hodgson | 1974, 58, 32 |
| Ion-exchange resin | Explosion risk | — | 1984, 107, 14 |
| Ion migration | HSE, ASE advice | — | 1990, 137, 28 |
| Ion-exchange resin | Hazards of soaking a dry resin | P. Rankin | 1976, 67, 15 |
| Iron | Steam on red-hot iron | C. W. W. Read | 1940, 83, 21, 976 |
| Iron | Filings, sulphuric acid: $FeSO_4$ prepn. | C. W. W. Read | 1940, 83, 21, 969 |
| Iron(III) oxide | See Ferric oxide | | |
| Jam pots | Caution against use in some experiments | — | 1981, 92, 43 |
| Jumpers | Hazards of wearing | — | 1989, 132, 18 |
| Kaowool | Disadvantages as asbestos substitute | D. A. Tawney | 1978, 79, 32 |
| Kaowool | Disadvantages of | M. Tingle, T. Goodfellow | 1978, 77, 21–22 |
| Ketene (ethenone) | Poisonous, but destroyed by water | J. W. Davis | 1952, 121, 33, 396 |
| Labelling | ASE advice | — | 1979, 82, 25–26 |

| Compound, Substance, Subject | Details, Reaction etc. | Author | Reference |
|---|---|---|---|
| Laboratory check list | *See* Safety check list | | |
| Laboratory Rules | Mnemonic | I. M. Carpenter | 1977, 205, **58**, 817 |
| Lassaigne test | Source of danger. Microtechnique to minimize danger; other precautions, *see* Sodium | J. T. Stock, M. A. Fill | 1956, 133, **37**, 346 |
| Lauroyl peroxide | Additive to render safer | — | *1967, 21, 26* |
| Lead bromide | Electolysis of molten. Hazardous. Bromine, lead bromide vapours. Precautions | C. A. Pryke | 1967, 166, **48**, 862 |
| Lead compounds | Toxic | C. G. Vernon | 1927, 34, **9**, 97 |
| Lead compounds | Poison | C. W. W. Read | 1940, 83, **21**, 972 |
| Lead nitrate | Potassium acetate: mixture explosive when heated | A. J. Mee | 1940, 85, **22**, 95 |
| Lithium | Explosion on heating | W. H. Lloyd | 1975, 196, **56**, 632 |
| Lithium | Explosion on heating | C. Holt | 1975, 198, **57**, 185 |
| Lithium | Explosion when heated on ceramic material | — | *1975, 62, 29* |
| Lithium | Explosion when heated on porcelain | A. Bullock | *1975, 62, 33* |
| Lithium | Explosion on heating | — | *1985, 113, 14* |
| Locust allergy | *See* allergy | | |
| Magnesium | Explosion when wrongly identified | — | *1984, 108, 14* |
| Magnesium | Beryllium fluoride: violently exothermic | H. L. Walker | 1954, 127, **35**, 348 |
| Magnesium | Oxygen: burning magnesium in oxygen | C. W. W. Read | 1940, 83, **21**, 968 |
| Magnesium | Potassium carbonate: explosive substance produced | J. G. F. Druce | 1926, 28, **7**, 261 |
| Magnesium | Potassium carbonate: Castellana fusion, possible explosion | G. Fowles | 1938, 77, **20**, 124 |
| Magnesium | Silica: denotation if silica not completely dry | W. B. Barker | 1938, 77, **20**, 150 |
| Magnesium | Powder, silver nitrate powder. Explosion with drop of water | D. J. Lyness K. Hutton | 1953, 125, **35**, 138 |
| Magnesium | Steam: method avoiding difficulties | J. D. Peterkin | 1934, 60, **15**, 524 |
| Magnesium | Steam: explosion possible with hydrogen if any undisplaced air in apparatus | T. A. Muir | 1936, 70, **18**, 283 |
| Magnesium | Steam | C. W. W. Read | 1940, 83, **21**, 976 |
| Magnesium | Steam: simple apparatus for burning in | E. A. Taylor | 1940, 84, **21**, 1143 |
| Magnesium | Sulphur | C. W. W. Read | 1940, 83, **21**, 977 |
| Magnesium | Sulphur. Heat: explosion | K. Hutton | 1950, 114, **31**, 265 |
| Magnesium | Explosive silicide on heating in porcelain crucible | R. B. Moyes *et al.* | 1975, 197, **56**, 819 |
| Magnesium | Explosive mixture with ammonium dichromate(VI) | — | *1972, 47, 24* and *1974, 56, 39* |
| Mains Leads | Hazards if uncoiled | W. K. Mace | 1977, 204, **58**, 587 |
| Manganese | Production by Thermit process | G. Fowles | 1940, 85, **22**, 6 |
| Manganese dioxide (manganese(IV) oxide) | Oxygen preparation: pure samples usable | H. Tattersall | 1956, 134, **38**, 132 |
| Marsh's test | Survey of its use | C. W. W. Read | 1940, 83, **21**, 976 |
| Mercuric oxide (mercury(II) oxide) | Hydrogen fluoride. Mercuric fluoride produced reacts with organic molecules highly exothermically | J. Ormston | 1944, 98, **26**, 32 |
| Mercuric sulphate (mercury(II) sulphate) | Preparation | C. W. W. Read | 1940, 83, **21**, 969 |

| Compound, Substance, Subject | Details, Reaction etc. | Author | Reference |
|---|---|---|---|
| Mercury | Harmful vapour | H. L. Walker | 1956, 132, **37**, 198 |
| Mercury | Toxic, high vapour pressure | J. A. Plewes | 1964, 157, **45**, 717 |
| Mercury | Continues to vaporize when covered with water | P. J. Weeks | *1977, 73, 24* |
| Mercury | Degree of hazard not to be overestimated | F. G. Scrawley | *1977, 74, 25* |
| Mercury | Advice on recovery of | D. Hodson | *1972, 46, 22–23* |
| Mercury | Precautions in use of | T. P. Borrows | *1977, 72, 20–21* and 1978, 209, 59, 750–2 |
| Mercury and compounds | Toxic | N. F. Hall | 1964, 158, **46**, 32 |
| Mercury compounds | Toxic | C. G. Vernon | 1927, 34, **9**, 97 |
| Mercury compounds | Poison | C. W. W. Read | 1940, 83, **21**, 972 |
| Mercury oxalate | Likely to explode on heating | W. E. Garner | 1933, 55, **14**, 247 |
| Methanal | *See* Formaldehyde | | |
| Methane | Fire, explosion | F. Briers | 1935, 65, **17**, 36 |
| Methane | Explosion danger | J. A. Stevenson | 1946, 102, **27**, 170 |
| Methane | Air, dangerously explosive mixtures | J. H. Wilkinson | 1962, 152, **44**, 4 |
| Methane | Chlorine: sometimes explosive violence | G. H. James | 1966, 164, **48**, 46 |
| Methane | Oxygen: explosive reactions possible | T. G. Pearson | 1940, 83, **21**, 923 |
| Methane | Oxygen, explosions with: precautions | T. A. H. Peacocke | 1964, 156, **45**, 459 |
| Methyl alcohol (methanol) | Air, mixture with: over Cu or Pt catalyst. Formaldehyde preparation. Explosion possible | P. H. Arnold | 1953, 120, **33**, 267 |
| Methyl alcohol | Air mixture with: over Cu. Safe expt. described | G. F. Hood | 1952, 121, **33**, 416 |
| Methyl alcohol | Air, mixture with: further details | D. T. Radford | 1953, 124, **34**, 426 |
| Methyl alcohol | Modifications of catalytic oxidation: 'harmless explosions' | D. T. Radford | 1956, 132, **37**, 258 |
| Methylbenzene | *See* Toluene | | |
| Methyl bromide (bromomethane) | Toxic. Precautions in preparation | S.M.A. Meeting report | 1956, 133, **37**, 408 |
| Methyl-2,4,6-trinitrobenzene | *See* Toluene and homologues and Trinitrotoluene | | |
| Microbiology | Details of advisory committee for schools | — | *1976, 67, 23* |
| Microbiology | Safety advice | — | *1981, 92, 19–27* |
| Millon's reagent | Hazards and possible substitute | — | *1979, 83, 19–20* |
| Millon's reagent | Sakaguchi test as substitute | — | *1979, 85, 31* |
| Naphthylamine (naphthalen-1-amine) | Inappropriate for phase rule studies | D. R. Browning | 1967, 166, **48**, 719 |
| Naphthylamines | Carcinogenic | D. R. Browning | 1967, 167, **49**, 278 |
| Natural gas | Problems of burning | P. Stone | *1977, 71, 21–22* |
| Natural gas | Explosion in air | T. P. Borrows | 1978, 209, **59**, 752 |
| Neutrons | Harmful effect of; from cyclotron | R. Pardoe | 1944, 97, **25**, 286 |
| Nickel, Raney | Precautions; pyrophoric when dry | A. Adair | 1963, 153, **44**, 417 |
| Nickel carbonyl | Formation and decomposition. Extremely toxic. 1 part in $10^6$ in air fatal | D. C. M. Waddell | 1966, 164, **48**, 167 |
| Nitric acid | Burns | C. G. Vernon | 1928, 38, **10**, 97 |
| Nitric acid | Poison | C. W. W. Read | 1940, 83, **21**, 972 |
| Nitric acid | Poison | D. R. Browning | 1968, 168, **49**, 606 |
| Nitric acid | Preparation | C. W. W. Read | 1940, 83, **21**, 976 |
| Nitric acid | Heat: decompose | C. W. W. Read | 1940, 83, **21**, 977 |
| Nitric acid | Oxidation of solids by | C. W. W. Read | 1940, 83, **21**, 976 |

| Compound, Substance, Subject | Details, Reaction etc. | Author | Reference |
|---|---|---|---|
| Nitric acid | Hazards of reaction with ether | C. Holt | 1976, 202, **58**, 159–160 |
| Nitric(V) acid | Explosion when added to rubber | T. R. Read | 1976, 200, **57**, 592 |
| Nitric oxide | Preparation | C. W. W. Read | 1940, 83, **21**, 976 |
| Nitric oxide | Carbon disulphide, burn with | C. W. W. Read | 1940, 83, **21**, 977 |
| Nitric oxide | Carbon disulphide, burns with blue flash | F. A. Hatton | 1963, 154, **44**, 701 |
| p-Nitroacetanilide | Sulphuric acid conc. 'Pharaoh's Serpent's' experiment; vigorous reaction at 200°C, mild explosion | R. E. D. Clark | 1934, 62, **16**, 271 |
| Nitrobenzene | Poison | C. W. W. Read | 1940, 83, **21**, 972 |
| Nitrobenzene | Poison: inhalation and absorption consequences | D. R. Browning | 1967, 166, **48**, 718 |
| Nitrobenzene | Preparation | C. W. W. Read | 1940, 83, **21**, 976 |
| t-Nitrobutane | Distillation. Explosion | A. J. Mee | 1940, 85, **22**, 95 |
| Nitro compounds | Aromatic. Poisonous, absorbed by skin | S. I. Levy | 1936, 68, **17**, 488 |
| Nitro derivatives of benzene | Toxic, absorbed by skin in some cases | C. G. Vernon | 1927, 34, **9**, 97 |
| Nitro explosives | A brief survey of explosive systems I | S. I. Levy | 1935, 67, **17**, 341 |
| Nitro explosives | A brief survey of explosive systems II | S. I. Levy | 1936, 68, **17**, 488 |
| Nitrogen | Preparation | C. W. W. Read | 1940, 83, **21**, 977 |
| Nitrogen dioxide | Poison | C. W. W. Read | 1940, 83, **21**, 973 |
| Nitrogen dioxide | Preparation | C. W. W. Read | 1940, 83, **21**, 976 |
| Nitrogen oxides | Toxic: attack lungs | C. G. Vernon | 1927, 34, **9**, 97 |
| Nitrogen oxides | Higher. Poisonous | A. J. Mee | 1940, 85, **22**, 95 |
| Nitrogen tetroxide (dinitrogen tetraoxide) | Dissociation in sealed tube. Beware of putting cold tube in hot water (>45°C), or explosion possible | L. Williams | 1958, 138, **39**, 291 |
| Nitrogen tetroxide | Dissociation of, poisonous nature of $N_2O_4$ | T. A. H. Peacocke | 1959, 141, **40**, 346 |
| Nitrogen triiodide | Unstable detonator | S. I. Levy | 1935, 67, **17**, 343 |
| Nitrogen triiodide | Preparation | C. W. W. Read | 1940, 83, **21**, 977 |
| Nitroglycerine | Explosive | W. E. Garner | 1933, 55, **14**, 250 |
| Nitroglycerol (propane-1,2,3-triyl nitrate) | Preparation | C. W. W. Read | 1940, 83, **21**, 977 |
| Nitrophenols | Poison | C. W. W. Read | 1940, 83, **21**, 972 |
| Nitrous acid (nitric(III) acid) | Preparation: sucking back danger | — | 1928, 38, **10**, 100 |
| Nitrous fumes | Can cause severe poisoning | D. R. Browning | 1968, 168, **49**, 606 |
| Nitrous oxide (dinitrogen oxide) | Preparation | C. W. W. Read | 1940, 83, **21**, 976 |
| Nylon fishing line | Hazard if snaps under tension | — | 1978, 78, 22 |
| Oil | Hazard of converting to gas | — | 1972, 46, 22 |
| Organic preparations | Small-scale, safer reactions | J. H. Wilkinson | 1955, 131, **37**, 91 |
| Organic preparations | Small-scale, safer reactions | J. T. Stock, M. A. Fill | 1961, 149, **43**, 130 |
| Organo-lead compounds | Survey of hazards | A. K. Holliday, W. Towers | 1974, 195, **56**, 417 |
| Organo-phosphorus compounds | Poisonous | R. S. Edmundson | 1963, 155, **45**, 112 |
| Osmic acid | Dangerous | A. R. A. Noel | 1967, 165, **48**, 479 |
| Overhead projector | Eye strain | G. L. Treglown | 1968, 171, **50**, 434 |
| Oxalic acid (ethanedioic acid) | Poison | C. W. W. Read | 1940, 83, **21**, 973 |

| Compound, Substance, Subject | Details, Reaction etc. | Author | Reference |
|---|---|---|---|
| Ozone (trioxygen) | Preparation | C. W. W. Read | 1940, 83, **21**, 976 |
| Ozonides | Decomposition of: ozonides highly explosive | G. N. Copley | 1944, 97, **25**, 293 |
| Peanut | Explosion in food calorimeter | I. Nuttall | 1977, 205, **58**, 817 |
| Pencil sharpener | Some contain magnesium and pose a hazard | — | 1975, 64, 16 |
| Pentyl nitrate | See Amyl nitrate | | |
| Perchlorates | Dangerously explosive: details | A. J. Mee | 1940, 85, **22**, 95 |
| Perchloric acid | Preparation | C. W. W. Read | 1940, 83, **21**, 977 |
| Perchloric acid | Dangerously explosive: details | A. J. Mee | 1940, 85, **22**, 95 |
| Perchloric acid | Advice on storage, ordering and use | — | 1967, 21, 48 |
| Peroxides, dialphyl } Peroxides, diethyl } | Explosive | G. N. Copley | 1939, 82, **21**, 871 |
| Pesticides | Use of in schools | — | 1979, 85, 26 |
| Petrol vapour | Experimental 'safe' explosions: details for performing | W. Railston | 1937, 74, **19**, 173 |
| Petroleum | Suspected carcinogen | — | 1975, 64, 16 |
| Phenol | Blisters on skin | G. Fowles | 1940, 85, **22**, 8 |
| Phenol | Beware of on skin | T. C. Swinfen | 1965, 160, **46**, 669 |
| Phenol | Absorbed through skin can cause death | D. R. Browning | 1967, 166, **48**, 918 |
| Phenol | Conc. sulphuric acid, Phenol sulphonic acid formed: add nitric acid; violent reaction, nitrous fumes | S. I. Levy | 1936, 68, **17**, 490 |
| Phenol sulphonic acids | See Phenol | | |
| Phenolic compounds | From fractional distillation of coal tar. Poisonous and corrosive | M. S. Parker | 1965, 159, **46**, 345 |
| Phenols | Poison | C. W. W. Read | 1940, 83, **21**, 972 |
| Phenylamine | See Aniline | | |
| Phenylene diamines (benzene diamines) | Poisonous | C. W. W. Read | 1940, 83, **21**, 972 |
| Phenylhydrazine | Toxic | C. G. Vernon | 1927, 34, **9**, 97 |
| Phenylhydrazine | Poisonous | G. Fowles | 1963, 153, **44**, 406 |
| Phosgene (carbonyl chloride) | Highly toxic impurity sometimes present in chloroform | P. F. R. Venables | 1942, 92, **24**, 26 |
| Phosgene | Preparation | C. W. W. Read | 1940, 83, **21**, 977 |
| Phosgene, benzene | Benzophenone preparation. Relatively safe on small scale | J. T. Stock, M. A. Fill | 1961, 149, **43**, 130 |
| Phosgene, diphosgene | Lung irritants | F. F. Crossley | 1940, 84, **21**, 1049 |
| Phosphine | | C. W. W. Read | 1940, 83, **21**, 969 |
| Phosphine | Toxic | C. G. Vernon | 1927, 34, **9**, 97 |
| Phosphine | Poison | E. A. Philpots | 1933, 56, **14**, 489 |
| Phosphine | Preparation | C. W. W. Read | 1940, 83, **21**, 976 |
| Phosphine | Preparation: 'safe' method | I. W. Williams | 1968, 168, **49**, 487 |
| Phosphorus | Yellow. Absorption effects. Ignites spontaneously | D. R. Browning | 1967, 166, **48**, 718 |
| Phosphorus | White. Burns | — | 1928, 38, **10**, 97 |
| Phosphorus | Burning; early reference | R. E. D. Clark | 1933, 58, **15**, 143 |
| Phosphorus | Yellow; don't handle | C. W. W. Read | 1940, 83, **21**, 973, 4 |
| Phosphorus | Burning dangers | E. H. Coulson, L. F. Ennever | 1942, 90, **23**, 230 |
| Phosphorus | Explosion possible | E. A. Philpots | 1933, 56, **14**, 489 |
| Phosphorus | Inflammable, dangerously spontaneous under warm, humid conditions | A. W. S. Watson | 1966, 164, **48**, 267 |

| Compound, Substance, Subject | Details, Reaction etc. | Author | Reference |
|---|---|---|---|
| Phosphorus | White, toxic | C. G. Vernon | 1927, 34, **9**, 97 |
| Phosphorus | Bromine, water. Danger of explosion | A. J. Mee | 1940, 85, **22**, 95 |
| Phosphorus | Carbon disulphide, solution in | C. W. W. Read | 1940, 83, **21**, 976 |
| Phosphorus | Chlorate: mixture explosive | H. K. Black | 1963, 153, **44**, 462 |
| Phosphorus | Ethyl bromide preparation | C. W. W. Read | 1940, 83, **21**, 976 |
| Phosphorus | Iodine, alcohol. Ethyl iodide preparation dangerous | C. W. W. Read | 1940, 83, **21**, 967 |
| Phosphorus | Metals, handling and disposal of phosphorus hazardous | P. D. Arculus | 1958, 140, **40**, 151 |
| Phosphorus | Oxygen, burn in | C. W. W. Read | 1940, 83, **21**, 977 |
| Phosphorus | Red; potassium chlorate. Explosive even without heat | — | 1923, 18, **5**, 112 |
| Phosphorus | Red; potassium chlorate. Explosive | — | 1928, 38, **10**, 97 |
| Phosphorus | Yellow; sodium hydroxide. 'Safe' method for phosphine details | I. W. Williams | 1968, 168, **49**, 487 |
| Phosphorus, red | Fire with plastic sinks | A. B. Newall | *1972, 47*, 24 |
| Phosphorus, white | Fire in outside brick store | R. J. Mitchell | *1979, 82*, 29 |
| Phosphorus chlorides | Avoid preparation | C. W. W. Read | 1940, 83, **21**, 976 |
| Phosphorus, organic compounds of | Poisonous | J. C. Curry | 1965, 160, **46**, 770 |
| Phosphorus trichloride | Possible fires etc. | — | 1928, 38, **10**, 100 |
| Phosphorus trichloride | Preparation | R. J. Kerr Muir | 1940, 83, **21**, 1007 |
| Phosphorus trichloride | Glacial acetic acid. Acetyl chloride preparation. Report of explosion | T. A. H. Peacocke | 1962, 152, **44**, 217 |
| Phosphorus tri- and pentachloride | Preparation | C. W. W. Read | 1940, 83, **21**, 969 |
| Phthalic anhydride (benzene-1,2-dicar-boxylic anhydride) | Anhydrous copper oxide. Explosive when heated | A. J. Mee | 1940, 85, **22**, 95 |
| Picric acid (2,4,6-trinitrophenol) | Poison | C. W. W. Read | 1940, 83, **21**, 972 |
| Picric acid (2,4,6-trinitrophenol) | Advice on disposal | — | *1985, 113*, 14 |
| Pipettes, mouth | Hazards of use | F. C. Brown | 1971, 181, **52**, 990 |
| Pipetting alkalis | Safe only for sixth formers | C. W. W. Read | 1940, 83, **21**, 977 |
| Pitch | Constituent of; producer of cancer | C. Dorée | 1937, 72, **18**, 498 |
| Plastic syringes, disposable | Not to be obtained from hospitals | — | *1976, 67*, 15 and 1976, 201, **57**, 784 |
| Plugs, electrical | Advantage of sleeved pins | — | *1990, 137*, 28 |
| Plutonium | Remote control handling. Critical mass | J. M. Thomas | 1959, 143, **41**, 33 |
| Plutonium 239 | DES advice to withdraw sources | — | *1974, 58*, 22 |
| Plutonium chemistry | Fitted glove box needed when handling | F. R. Paulsen | 1955, 131, **37**, 49 |
| Poisons | Solid and gas | — | 1929, 41, **11**, 22, 23 |
| Poisons | Storage of | E. A. Philpots | 1933, 56, **14**, 489 |
| Poisons | Note on Scheduled Poisons | C. W. W. Read | 1940, 83, **21**, 971 |
| Poisons | 'Their Properties, Chemical Identification, Symptoms and Emergency. Treatment'. Review | V. J. Brookes, H. N. Alyea | 1948, 110, **30**, 132 |
| Polonium | Body tolerance $10^{-12}$ g | T. A. H. Peacocke | 1953, 127, **35**, 355 |
| PTFE (polytetrafluoroethene) | Toxic fumes above 350°C | — | 1958, 140, **40**, 208 |
| PTFE | Toxic fumes (highly) on heating | J. L. Latham, W. F. Tyler | 1961, 149, **43**, 151 |
| Polypropylene sinks | *See* Sinks | | |

| Compound, Substance, Subject | Details, Reaction etc. | Author | Reference |
|---|---|---|---|
| Polystyrene sinks | *See* Sinks | | |
| Polyurethanes | *See* Di-isocyanates | | |
| Potassium | To be used only by teachers | C. W. W. Read | 1940, 83, **21**, 976 |
| Potassium | Do not handle, avoid contact with water | C. W. W. Read | 1940, 83, **21**, 973, 974 |
| Potassium | Explosion on cutting: metal was stored in naphtha | D. P. Pomeroy | 1946, 103, **27**, 422 |
| Potassium | Preparation by Brunner's method ($K_2CO_3+C$): product contains explosive potassium carbonyl | J. G. F. Druce | 1926, 28, **7**, 261 |
| Potassium | Hydrogen equivalent, measurement of. Danger of explosion | D. M. T. Casey | 1964, 156, **45**, 411 |
| Potassium | Water. Explosion danger; minimization | W. W. Allen | 1937, 72, **18**, 600 |
| Potassium | Water | C. W. W. Read | 1941, 87, **22**, 340 |
| Potassium | Water. Explosion when restricted | L. H. Angus | 1950, 115, **31**, 402 |
| Potassium | Water. Safer method of collecting hydrogen, using liquid paraffin | K. I. P. Adamson | 1964, 158, **46**, 178 |
| Potassium acetate (ethanoate) | Lead nitrate. Explosion when heated | A. J. Mee | 1940, 85, **22**, 95 |
| Potassium antimonyl tartrate | Effect of swallowing | — | 1928, 38, **10**, 102 |
| Potassium carbonate | Magnesium. Explosive substance formed | J. G. F. Druce | 1926, 28, **7**, 261 |
| Potassium carbonate | Magnesium. Castellana fusion: possible explosion | G. Fowles | 1938, 77, **20**, 124 |
| Potassium chlorate | Preparation | C. W. W. Read | 1940, 83, **21**, 977 |
| Potassium chlorate | Heat. Possible explosion | — | 1928, 38, **10**, 99 |
| Potassium chlorate | Heat | C. W. W. Read | 1940, 83, **21**, 976 |
| Potassium chlorate | Manganese dioxide. Possible explosion on heating | — | 1928, 38, **10**, 99 |
| Potassium chlorate | Phosphorus, red. Explosion, even without heat | — | 1923, 18, **5**, 112 |
| Potassium chlorate | Phosphorus, red | — | 1928, 38, **10**, 97 |
| Potassium chlorate | Sugar, conc. sulphuric acid. Explosive precautions | — | 1923, 18, **5**, 112 |
| Potassium chlorate | Sulphur. Explosion | C. W. W. Read | 1940, 83, **21**, 969 |
| Potassium chlorate | Sulphur | C. W. W. Read | 1940, 83, **21**, 976 |
| Potassium chlorate | Sulphuric acid | C. W. W. Read | 1940, 83, **21**, 976 |
| Potassium cyanide | Teachers only should use it | C. W. W. Read | 1940, 83, **21**, 976 |
| Potassium cyanide | Antidote for | E. J. Williams | 1937, 74, **19**, 308 |
| Potassium cyanide | Poison, deadly. Technique to avoid in analysis | R. Chandra | 1962, 150, **43**, 451 |
| Potassium cyanide | Further notes on avoidance in analysis | G. Fowles | 1963, 153, **44**, 406 |
| Potassium dichromate dust | Suspected carcinogenic | D. R. Browning | 1967, 167, **49**, 278 |
| Potassium hydroxide | | C. W. W. Read | 1940, 83, **21**, 972 |
| Potassium hydroxide | Caution when solution used in syringe | — | 1976, 69, 29 |
| Potassium nitrate | Sulphur, charcoal, explosion when ground | — | 1923, 18, **5**, 112 |
| Potassium permanganate | Hydrochloric acid drops. Explosion reported | J. C. Curry | 1965, 160, **46**, 770 |
| Potassium permanganate | Sulphuric acid conc. Explosion when warmed | L. R. Wheeler | 1929, 39, **10**, 274 |

| Compound, Substance, Subject | Details, Reaction etc. | Author | Reference |
|---|---|---|---|
| Potassium permanganate | Sulphuric acid conc. Manganese heptoxide explodes violently on warming | — | 1930, 46, **12**, 178 |
| Propane-1,2,3-triol | *See* Glycerol | | |
| Propane-1,2,3-triyl nitrate | *See* Nitroglycerol | | |
| Propanone | Explosion on mixing with trichloromethane | E. H. Coulson | 1974, 192, **55**, 596 |
| Propanone | Explosive mixture with chloroform | — | *1974, 57, 38* |
| Propenoates | *See* Acrylic esters | | |
| Prop-2-en-1-ol | *See* Allyl alcohol | | |
| Proscribed chemicals | Difficulty of producing a satisfactory list | — | *1978, 78, 22–23* |
| Protoactinium | Uranium cow experiment. Contamination avoided by means of tray | T. A. H. Peacocke | 1962, 152, **44**, 137 |
| Prussic acid (hydrogen cyanide) | Preparation. (*See also* Cyanides) | C. W. W. Read | 1940, 83, **21**, 977 |
| Pyridine | Danger to eyes, heart. Details | D. R. Browning | 1967, 166, **48**, 718 |
| Pyrotechnics | Case for and against | — | *1963, 5, 53–54* |
| Radiation | Precautions with radioactive materials | R. M. Fishenden | 1949, 112, **30**, 306 <br> 1949, 112, **30**, 311 <br> 1949, 112, **30**, 314 |
| Radiation | Dangers; effect on man | F. W. Spiers | 1958, 139, **39**, 450 |
| Radiation | Hazard, details | Min. of Ed. | 1959, 141, **40**, 363 |
| Radiation | 'Radiation. Dangers and what they mean to you': review of book | H. W. Heckstall-Smith | 1959, 141, **40**, 394 |
| Radiation | Effects of | P. A. Barker | 1959, 143, **41**, 169 |
| Radiation | Biological effects of | P. J. Lindop | 1961, 147, **42**, 223 |
| Radiation | 'Radiation, Genes and Man': review of book | B. Wallace, T. Dobzhansky | 1961, 149, **43**, 235 |
| Radiation | 'Radiation, Hazards and Protection': review of book | D. E. Barnes, D. Taylor | 1963, 155, **45**, 274 |
| Radioactive isotopes | Hazards and precautions | UKAEA | 1958, 140, **40**, 179 |
| Radioactive materials | Safe transport of: film review | UKAEA | 1966, 162, **47**, 582 |
| Radioactive sources | Precautions: $Ra^{226}$, $Co^{60}$, $Sr^{90}$ etc. | J. W. Lucas | 1966, 164, **48**, 19 |
| Radioactive substances | Report of ASE sub-committee | — | 1959, 143, **41**, 173 |
| Radioactive tablet scheme | Details of sources and how to obtain them | UKAEA | 1967, 165, **48**, 571 |
| Radioactivity experiments | Precautions | K. Forster | 1965, 159, **46**, 397 |
| Radiochemistry | Some experiments for schools | T. A. H. Peacocke | 1954, 127, **35**, 354 |
| Radiochemistry | Suggested experiments for schools | N. H. Davies | 1965, 161, **47**, 152 |
| Radiochemistry | Experiments, precautions, disposal | T. A. H. Peacocke | 1964, 157, **45**, 597 |
| Radiochemistry | Solution, chemical systems in: generally not safe to handle in lecture theatre | P. A. Murfin | 1957, 137, **39**, 39 <br> 1957, 137, **39**, 41 |
| Radiochemistry, practical | Review of book: stresses health precautions | M. F. C. Ladd, W. H. Lee | 1964, 158, **46**, 257 |
| Radio-isotopes | 'The measurement of Radioisotopes': review. Chapter on health hazards | D. Taylor | 1952, 120, **33**, 283 |
| Radon | Radiation danger | C. G. Ferguson | 1946, 102, **27**, 179 |
| Ragwort | *See Senecio* sp. | | |
| Resorcinol | Formaldehyde resin: explosion | — | *1971, 45, 36* |
| Rocksill | Hazards of oxidizable impurities | — | *1976, 70, 29* |
| Rocksill wool | Explosions with manganate(VII) | B. J. Hallam, M. Armstrong | 1975, 197, **56**, 82 |

| Compound, Substance, Subject | Details, Reaction etc. | Author | Reference |
|---|---|---|---|
| Safeguards in School Laboratories | Comments on LEA Regulations | G. Fowles | 1940, 85, **22**, 3 |
| Safety | Carcinoma-inducing compounds | D. R. Browning | 1967, 167, **49**, 278 |
| Safety | The teacher's duty | D. R. Browning | 1967, 166, **48**, 918 |
| Safety | Accidents with Tollen's reagent | D. R. Browning | 1968, 168, **49**, 605 |
| Safety | DES advice | — | 1976, 69, 20–21, 1976, 68, 9 and 1978, 79, 22–23 |
| Safety | Checklist | — | 1977, 75, 18–19 |
| Safety | Need for positive advice | B. D. Sorsby | 1978, 77, 22 |
| Safety | And professional judgement | L. J. Campbell | 1977, 71, 22 (and 1976, 68, 20–21) |
| Safety | Check list | — | 1986, 120, 24–5 |
| Safety equipment | Responsibility for providing | — | 1976, 67, 14 |
| Safety goggles | A new hazard? | — | 1982, 99, 20 |
| Safety in the Chemical Laboratory | Book by H. A. J. Pieters and J. W. Creyghton | Review | 1951, 118, **32**, 411 |
| Safety in the Laboratory | Book by J. N. Friend | Review | 1958, 140, **40**, 233 |
| Safety in School Chemistry | How do textbooks deal with hazards? | D. R. Browning | 1967, 166, **48**, 717 |
| Safety Precautions in Schools | M. of Ed. Pamphlet | Review | 1961, 148, **42**, 582 |
| Safety Rules for pupils | Sample rules | — | 1979, 83, 19 |
| Safety spectacles | *See* Eye protection | | |
| Sealing tube ends | Accidental | — | 1928, 38, **10**, 101 |
| Selenium compounds | Biological methylation of | F. Challenger | 1936, 68, **17**, 575 |
| *Senecio* spp. | Toxic and carcinogenic alkaloids of these spp. | J. R. Martin | 1975, 199, **57**, 391 |
| Silica | Magnesium. Detonation if silica not completely dry | W. B. Barker | 1938, 77, **20**, 150 |
| Silicate | Sodium hydroxide: fused bead. When hot, explosion may take place when bead dipped into water | P. Heath | 1956, 132, **37**, 250 |
| Silicon(IV) chloride | Explosion of stock bottle | — | 1971, 41, 34 |
| Silicon(IV) chloride | Explosion | J. A. Kirk | 1969, 34, 49 |
| Silicon (IV) chloride | Explosion (by hydrolysis?) | A. J. Maclean | 1969, 35, 38 |
| Silicon(IV) chloride | Bursting of bottle | — | 1970, 37, 42–43 |
| Silicon tetrachloride | *See* Silicon(IV) chloride | | |
| Silicon tetrachloride | Storage and handling advice | — | 1979, 85, 31 |
| Silver acetylide (silver(I) dicarbide) | Unstable detonator | S. I. Levy | 1935, 67, **17**, 343 |
| Silver ions | Ammonium ions. Substance heated to expel ammonia; Devarda's alloy added: violent explosion | J. Baldwin | 1967, 165, **48**, 586 |
| Silver nitrate | Powder, magnesium powder. Explodes immediately on adding drop of cold water | D. J. Lyness, K. Hutton | 1953, 125, **35**, 138 |
| Silver oxalate | Heat: likely to explode | W. E. Garner | 1933, 55, **14**, 247 |
| Silver oxide ppt. | Ammonia. When hot, explosion. Fulminate possibly formed | J. R. Morse | 1955, 131, **37**, 147 |
| Silver oxide ppt. | Ammoniacal, caustic soda. Explosion on standing | E. Green | 1965, 161, **47**, 231 |
| Silver oxide ppt. | Ammonia, dissolved in; pptd. by $AgNO_3$. Solution exploded on standing | D. R. Browning | 1968, 168, **49**, 605 |
| Sinks | Fire with phosphorus | A. B. Newall | 1972, 47, 24 |

| Compound, Substance, Subject | Details, Reaction etc. | Author | Reference |
|---|---|---|---|
| Sinks, polypropylene | Hazards of | — | *1971, 43, 24* and *1971, 45, 35* |
| Sinks, polystyrene | Hazards of | — | *1971, 43, 24* |
| Soda | Molten, dry chlorine | J. Bradley | 1968, 168, **49**, 454 |
| Sodium | Metal | C. W. W. Read | 1940, 83, **21**, 976 |
| Sodium | Wire | May & Baker | 1956, 133, **37**, 446 |
| Sodium | Burns | — | 1928, 38, **10**, 97 |
| Sodium | Explosion possible | E. A. Philpots | 1933, 56, **14**, 489 |
| Sodium | Do not handle, or allow in contact with water | C. W. W. Read | 1940, 83, **21**, 973, 974 |
| Sodium | Handling dangers | J. Allsop | 1949, 113, **31**, 133 |
| Sodium | Preparation. Davy's isolation of, from caustic soda. Spitting. Screen | E. R. Martin | 1925, 25, **7**, 39 |
| Sodium | Hydrogen equivalent measurement of. Explosion danger | M. T. Casey | 1964, 156, **45**, 411 |
| Sodium | Lassaigne's test. Some compounds explode when heated with sodium in organic analysis | G. Fowles | 1938, 77, **20**, 124 |
| Sodium | Water. Violent explosion | — | 1922, 14, **4**, 97 |
| Sodium | Water. Possible explanation and avoidance of explosion | — | 1922, 16, **4**, 216 |
| Sodium | Water. Reason for possible explosion; precautions | J. A. Cochrane | 1928, 35, **9**, 234 |
| Sodium | Water. Explosion possible, particularly in confined space | — | 1928, 38, **10**, 100 |
| Sodium | Water. Explosion with | C. Baily | 1935, 65, **17**, 146 |
| Sodium | Water. Explosion danger; minimization | W. W. Allen | 1937, 72, **18**, 600 |
| Sodium | Water. Teacher demonstration | C. W. W. Read | 1940, 83, **21**, 976 |
| Sodium | Water. A method of minimizing danger using metal apparatus | M. T. Casey | 1957, 136, **38**, 424 |
| Sodium | Use of metal | — | 1970, 176, **51**, 707 |
| Sodium | Water. Explosion risk; further comment | L. H. Angus | 1958, 138, **39**, 321 |
| Sodium | Water. Safer method of collecting hydrogen | K. I. P. Adamson | 1964, 158, **46**, 178 |
| Sodium | Water. Method of performing demonstration | C. Holt | 1966, 164, **48**, 171 |
| Sodium | Water. A class experiment with care | J. P. C. Watson | 1967, 166, **48**, 924 |
| Sodium | Violent reaction with a detergent solution | M. A. Shaw | *1979, 82, 33* |
| Sodium azide | Nitrogen source. Detonates on rapid heating. Demonstration | B. Lambert | 1927, 31, **8**, 218 |
| Sodium chlorate(I) | *See* sodium hypochlorite | | |
| Sodium fluoride | Poison | C. W. W. Read | 1940, 83, **21**, 972 |
| Sodium fusions | Performed by teacher only | C. W. W. Read | 1940, 83, **21**, 976 |
| Sodium fusions | Middleton's procedure is safer | G. Fowles | 1940, 85, **22**, 6 |
| Sodium hydroxide | Poison | C. W. W. Read | 1940, 83, **21**, 972 |
| Sodium hydroxide | Skin, dangers to | T. C. Swinfen | 1965, 160, **46**, 670 |
| Sodium hydroxide | Ammonium compound, boiling with | C. W. W. Read | 1940, 83, **21**, 968 |
| Sodium hypochlorite | Explosion of bottle | — | *1971, 43, 24* |
| Sodium nitrate | Sodium thiosulphate. Mixture exploded when heated | — | 1947, 107, **28**, 386 |
| Sodium nitrate | Sodium thiosulphate. Mixture exploded when heated | A. J. Mee | 1940, 85, **22**, 95 |
| Sodium nitrate(III) | Toxicity | G. C. Britton | 1975, 198, **57**, 186 |

| Compound, Substance, Subject | Details, Reaction etc. | Author | Reference |
|---|---|---|---|
| Sodium peroxide | Substance blown out of bottle on releasing stopper | N. F. Watterson | 1935, 64, **16**, 569 |
| Sodium peroxide | Explosion: possible explanation | C. Baily | 1935, 65, **17**, 146 |
| Sodium peroxide | Explosion: explanation; air and organic substances react causing ignition | F. L. Swift | 1935, 66, **17**, 310 |
| Sodium peroxide | Dangerous | G. Fowles | 1955, 130, **36**, 417 |
| Sodium peroxide | Hydrogen sulphide ignited by trace of $Na_2O_2$ | A. J. Mee | 1940, 85, **22**, 95 |
| Sodium peroxide | Water. Oxygen preparation. Beware excess sodium present: explosive hydrogen-oxygen mixture likely | W. B. Barker | 1935, 63, **16**, 438 |
| Sodium peroxide | Water: denial of explosion | A. Adair | 1935, 67, **17**, 439 |
| Sodium silicofluoride | Poison | C. W. W. Read | 1940, 83, **21**, 972 |
| Sodium thiosulphate | Sodium nitrate. Mixture exploded when heated | — | 1947, 106, **28**, 386 |
| Sodium thiosulphate | Sodium nitrate. Exploded when heated | A. J. Mee | 1940, 85, **22**, 3 |
| Solids | Decomposition and detonation of | W. E. Garner | 1933, 55, **14**, 244–51 |
| Soxhlet extraction | Undesirable in schools | C. W. W. Read | 1940, 83, **21**, 977 |
| Spirit burners | Fire hazards | — | 1979, 85, 30–31 |
| Steam engines | Flash fires | — | 1984, 108, 112–13 |
| Steam engines | Advice on use | — | 1986, 116, 15–16 |
| Storage | Safety hazards if inadequate | — | 1970, 37, 47 |
| Storage | Advice on chemical storage | — | 1980, 89, 16–22 |
| Sugar | Chlorate mixture: explosive | H. K. Black | 1963, 153, **44**, 462 |
| Sugar | Potassium chlorate, sulphuric acid conc. Explosive: precautions | — | 1923, 18, **5**, 112 |
| Sulphamic acid (amino-sulphonic acid) | Skin, precautions with | J. G. Stark | 1965, 161, **47**, 171 |
| Sulphonal | Poison | C. W. W. Read | 1940, 83, **21**, 972 |
| Sulphur | Aluminium | C. W. W. Read | 1940, 83, **21**, 977 |
| Sulphur | Carbon disulphide, solution in | C. W. W. Read | 1940, 83, **21**, 976 |
| Sulphur | Charcoal, potassium nitrate. Grind: explosive | — | 1923, 18, **5**, 112 |
| Sulphur | Chlorate mixture: liable to spontaneous ignition, detonation | H. K. Black | 1963, 153, **44**, 463 |
| Sulphur | Magnesium | C. W. W. Read | 1940, 83, **21**, 977 |
| Sulphur | Magnesium. Heat: explosion | K. Hutton | 1950, 114, **31**, 265 |
| Sulphur | Oxygen, burn in | C. W. W. Read | 1940, 83, **21**, 976 |
| Sulphur | Potassium chlorate. Explosion | C. W. W. Read | 1940, 83, **21**, 969 |
| Sulphur | Potassium | C. W. W. Read | 1940, 83, **21**, 976 |
| Sulphur | Zinc | C. W. W. Read | 1940, 83, **21**, 976 |
| Sulphur chlorides | Preparation | C. W. W. Read | 1940, 83, **21**, 977 |
| Sulphur dioxide | Poison | — | 1929, 41, **11**, 22 |
| Sulphur dioxide | Poisonous, corrosive; disadvantages as refrigerant | V. A. Carpenter | 1952, 120, **33**, 173 |
| Sulphur dioxide | Preparation | C. W. W. Read | 1940, 83, **21**, 976 |
| Sulphur dioxide | Explosion danger in critical temp. expt. | B. J. Bedell | 1938, 77, **20**, 148 |
| Sulphur dioxide | Hazard in contact process | — | 1981, 93, 21 |
| Sulphur trioxide | Water. Violent reaction | E. S. Dewing | 1955, 131, **37**, 27 |
| Sulphuric acid | Conc. Burns. Antidote. | H. Garnett | 1929, 40, **10**, 350 |
| Sulphuric acid | Poison | C. W. W. Read | 1940, 83, **21**, 972 |
| Sulphuric acid | Preparation. Chamber, contact processes | C. W. W. Read | 1940, 83, **21**, 969 |

| Compound, Substance, Subject | Details, Reaction etc. | Author | Reference |
|---|---|---|---|
| Sulphuric acid | Preparation. Chamber process model | C. W. W. Read | 1940, 83, **21**, 976 |
| Sulphuric acid | Preparation. Contact process demonstration | C. W. W. Read | 1940, 83, **21**, 977 |
| Sulphuric acid | Collection of gases over: dangerous | — | 1963, 154, **44**, 740 |
| Sulphuric acid | Conc. Use in Dreschel bottles | C. W. W. Read | 1940, 83, **21**, 977 |
| Sulphuric acid | Conc. Desiccant in chlorine prepn.: suck back danger | A. Adair | 1962, 152, **44**, 159 |
| Sulphuric acid | Conc. Expansion of gas measurement with: dangerous | E. B. Rodmell | 1961, 149, 343, 199 |
| Sulphuric acid | Conc. Copper. Caution when adding Cu to hot acid: violent reaction | G. Fowles | 1927, 34, **9**, 90 |
| Sulphuric acid | Copper. Preparation of $SO_2$ dangerous | D. A. Campbell | 1939, 80, **20**, 631 |
| Sulphuric acid | Copper. Preparation of $SO_2$ dangerous | C. W. W. Read | 1940, 83, **21**, 969 |
| Sulphuric acid | Heat to decompose | C. W. W. Read | 1940, 83, **21**, 977 |
| Sulphuric acid | Iron filings. $FeSO_4$ preparation | C. W. W. Read | 1940, 83, **21**, 969 |
| Sulphuric acid | Potassium chlorate | C. W. W. Read | 1940, 83, **21**, 976 |
| Sulphuric acid | Treatment of burns | J. T. Burton | 1976, 67, 16 |
| Syringes disposable | Potential hazard | A. Farmer | 1971, 182, **53**, 231 |
| Syringes disposable | See Plastic syringes | | |
| | | | |
| Tetrachloromethane | See Carbon tetrachloride | | |
| Thallium | Poison | C. W. W. Read | 1940, 83, **21**, 972 |
| Thallium | Element and compounds too toxic for schools. | A. W. Bamford | 1976, 201, 57, 784 |
| Thermit process | Fusing: safe method | E. Walker | 1956, 133, **37**, 435 |
| | Fusing: dangerous methods | A. D. Macdonald | |
| Thermit process | Magnesium, sodium peroxide; potassium chlorate, sulphur | O. J. Elphick | 1957, 135, **38**, 295 |
| Thermit process | Fusing. Aluminium, iodine fuse recommended | C. M. Hammerton | 1957, 136, **38**, 459 |
| Thermit process | Ignition, further comment | C. Chittock | 1958, 138, **39**, 323 |
| Thermit process | Ignition, further comment: sodium peroxide, magnesium ignition possibly dangerous | L. H. Angus | 1958, 140, **40**, 154 |
| Thermit process | Ignition: match heads safe | E. C. Weaver | 1959, 142, **40**, 555 |
| Thermit process | Fuse, discussion: possible danger of chlorate mixtures | Editors of Science Masters' Book IV, 2 | 1966, 162, **47**, 560 |
| Thermit process | Fuse | N. Le Poidevin | 1966, 164, **48**, 243 |
| Thermit process | Explosion with copper oxide | T. E. W. Browne | 1967, 166, **48**, 921 |
| Thioacetamide | Skin: may be harmful if absorbed through | B. E. Dawson | 1961, 147, **42**, 220 |
| Thiocyanates | Danger of HCN when oxidized | G. J. Cooper | 1967, 24, 33 |
| Thorium | Uranium cow experiment. Avoid contamination by means of tray | T. A. H. Peacocke | 1962, 152, **44**, 137 |
| Thorium hydroxide | Salt preparation from. Fume cupboard, gloves | T. A. H. Peacocke | 1954, 127, **35**, 356 |
| Tin(IV) chloride | Preparation to be avoided? | C. W. W. Read | 1940, 83, **21**, 969 |
| Tollen's reagents | Exploded after leaving | E. Green | 1965, 161, **48**, 231 |
| Tollen's reagent | Exploded while being prepared | D. R. Browning | 1967, 166, **48**, 920 |
| Tollen's reagent | Explosions recorded | D. R. Browning | 1968, 168, **49**, 605 |
| Toluene (methylbenzene) and some homologues | Toxic | C. G. Vernon | 1927, 34, **9**, 97 |

| Compound, Substance, Subject | Details, Reaction etc. | Author | Reference |
|---|---|---|---|
| Toxic agents | *Laboratory Handbook of Toxic Reagents* (C. H. Gray) | Reviews of this book | 1961, 148, **42**, 581 <br> 1967, 165, **48**, 614 |
| Toxic chemicals | Inorganic and organic | C. G. Vernon | 1927, 34, **9**, 97 |
| Trichloromethane | *See* Chloroform | | |
| Trifluoracetic acid (trifluoroethanoic acid) | Vesicant | J. Ormston | 1945, 99, **26**, 151 |
| Trinitrotoluene | Explodes with detonator | S. I. Levy | 1935, 67, **17**, 343 |
| Trinitrotoluene | Vapour volatile in steam: poisonous | S. I. Levy | 1936, 68, **17**, 495 |
| Tripods | Dangers when hot; storage | C. Holt | 1968, 168, **49**, 492 |
| Turpentine | Inflammable | C. W. W. Read | 1940, 83, **21**, 973 |
| Ultra-violet light | Absorption: glass containing 5% nickel oxide absorbs U.V. light, produces fluorescence | W. J. R. Calvert | 1921, 7, **2**, 258 |
| Ultra-violet light | Goggles needed to work with | F. H. Pollard *et al.* | 1952, 122, **34**, 34 |
| Vacuum pump | Hazards of older models | — | *1990, 137, 28* |
| Waste disposal | ASE advice | — | *1982, 97, 29–37* |
| Water | Composition of, by volume. Dangers of amyl alcohol vapour surrounding eudiometer tube (inflammable vapour) | W. B. Barker | 1935, 63, **16**, 415 |
| Water | Composition of, by volume. 'Safe method' | W. V. Lloyd, F. J. Knight | 1940, 84, **21**, 1144 |
| Wet asbestos technique | Avoid | D. H. Mansfield | *1967, 25, 26* |
| X-rays | Apparatus dangers. Radiation. High potential | H. Mason | 1938, 76, **19**, 532 |
| X-rays | Hazards from 'maltese cross' experiment | — | 1959, 143, **41**, 173 |
| Xylyl bromide | Lachrymator | F. F. Crossley | 1940, 84, **21**, 1049 |
| Ziegler process | Polyethylene preparation. Precautions with spontaneously inflammable aluminium triethyl, also highly toxic | T. A. H. Peacocke | 1962, 150, **43**, 453 |
| Zinc | Dust. Explosion risk | S. Robson | 1934, 62, **16**, 165 |
| Zinc | Sulphur | C. W. W. Read | 1940, 83, **21**, 976 |

# INDEX